Resisting
Bodies

Kritik:
German Literary Theory and Cultural Studies
Liliane Weissberg, editor

*A complete listing of the books in this series
can be found at the back of this volume.*

Resisting Bodies

The Negotiation of Female Agency in
Twentieth-Century Women's Fiction

Helga Druxes

WAYNE STATE UNIVERSITY PRESS
DETROIT

LIBRARY OF CONGRESS CATALOGING-IN-PUBLICATION DATA

Druxes, Helga, 1959–
    Resisting bodies : the negotiation of female agency in twentieth-
century women's fiction / Helga Druxes.
       p.   cm. — (Kritik : German literary theory and cultural
studies)
    Includes bibliographical references and index.
    ISBN 0-8143-2534-3
    1. Literature, Modern—Women authors—History and criticism.
2. Literature, Modern—20th century—History and criticism.
3. Women in literature. 4. Women and literature.   I. Title.
II. Series: Kritik (Detroit, Mich.)
PN471.D78   1996
809.3'9352042—dc20   96-11414

DESIGNER

Mary Krzewinski

CONTENTS

ACKNOWLEDGMENTS

I would like to thank those who read versions of the manuscript when it was in its formative stages. For their rigorous readings, critical suggestions, and sustained interest I am indebted to my colleagues and friends Angela Zito and John Calagione, Alex Mihailovic, Diane Shooman, Holly W. Fils-Aimé, Sally Shafto. My colleagues at Williams College, Mark Taylor, Gail Newman, Bruce Kieffer, Jana Sawicki, and Jeanne Bergman provided helpful responses to earlier drafts. I would also like to thank Art Evans; Liliane Weissberg, the series editor; and the readers at Wayne State University Press for their useful and perceptive comments and their patience. For his unflagging support, I am once again grateful to Alex, whose conversation, humor, and cooking have proved invaluable.

INTRODUCTION
Transaction, Exchange, and Female Agency

It has become fashionable in recent literary and social criticism to assert that the subject and agency (its *modus operandi*) are dead. This debate began in the seventies and may be divided roughly into two camps: voluntarists, who subscribe to a notion of the subject as autonomous and led by free will, and constructionists, who conceive of the subject as determined by social forces. For instance, in the first group there are liberal humanists such as the American philosopher Richard Rorty. He argues for an ironic distance to social constructions combined with a pragmatist approach that would allow the subject to recognize its contingency, yet still empower the individual to act.[1] Marxist constructionists, such as French sociologist Jean Baudrillard[2], describe advertising practices and mass consumption as controlling human behavior through the creation of false needs and the proliferation of objects that, in turn, supplant all personal interaction with mechanistic technologies, commodity fetishism, and instrumental acts. The speedy recycling of ever-new commodities leaves in its wake insecure, politically unengaged individuals whose only goal is to appropriate new lifestyles, technologies, and so on, so that they may preserve the status quo. The work of French philosopher Michel Foucault traces the reproduction of power through such confining social institutions as schools, hospitals, and prisons.[3] Because power is present everywhere in society, the individual internalizes various control regimes and risks becoming no more than a docile body, unconsciously reproducing repressive power relations. Another example in the constructionist group is the Frankfurt-school philosopher and social theorist Jürgen Habermas.[4] In his view, late capitalist society has naturalized its own systemic operations. "The market" then appears as a given, not as a man-made, therefore changeable, construct; its own increasingly complex operations justify its existence. As the Marxist literary critic Terry Eagleton sees it, "the system of late capitalism can be said to operate 'all by itself,'

9

without any need to resort to *discursive* justification. It no longer . . . has to pass through consciousness; instead, it simply secures its own reproduction by a manipulative incorporative logic of which human beings are the mere obedient effects."[5]

Resistance in these circumstances becomes practically impossible. Many of these constructionist scenarios share a distopian and deterministic viewpoint. If they envision resistance at all, it is against a system, from a standpoint somewhere outside it. Alternatively, social change would be produced by the revolution of an oppressed class in the system. How would it be possible for critical consciousness to arise in the closed system as traditional Marxism described capitalist society? Several years later the British Marxist Raymond Williams argued that no hegemony is ever absolute because in any given historical period different forms of "dominant," "residual," and "emergent" consciousness coexist and contradict each other. Social class is also a factor in resistance, because not all classes are equally vulnerable to the same ideology.[6] This debate about agency has, in fact, roots in leftist criticism that arose after World War I (the Great War). In the opinion of György Lukács, only the proletariat can attain a total overview of the functioning of capitalism and its own commodity role in it. Only from the vantage point of this class can a plan for the reorganization of society be imagined because the bourgeoisie has a stake in maintaining the old order.[7] Implicit in his analysis is the presupposition of a certain type of crisis that pits two classes against each other over a concrete crucial issue, as happened, for instance, in the 1917 Russian Revolution; or, again, who owns the production mechanisms versus who gets killed on the battlefields, as happened, for example, during World War I when many of the upper-class war strategists remained safely behind the front lines, whereas the working class supplied soldiers as cannon fodder. Lukács believed that periods of crisis would act as catalysts in facilitating systemic insight into the arbitrariness of seemingly "natural" social laws: "At such times we can see how the immediate continuity between two partial systems is disrupted and their independence from and adventitious connection with each other is suddenly forced into the consciousness."[8] Suddenly a hidden truth about social mechanisms is revealed, critical consciousness is born and leads to "the practical interaction of the awakening consciousness and the objects from which it is born and of which it is the consciousness."[9] We can see here how Lukács idealizes consciousness as inevitably leading to revolutionary agency. Seven decades later we now know that the abolition of wage labor and capitalism did not entail the demise of exploitive class structures; within socialism new elites formed in the party bureaucracy that accumulated private capital and special privileges to the detriment of the other citizens. The very structure and frequency of crises have changed—

what used to be discrete events are now, in our televisual culture, proliferated and sensationalized spectacles. Crises become staged events in themselves. The psychic numbing that results from overexposure to such *dramatizations* discourages systemic analysis or active engagement with these crises. The 1989 peaceful revolution in East Germany showed that intellectuals, workers, and even party officials banded together to overthrow the Honecker regime—this proves that a revolution is not always carried out by one class only. A more flexible, inclusive concept of agency thus might allow for the formation of alliances across social classes.

In spite of recognizing the importance of consciousness, Lukács still tended to see empowerment in terms of one class. If we shift Lukács's discussion of oppression from workers to women as a gender in patriarchy, we have to take into account the historical specifics of the oppression of a particular group. Race and gender were not categories that concerned Lukács in his indictment of capitalism, but in the waning days of imperialist colonialism after World War I, they become important foci to express modernist alienation from bourgeois society. Lukács as a transitional thinker who emphasized consciousness paved the way for the realization that not *only* the proletariat could liberate itself. The middle-class woman is not a worker and she cannot have the relation to the production process that Lukács describes. However, the experience of World War I thrust such women (more aggressively than ever before) into a situation in which they became more overtly commodities, abruptly reaching the same conclusions as the workers in Lukács's scheme. Women were suddenly surplus, so many unwanted goods. It was a situation that pointed up their existence *as* commodities, a state somewhat concealed in bourgeois family life before World War I. The parallel plight of working-class women perhaps reinforced this conclusion. If a woman becomes conscious of her commodity status—that the only public viability she has is as an exchange commodity among men—she can either try to exploit her commodity status by marketing herself to the men with the most social prestige or seek for some other form of currency for her presence in the public sphere. As a woman worker she may gain economic independence and a sense of subjecthood, but her physical presence as a body to be seen in the streets will still reduce her to the status of a visual commodity for the male gaze and guarantee her alienated subjectivity. This might lead from perceived discomfort with a social injustice to critical consciousness and, moreover, from there to innovative agency. For Lukács, this pragmatic step followed out of recognition: "his immediate existence integrates him as a pure, naked object into the production process. Once this immediacy turns out to be the consequence of a multiplicity of mediations, . . . then the fetishistic forms of the commodity system begin to dissolve: in the commodity the worker recognizes

11

himself and his own relations with capital."[10] In addition to selling their labor power as a commodity, workers produce commodities. They are the simulacra of commodities; women (post World War I), in fact, *constitute* commodities in themselves. They represent in an even more exacerbated form that which Lukács describes in the plight of the worker. Even though a woman might recognize her existence as a female body as mediated, she may still be vulnerable to internalized self-surveillance and long-ago learned fetishizations. This may be partly the case because from the mid-nineteenth century on, female social presence was associated with the private sphere, with the home and the family. This meant that a woman's experiential world was more circumscribed and that she would be more prone to see herself in isolation rather than as participating in a systemic social critique. The dissemination of Marxist tracts through newspapers and political meetings for workers may have changed this for some working-class European women, who became politicized and actively organized to change their condition.[11] But the "fallen" and "displaced" middle-class women the modernist writer Jean Rhys describes never attain radical agency; yet in their attempts to express rebellion against their commodification, they can be seen to have some form of agency. Such displaced women gravitated naturally towards the city.

Unless such a protagonist can enter into nonexploitive relationships with others who do not treat her as a passive voiceless commodity, she will not be able to translate consciousness into social engagement. In this study, I do not ascribe to the voluntaristic view of the self as a monad, making choices that are free and transcendent. I believe that we are inscribed in social practices and institutions. I also believe, however, that we can reposition ourselves within these practices and change them. In the novels I analyze in this study, the city as the epitome of the commodity marketplace becomes the catalyst for critical self-consciousness, and I trace a progression from female protagonists as mute exchange objects to vocal agents in the exchange.

Perhaps the most valuable rethinking of the problematic of subjectivity and agency has come from feminist critics. The American philosopher Judith Butler investigates the construction of gender and the attribution of social power as processes. She reinvests these processes with a temporal dynamic, focusing on repetition in its destabilizing, not merely in its consolidating effects. She states: "Construction is neither a subject nor its act, but a process of reiteration by which both 'subjects' and 'acts' come to appear at all. There is no power that acts, but only a reiterated acting that is power in its persistence and instability."[12] Her approach strikes me as offering a solution to the problematic of agency: Where in the social network can it locate itself? Contestation is always possible, but from *within* the very norms and gender identities that have influenced and are still shaping the subject. Fundamentally, this is a paradox, as Butler goes on to explain: "The paradox of subjectivation (assujetissement) is precisely that the subject who would resist such norms is itself enabled, if not produced, by such norms. Although this constitutive constraint does not foreclose the possibility of agency, it does locate agency as a reiterative or rearticulatory practice, immanent to power, and not a relation of external opposition to power."[13] This responsive origin of agency is a more plausible rethinking of how this practice occurs—it is not a spontaneous or purely voluntaristic act, but rather a sustained and varied reshaping of power relations from which the agent can never free herself. While acting, we are at the same time acted upon; we are implicated in and help to reproduce even through our innovative interventions a whole network of social norms. Butler does allow for a loophole in the formation of agency—power may engender its own enemy and critic.

Analogously, there exists a reciprocal and dynamic relationship between critical consciousness and the gendered body as its material matrix. I show how it is only after the female body is exposed to the censorship/ appraisal of the public gaze in the urban marketplace that critical consciousness becomes translated into self-authored physical mobility within the city. This in turn may cause a different embodied awareness that seeks out experimentation, mimicry, and parody through dress, behavior, and speech. These are the roots of the subversion of existent norms governing the female body in the public sphere. I am not suggesting, however, that subversion can be accomplished by a lone heroic subject. Although the female subject partially constitutes herself through being seen by others, in the city she also observes others who may be in similar situations as herself or who may have moved beyond her particular position in society and then seeks out these others for friendship, mentoring, and support. We find a thwarted desire for such connections to other women in Jean Rhys's modernist work that presents us with an alienated protagonist whose tentative public self-expression is misunderstood or goes unheard by its addressees. As women entered the public sphere in ever-greater numbers in the period between the two world wars, opportunities for encountering them in nontraditional roles grew. The mass media (especially films made for a largely female audience, whose plots often grotesquely overemphasized the woman as a passive male appendage) could, through repeated viewings, paradoxically spawn a critical awareness of the artificiality of this role and foster a desire to explore women's other options in society beyond marriage. Butler implies this possibility in her discussion of how agency is generated.

Although repetition in Jean Rhys is a trap for the protagonist, repetition in Marguerite Duras is a transformational opportunity. This interest in the innovative potential of repeated acts, including speech-acts, links

Duras to modernist writers like Gertrude Stein. Self-knowledge is birthed in the conversational reenactment and reflection of daily experience between two female interlocutors. But unconstrained, noncompetitive communication between women about their options could not at that time be taken for granted in the absence of a feminist movement. It is therefore only in the work of women writers who write after feminism that such female relationships become integral to the plot and are even sustained over several novels.

In the work of these authors, the city represents the only possible site for such communication. The architectural historian Elizabeth Grosz argues for the importance of the city as a cultural, economic, and spatial matrix for the bodied subject. She writes: "The city is one of the crucial factors in the social production of (sexed) corporeality: the built environment provides the context and coordinates for most contemporary Western and, today, Eastern forms of the body, even for rural bodies . . . [if we consider 'the rural'] as the underside or raw material for urban development. . . . It is the condition and milieu in which corporeality is socially, sexually, and discursively produced."[14] Mindful of the subject's *interactive* relationship with the city matrix, we can investigate how the subject receives perceptions about her place in this power network, reacts to them with somatic speech, and finally transforms them into public verbal speech acts. The disjunctive speech acts by women within the city are parallel; subsequently, it is no wonder that a community is eventually formed as the knowledge of other alienated experiences is spread. Community is formed by increased verbalization, which inevitably seeks out its own interlocutors. Verbalizing on its own does not constitute innovative agency; nonetheless, it is a conscious activity that presupposes the give-and-take of a community and can be the germ of a communal agenda.

Grosz characterizes the city as "a complex and interactive network which links together, often in an unintegrated and de facto way, a number of disparate social activities, processes, and relations . . . brings together economic and informational flows, power networks, forms of displacement, management, and political organization".[15] The suburbs and the contemporary shopping mall are different from the city in that they are less accessible (a car is needed to reach or traverse them); moreover, they structure the individual's presence in their space more stringently. Because disjuncture is more readily apparent in the city, it can provoke contestations of the ways in which we live. According to Grosz, the city is "the site for the body's cultural saturation, its takeover and transformation by images, representational systems, the mass media and the arts—the place where the body is representationally reexplored, transformed, contested, reinscribed."[16] I believe that the image of this body is

14

essentially female: initially fought over as an exchange object, perhaps violated, but ultimately transcending its initially highly circumscribed bounds. The search for agency attains its focus in the city. First, the city is an emblem of deracination. Rhys's London and Duras's colonial city are capitals of empire; moreover, the protagonists move back and forth between center and periphery, capital and provincial town. Through a series of voluntary displacements, they gain insight into the constructedness of the city as the emblem of a particular kind of alienating social organization. This awareness of the constructedness of the city engenders a new desire for, and consciousness of, community. The formation of urban female communities is aided by the greater presence of single women in the public sphere. Their differences in age, class, and—in some cases—race become productive differences, that is, they are not erased or entirely ignored. It must, however, be noted as a caveat that the authors whose urban fiction I analyze do not explore radical difference, nor do they put center stage the lives of protagonists who are much different from themselves. Both the contemporary British writer Margaret Drabble and the East German author Monika Maron romanticize urban working-class areas and their denizens, a well-intentioned stance that barely conceals a certain condescension and its tendency to posit them as radically other. The protagonists of these latter two authors are therefore held back by inherited class and group prejudices that occasionally undercut their impulse towards social change.

Alienation and Spectatorship in Modernism versus Postmodernism

The Marxist critic Fredric Jameson gives voice to these qualms about the politics of urban space in his contention that postmodern architecture distorts and distends the spectator's perception of the cityscape and his own location within it by creating monolithic buildings that exist in "disjunction from the surrounding city."[17] According to Jameson, postmodernism "looks for breaks, for events rather than new worlds," "for shifts and irrevocable changes in the *representation* of things and of the way they change," and lastly, "it only clocks the variations themselves, and knows only too well that the contents are just more images."[18] This turning away from a content-based search for meaning results in an overprivileging of the surface and exteriority.

Although modernism was also interested in chronicling the new and registering alienation, Jameson radically opposed the modernist attitude to the new and to the postmodernist fascination with the *formal* aspects of change, an understanding of change that has become more vast in spatial terms but more shallow in philosophical terms. In opposition

15

to postmodernist theorists, I understand agency today as rooted in a political ethics of sociality that is content based and not primarily or exclusively image based. Like the postmodernists Jameson mentions, I do understand cultural life to be part of the commodity process. It is a socially manufactured construct, but, I also believe, it can consist of more than shared consumption processes engineered by marketing strategies. I do not see culture exclusively as an infinitely malleable *commodity* whose purpose it is to inspire "a prodigious exhilaration with the new order of things, a commodity rush, our representations of things tending to arouse an enthusiasm and a mood swing not necessarily inspired by the things themselves."[19] Even though the media in our televisual age often describes social life as manufactured out of newsbiteworthy events, I believe there is more political depth to social transactions. For example, when late twentieth-century feminist women authors write about exchange processes in urban space, they focus on local coalition building as an alternative strategy to bring about individual and communal transformation. Writers like Drabble and Maron and theorists like the French feminist philosopher Luce Irigaray still use utopia as a political term, they want to effect social transformation in real content-based terms. They imagine female subjects who approach their roles as transactors of exchanges with greater wariness than their male counterparts and who develop a dialogic concept of social participation.

The monumentality of postmodern architecture can have a profoundly alienating effect. It disallows agency, which I understand ideally—along with cultural theorist W. J. T. Mitchell—as "full economic participation in the public sphere by equal citizens."[20] The spatial distortion characteristic of postmodern urban architecture leads to the proliferation of seemingly autonomous miniature city-fortresses whose reflecting glass exteriors further disorient the individual human being by giving no clue to the interior use of the building. They even dissolve city space altogether because such miniature cities (malls, office towers) are no longer predicated on existing only in inner cities—they proliferate through urban sprawl to suburbs and the countryside. The place these spaces assign to the human body is merely to be part of a mass of bodies being transported on speeded-up people movers into and within the building cluster. The resulting loss of self-initiated individual mobility at a human pace is concomitant with spatial and cognitive disorientation. According to Jameson, the only forms individual participation in exchange processes can take under such alienating circumstances are a frenzied consumption of ever-new commodities—the pursuit of consumer trends to fit constantly new lifestyles—or a dazed touristic spectatorship of glossy surfaces and disembodied televisual images.

Both of these forms can produce a euphoria, but it is a euphoria of the diffused and transcended body, of images and surfaces, of a continuously new present. In the Calvinist strain that runs especially strongly through contemporary American public discourse about the body, the body is seen as an amorphous trap for free will that either needs to be disciplined or eschewed. Virtual-reality technologies as well as a commodity culture intent on selling hard, smooth surfaces allow the spectator/consumer to fantasize an escape from the limitations of his or her own imperfect body for a time or to regard the body as burdensome flesh that needs to be reshaped into a seemingly inviolable muscled and taut machine.

The feminist philosopher Susan Bordo argues compellingly in her recent *Unbearable Weight: Feminism, Western Culture, and the Body* that contemporary culture continually suggests to us that working on and reshaping our bodies is an expression of free will, creative agency, and individual choice, not a matter of systemic pressure to conform to normalizing practices.[21] Bordo advocates an alternative strategy of feminist consciousness-raising to allow for both systemic criticism and informed individual choice

> simply becoming *more conscious* is a tremendous achievement. (As Marx insisted, changes in consciousness are changes in life, and in a culture that counts on our remaining unconscious they are political as well.) Feminist cultural criticism cannot magically lift us into a transcendent realm of immunity to cultural images, but it ought to help guard against the feeling of comfortable oneness with culture and to foster a healthy skepticism about the pleasures and powers it offers.[22]

Bordo interprets the contemporary slender, taut female body ideal as so compelling to many women because women *themselves* may want to emphasize the nonreproductive functions of their bodies. More social prestige is accorded a person who overcomes the materiality of the body, transforming it into a tough, inviolable machine through body work. Body fat in the belly, thigh, and upper arm areas is feared as unsightly evidence of a flabby, bulging feminized body that in turn becomes symbolic of excessive desire, lack of self-control, a sedentary lifestyle, and so on, all of which connote limited upward mobility and opportunity for self-realization. "The quest for firm bodily margins"[23] betrays our current anxiety about the individual body's coherence and functionality in the perceptually distended space around it. Strict body management, it is hoped, will equal gaining control, detachment, and the physical stamina and energy needed to get through a workday. Its potentially self-liberatory impulses for women are overshadowed by the misery of internalized monitoring and dieting regimes, which occupy a good part of women's everyday life.

17

Female rebellion against the maternal feminized body is not original to contemporary Western culture: in the twenties, roughly equivalent to the period of modernism, the slender androgynous body of the *gamine* became a new standard. In the fiction of Jean Rhys, we can trace excessive self-monitoring against unsightly bulges in the wrong places (a belly swollen by pregnancy, the buttocks area in a too-short dress). The beauty regimes Rhys chronicles so bitterly isolate and almost enslave her female characters and prevent them from focusing their energies on the pursuit of emancipatory goals, such as professional skills, financial security, and self-esteem.

Even though Rhys is very sensitive to gender bias in ex-colonial societies, she never fully overcomes class bias. The author and her characters remain trapped in a love-hate relationship towards the ideal of the "lady." This fetish prevents systemic critique based on political categories such as race and class. Agency for Rhys can only come out of a radical sense of alienation from, and contempt for, social hypocrisy. She shows that men colonize women just as the British colonized "the natives." But she exhausts her emotional energy in lashing out against an exploitive system. Her characters rebel alone, and their verbal statements are not heard or given credence. Nonetheless, one can see the beginnings of subversive agency in the *somatic* language Rhys's protagonists speak. The hysterical body acts out the violent critique of colonialist practices.

One of the consequences of having a thinner body is increased mobility. For a woman, her mobility in public implies commodification. Her appearance in the urban marketplace invites the acquisitive gaze of male passers-by. In describing his urban peregrinations, Baudelaire would pause to wonder about this or that woman on the street—her background, possible destination, and sometimes the prospect of a liaison with him. For Baudelaire, it is a fleeting moment rife with erotic potential all the more mysterious for being unrealized. The members of the urban crowd are characterized by their mutual unknowability. Rhys's fascination with alienation and the urban crowd is not new, it can be traced at least as far back as Walter Benjamin's essay on Baudelaire. For Benjamin, the modern city becomes the space of production and of crowds of workers rushing about frenetically. The urban flâneur is an anachronism in that industrialized, regimented space because he stands for contemplation, independent means, leisurely pleasure-walking. Benjamin observes that "the man of leisure can indulge in the perambulations of the flâneur only if as such he is already out of place. He is as much out of place in an atmosphere of complete leisure as in the feverish turmoil of the city."[24] He occupies a unique privileged, albeit isolated, position and is quickly supplanted by the "man of the crowd" who makes fewer individual demands on public space and who seems indistinguishable from the mass. Benjamin is fascinated by modern mechanical reproduction technologies (e.g., like the camera and the movie), and he compares the pedestrian's immersion in the jostling urban crowd with the repeated "optic shocks" they produce in the viewer. His concern is that an independent critical consciousness can no longer be maintained because the urban dweller moves about and functions with reactive mechanical precision like an automaton. Experience, skill, and practice count for nothing and are replaced by drill, mindless repetition, and speed.

When we look at urban writing by women in late modernity, we find that their female characters come to the city to experience not only fragmentation and alienation, but also to begin to witness women fulfilling public roles in the workplace as managers rather than disenfranchised unskilled factory workers. They observe other women manipulating and controlling the traffic of urban consumption, they come into contact with female professionals who represent social status and economic power in the public sphere. Benjamin's flâneur had attained economic independence prior to entering the urban crowd, his sojourn in it is a temporary distraction of consuming images in carefully managed encounters, a staging of his leisured superiority to the crowd's frenetic pursuit of basic subsistence. As the archetypal figure of modernity, Benjamin's urban flâneur records modern life via his strolling and meandering through the city. Unlike the postmodern worker/consumer ferried between home, workplace, and temples of consumption, he sets the pace and itinerary of his perambulations. Benjamin still sees culture and the cultural critic as residually outside commodification processes. By contrast, Jameson argues that in postmodernity culture itself has become part of the marketplace. This means that culture is not exempt from commodification and that it cannot be a safe vantage point for systemic and potentially subversive criticism. Rather, resistance and systemic change can come from humans within the commodity exchange system who refuse their assigned roles as passive consumer/spectators.

Benjamin's flâneur epitomizes the cultural critic, whom he sees as having been replaced by the photographer and filmmaker as images of modern urban life. He is ambivalent about the evaluative dimension of their chronicles. Benjamin has a certain morbid fascination with the precision and speed of mechanical processes, but he does not see a possibility for critical evaluation of these urban phenomena. Beginning with Jean Rhys, women writers as critics of modernity redeem this critical consciousness. They stress the importance of cinema as providing examples of current gender roles to female audiences. For the female protagonists of Rhys's and Duras's texts, cinema plays a redemptive role, whereas for Benjamin, cinema exacerbates the freneticism of modern life.

The disenfranchisement women suffer coupled with their mobility

19

between the interstices of urban power nodes leads to a growing awareness of their condition, which in turn can provoke subversive agency. With the awareness of themselves as alienated subjects comes the desire to integrate and to define their place in a community of some sort. I believe that postmodern urban fiction by women writers explores the possibilities for female agency in the context of democratic social innovation. It is fueled by a desire to rethink what social practices would sustain and guarantee a pluralistic society. Its scope is more inclusive, its systemic critique reaches farther than that of their predecessors.

The flâneur comes to symbolize mobility and critical consciousness of social institutions and one's interactions with them. The female flâneur (flâneuse) however, wishes to remain less aloof from the crowd's daily concerns—they are hers, too. Women entering the city mimic someone who has power—the flâneur—just as the flâneur mimics someone who is marginalized. Their mimicking men who are mimicking women exemplifies a double remove from feminity as performance. They enter into the role of the flâneur with a profound awareness of gender. In freely circulating through urban space, they gain knowledge by overcoming the spatial barriers that had sequestered the middle-class woman from full participation in the public sphere.[25] Although Benjamin sees the flâneur as someone who preserves his observer status through the erection of spatial barriers, this voluntary distancing may skew his point of view. By shielding himself from close contact with the masses, the often stationary flâneur misses out on the reality of the crowd's experience. He is tempted to categorize them precipitately.

The female characters in these novels gravitate towards the ideal of the flâneuse, but they immediately realize its problematical nature as an ethical paradigm. Rather than looking up to the flâneuse as a lofty and insouciant figure, they recontextualize her as a role model. Female characters seek out movement and immersion in the mass as a kind of disguise that frees them to become observers. Their attention embraces the kind of people who had been anathematized for them: the prostitute in Rhys, the colonizer in Duras, the working class in Drabble, the intellectual in Maron's socialist Germany. The architectural historian Daphne Spain analyzes, "spatial segregation does more than create a physical distance; it also affects the distribution of knowledge women could use to change their position in society."[26] Change in women's roles occurs collectively, women become politicized subjects as they begin to take up public space actively. As they move through the city, they seem to look for identification with others rather than acute differentiation, which helps them build coalitions to effect local change. In the case of Drabble's and Maron's novels, these female coalitions shift but last over time, providing the stability otherwise missing in urban flow. These authors and their characters come to the realization that mere spectatorship or voyeurism cannot provide the basis for such social affiliations. By cutting across class and cultural lines, gender emerges as the driving force behind agency.

Recent critics of urban fiction follow in Benjamin's footsteps by describing the city as the paradigmatic site of late modern alienation. For instance, William Sharpe and Leonard Wallock in their anthology *Visions of the Modern City* claim that the contemporary city is experienced as decentered and confusing in the multiplicity of its signs.[27] They especially see American fiction of the eighties as depicting a transient city culture, focused, on the one hand, on constantly shifting delocalized hot spots for consumerism and, on the other hand, on its byproducts: the urban junkyard, abandoned spaces, used-up derelicts.[28] In the postmodern urban landscape, spectatorship has displaced agency: ubiquitous televised images, the electronic interface, mediate all human contact. Speeded-up simulated realities displace each other in quick succession and create a saturated and ever-present environment in which history is nonexistent. This surfeit of stimuli inscribes the individual as a reflex consumer blindly struggling to meet externally posited needs. Although some of the recent texts I analyze also paint the city as an apocalyptic battleground—for instance, Margaret Drabble's London in *The Radiant Way* (1987) or the East German writer Monika Maron's Berlin in *The Defector* and *Silent Close 6*—it is significant that they do not subscribe to an unmitigatedly bleak view of the city's potential for renewal. The successfully integrated characters in city culture tend to be female, part of a network of either very similarly educated and politically left-oriented women friends (Drabble's triad of Alix, Liz, and Esther) or they tend to be vastly disparate male and female characters who are united in their quest for escape from the strictures of an oppressive urban political apparatus, such as the characters of Rosalind, Martha, Klärchen, Bruno, and the Count in Maron's *The Defector* (*Die Überläuferin*) (1986) or Rosalind, Thekla, and Bruno in her *Silent Close 6* (*Stille Zeile 6*) (1991).

Women as agents especially risk omission in postmodern representations of the city as the site of consumption. In a culture that emphasizes surfacity and constructs the woman's physical presence as largely ornamental, female roles appear limited to being a consumer or, worse, a mere accessory to, or object of, male consumption. The consumer's immersion in a hyperreality made up of speeded-up image sequences evoking ever-new present moments further precludes historical consciousness. There will be no perception of distance or interiority, either towards the body or the world at large. Jameson argues that under these circumstances, any attempt to organize external reality is given up, any cognitive mapping of one's own location via systemic analysis of sociopolitical processes becomes impossible and undesirable.

21

All of this, however, differs from agency that requires as one of its prerequisites the formation of an individual critical consciousness. Attaining critical consciousness has become far more difficult in postmodernity than it was in modernity. Modernist writers like Rhys were quick to recognize and express alienation; in today's more globalized and dispersed economic network of interdependence and interpenetration, many of us are unable to recognize alienation or commodification when and where they occur. Moreover, commodity circulation in modernity followed simpler paths that could be observed by studying the links between colonies and colonial powers or by analyzing technical innovations, such as photography and filmmaking, and capitalist conversion processes were less refined than today.

For instance, in the writings of Rhys and Duras, the marginalized subject (Rhys's Creole female protagonist who journeys back to the colonial homecountry or Duras's white, impoverished middle-class female protagonist at the lowest end of the French colonial hierarchy in Indochina) is more easily able to recognize the fact and sources of its commodification. The exchange of commodities in late colonialist societies like those Rhys and Duras describe progressed more crudely, exploitation and commodification became more palpably obvious to its victims because, for instance, the conversion of raw commodities from the colonies into industrial products in the home country was a virtually self-evident process, more discernible than the interconnected and proliferated global network of industry and technology conglomerates that are responsible for postmodernism. In Drabble's writing of the eighties, London has decayed into a postmodern urban wasteland dissected by motorways, but the culprits are hard to make out. The policies of the Thatcher government, ruthless real estate speculators, a complacent white middle class who simply retrenches itself in the suburbs, all contribute to, but by no means exhaustively account for, the erosion of community that Drabble decries. Nor are the links between these factors explored. In Maron's fiction about late-stage Socialist Berlin, its inhabitants initially feel paralyzed and cut off from each other by government surveillance without being able to name the sources of their repression. Josefa and Rosalind are so caught up in alienating daily work routines that they only begin to reflect when these routines are interrupted by an accident. Nonetheless, the consequences of female agency in the work of these two contemporary writers are more far-reaching than in the work of Rhys and Duras. Agency leads to female coalition building that enables a shared systemic critique, and this in turn fosters collective acts of civil disobedience against undemocratic social practice. Such local political involvement may attempt to undo the creation of, and subsequent marginalization of, an underclass in the Thatcher era in an effort to reintegrate them into social discourse—Drabble's examples are prison inmates, a young runaway woman, a murderer, the elderly, the mentally ill. Or, in Maron's work acts of civil disobedience are directed against Stalinist practices that destroyed freedom of speech, falsified history by selective rewriting, limited citizens' freedom to travel and associate with others who were deemed enemies of the state. Maron's protagonists successfully confront not only the perpetrators, but also a larger audience, with the true state of affairs in their society: They attack environmental pollution and its cover-up, they point out the victimization of individuals whose careers are ruined by arbitrary political labeling, they criticize the militarization of everyday life and the creation of a privileged elite of Stalinist functionaries. Even though these truths are more difficult to discern in the postmodern state than female commodification and the exploitation of the colonized were in earlier times, they can still be recognized; furthermore, they are critical to any sustained attempt at social inclusion and innovation. The political awareness and involvement shown by Drabble's and Maron's female coalitions is broader based, more effective, and even surpasses both the indictment of female commodification in Rhys's work as well as the eventual rejection of female commodity status through the manipulation of its parameters in Duras's work.

There is a certain progression from Rhys to Maron, a movement from isolated acts of rebellion towards an activist collective agency for social innovation and democratization. Rhys's protagonists recognize their victimization as exchange objects between men but are still so implicated in disciplinary body regimes that they cannot break free from commodification practices. Their energy for rebellion exhausts itself in brief furious physical and verbal lashing out. Duras's protagonist Suzanne learns to play with the concept of women as exchange objects by taking over her own marketing without ever having to give herself up. Through trial and error and through mimicking the male seeker role, she learns to parody and ultimately opt out of the commodification of women, choosing to leave the exploitive colonial society. Drabble's protagonists have an advantage over those of Rhys and Duras because they are better educated and supported by shared middle-class values and a liberal feminist movement. They are limited in their coalition building, however, by their sharing a particular class and generational identity. They alternatively romanticize the working class as in need of redemption and demonize it as ungratefully reluctant to be redeemed. In Drabble's work we move towards a moral agenda for social justice, but the characters for long stretches feel alienated from public life and political processes, and they labor under a class bias similar to that of Rhys's protagonists. Finally, in Maron's work, we find female protagonists who form alliances across age and class lines and who confront representatives of a repressive socialist regime directly. They struggle to formulate their resistance both imaginatively and actively. They reclaim personal and collective memory by unwriting and analyzing the falsification of history that Stalinist politicians and party functionaries committed. They reach a dialogic understanding of human connection in the present and the connection of places and events in historical time and space that enables them to attain a more informed perspective on self and community, which in turn is the basis for effective agency.

Resistance Strategies and the Urban Underground

In analyzing the urban fiction of Rhys and Duras, Drabble and Maron, I employ a double theoretical focus: I use recent psychoanalytic research into female identity formation as well as anthropological theories about social ritual. In the Duras chapter, for instance, I contrast gift economies to the capitalist economic cycle of production–accumulation–circulation, and I use the Kwakiutl potlatch ritual as an example of women participating actively in their own marketing to acquire social prestige. On the one hand, I analyze commodification and how public spaces affect female identity formation, on the other hand, I investigate embodied living for women and the positive and negative aspects of that. New anthropological research on exchange rituals parallels the findings of recent psychoanalytic research on identity formation; both describe self-in-society as processual and establishing itself in the interplay of spatial movements and transactions. Commodities and gifts become important mediators in expressing self-in-society. I do not believe that the subject's relationship to the modern city is fully expressed by, or limited to, its transactions as a consumer. Rather, I reinvestigate the more flexible processual restructuring of female consumer roles that occurs by means of mimicking, parody, trial and error, and through the conversion of commodities into gifts; all of these repositionings are techniques female consumers learn on urban ground that help to foster a sense of agency and interconnectedness in social life.

Good examples of mimicry and parody as sources of a social critique of women's place are Suzanne's wanderings in the colonial city. In moving back and forth freely between the two segregated spaces of the "upper" city of the whites and the "lower" city of the natives, Suzanne obtains a critical awareness of colonialist exploitation. She enters into the role of the flâneuse in borrowed "used" clothes—the hotel owner's daughter lends her a garishly colored dress, her mother lends her an old scuffed handbag. She becomes gradually aware that her strange outfit attracts stares—the residents of the upper city do not know what to make of a young woman looking like a mix of prostitute and lady. Although she attempts to mimic city chic through her dress choices, Suzanne unwit-

24

tingly creates a parody of the urban codes that distinguish women accordingly to their class and social function. She further refuses to stay in the company of men—her brother Joseph, who might ordinarily act as her chaperone, leaves her to her own devices, and she rejects her former suitor M. Jo. Aided by her playful shifting identifications with male and female screen icons in the city cinemas, Suzanne gradually develops a defiant pride in her flânerie. She transgresses traditional class and gender barriers and chooses spatial mobility as her means of fostering a critical awareness of herself as a female subject.

In categorizing city spaces in the work of Rhys and Duras, Drabble and Maron, I distinguish three types of cities—the labyrinthine colonial city in Duras and Rhys, the city as palimpsest in Drabble's London and to some extent Maron's Berlin, and the divided city in which two political systems oppose each other, sharing a common but submerged city past. The three types of city spaces all reflect more or less stringently organized hierarchical societies, and I am interested in the factors that allow female subjectivity and agency to be established despite these unequal conditions. With the exception of Rhys's London and Paris, these cities all occupy tenuous border spaces, either because of their geographical location in a colony far removed from the mother country (Duras's fictional Kamlong and Saigon); or through their highly visible splitting into two opposing political halves, near the border of one country and on the vulnerable perpihery of the other (Maron's Berlin); or because of their characterization as a multiethnic battleground (Drabble's London). The precariousness of their existence as cities seems to facilitate a shift in the female characters from mute and trapped exchange objects to women who become mobile and vocal agents in the exchange, and who, in the novels of Drabble, Maron, and to some extent in those of Duras, forge subversive social relationships with each other.

Duras takes a structural approach to the issue of commodification and sees it as part of a system she is outside of. Rhys feels compelled to tell female commodification anecdotally by creating a specific scenario of exploitation over and over again. Duras tells it structurally, from the critical perspective of the anthropologist studying a tribe among whom she once belonged, thus opening up the structure for subversion. Rhys privileges the city as symbolic center, Duras does not. Whereas Rhys and Duras present the city primarily as a site of commodification and individual disintegration, Drabble and Maron tend to view the city as a place of educational opportunity for their female characters. They also claim the city as an appropriate habitat for their politicized female subjects, but remain attentive to its alienating, even destructive potential. By contrast, Rhys's protagonists, and to a lesser extent Duras's female characters, still feel themselves to be trespassers on alien ground. They experience city

25

space as a closed system, that, in the case of Duras's Suzanne, they have to leave behind for an 'other' city of greater possibility.

Commodification and Transitional Female Roles in Jean Rhys

In the case of Rhys's characters, escape from the city's commodifying practices becomes virtually impossible because they have internalized its precepts. Although her characters remain trapped in a Darwinian urban struggle for survival through adaptation to the exploitive scheme, Rhys the author/narrator gains emotional distance from, and control over, her own status as a victimized female by projecting out her own experiences onto younger fictional selves. I compare colonial society and its disciplinary effects on the female child in Rhys's fragmentary autobiography *Smile Please: An Unfinished Autobiography* (1979) with the more overtly fictionalized form of these experiences in *Voyage in the Dark* (written in 1924 but published a decade later), *After Leaving Mr. Mackenzie* (1930), and *Good Morning, Midnight* (1939).

As Michel Foucault has shown in *Discipline and Punish: The Birth of the Prison* (1977)—a genealogy of carceral institutions in France—body regimes are linked to constant surveillance, at first by others, later practiced as self-monitoring. It is the mother who first teaches bodily control in the home and who—in the case of Rhys and her mother, herself a product of a restrictive upbringing—is experienced by her daughter as both aloof and severe. Rhys as an author who "mothers" fictional daughters reproduces that relationship because she does not let her daughters grow into full subjecthood. They manage to perform brief transgressive gestures to protest their commodification, but then their rebellion collapses—it never has enough force to propel them beyond. The somewhat sadistic repetition of these scenarios maintains the author's feeling of power; she indicts male colonialism of the female body while maintain a similarly exploitive hold over her characters. Narrating female commodification provides a release, but it remains a compensatory practice for the author because she cannot shake off class and gender biases, despite rebelling against class and gender prejudice in her writing. I investigate the relationship between author and female character with the help of Judith Kegan Gardiner's concept of empathy[29] and Anthony Giddens's concept of constituting the self through narrative.[30]

Rhys documents the limitations as well as the opportunities for class change to be found in city life between the two wars. I analyze the subversive potential of laughter and hysterical speech as expressions of dissatisfaction with female commodification in *Voyage* and *Mr. Mackenzie*. The city brings the female newcomer into contact with women in new, no longer wholly traditional roles; it is the site of activity for the professional woman, such as nurse Wyatt in *Mr. Mackenzie*, the masseuse and manicurist Ethel Matthews in *Voyage*, or the portrait painter for whom Julia sits in *Mr. Mackenzie*. Less socially respectable are professional prostitutes like Laurie and Germaine who expose commodification's pretenses and use femininity in dress, hairstyle, and speech consciously as masquerade to attract a wider range of clientele. They exemplify a more parodic form of what Judith Butler terms "gender as performance." They are able to manipulate their appearance and thus enhance their value as a commodity, but they are unable to transcend the status of a commodity. They provide learning models for the naive female newcomer to the city insofar as they expose the machinery of exploitation, but the solidarity they provide in the Darwinian struggle for economic survival is limited.

The city makes available mass-produced goods to the female consumer, giving her the illusion that she may raise her status by consuming the right products—whether it is a cream to make the neck more voluptuous, a new dress, or make-up. The accessibility of secondhand clothing gives even the poorer woman the opportunity to disguise herself as a "lady"—all of Rhys's female characters are caught up in the obsessive monitoring of their appearance, they were taught to aspire to ladyhood as the pinnacle of female existence, and they will pursue it unhappily but determinedly as long as they live. The only woman who takes herself out of the competition for physical femininity and daintiness is the lesbian, but even she chooses a "ladylike" woman as her mate. Rhys can only figure their relationship as vampiric on pecuniary motives—Norah and Wyatt form a couple not out of love, it seems, but to exclude and deny the financial and emotional demands of Julia.

I turn to the colonial background of Dominica for an analysis of the zombie as a representative metaphor of the socially silenced body whose memory has been erased as well as of the condition of being trapped inside a (female) body that one does not own. Vodoun beliefs about identity need to be contrasted with modern Western concepts of identity because they incorporate the body in a different way. Rhys locates the process of zombification in the city because the city space is where the body becomes possessed, its boundaries violated. The female body becomes a symbol of contagion, and can only react against this perception by speaking somatically. The epidermalizing of female experience as Iris Marion Young calls it, is a sign of a society in transition, with a dominant minority who feels its hold on power threatened, and therefore resorts to scapegoating.[31] I analyze this process in the context of British society in the aftermath of World War I. As an urban institution, cinema's innovative power lies in presenting female spectacles to the female gaze. In this context, I analyze the urban economy of seeing and being seen as a form of social recognition and control. Finally, I evaluate somatic speech as a more effective—thought still highly problematic—means of protest than verbal expression for Rhys's female characters. Rhys describes the city as the paradigmatic site where female imprisonment in commodifying practices is made public, and she challenges her readers to speak out against these practices where her characters cannot.

Transformation via Mimicry and Gifting in Marguerite Duras

In my second chapter, I investigate the possibilities for female social innovation and self-expression by referring to Marcel Mauss's theory of the gift and the potlatch; then I go on to more recent anthropological theories about exchange processes, such as Chris Gregory's contrasting of gift and commodity exchanges and Sherry Ortner's emphasis on prestige structures, which are produced through the interplay between centrifugal and centripetal processes. The character Suzanne in *The Seawall* actively takes on a centripetal role when she decides to "pull in" M. Jo into her family. She raises her family's prestige, and this fosters a sense of personal agency for her. I analyze how far permeable borders or walls condition a more flexible concept of the self in space, ultimately allowing for play with solid obstacles/objects. Suzanne learns from the breakdown of the family's economic enterprise—the building of a seawall to cultivate farm-land and extract profit from it—that she has to be more distrustful of the colonialist elite than her mother. She begins to manipulate as a sort of game her own status as an exchange object even before she arrives in the colonial capital. The border zone in which the family ekes out a living is both a space in which public and private areas merge, often destructively, as well as a place where rhythms of nature (the periodic flooding by the sea, the epidemic deaths of the native children) disturb cultural commerce (parceling off land, cultivating it, and transporting its products away on the road between the colonial port city and the capital). These experiences allow the female protagonist to recognize the constructed-ness of the colonial enterprise, so that on entering the colonial city, she quickly comes to understand its artificiality, corruption, and ephemerality, despite its presentation as an immutable sepulchre.

The existence of a different city—Paris—to which the mother dreams of returning holds out a vision of a better urban reality. The older brother, Joseph, serves as a role model for his sister because he verbalizes his belief in change and then translates his desire for change into action. In addition, Suzanne forms a bond of friendship with Carmen, the brothel keeper, whom she imitates for a time, just as she had imitated her brother and certain behaviors of her suitor M. Jo. I argue that mirroring the self in others breaks the familial bonds of sameness and contiguity. An economy of sound and hearing counteracts the paralyzing effects of a purely visual economy that forms a large part of city culture; we already witnessed this in Rhys's cities. Narcissistic desire needs to be voiced for the self by an other in order to set the subject free from the specular gaze. Instead of the mother's strategies for mediating alterity through appropriation and incorporation, Joseph and Suzanne use distancing and recontextualizing practices. At first they learn to manipulate objects in space in this way, later they apply these strategies in an abstract sense. The record player and the diamond ring are both bridge objects, around which a vision of urban culture can be fashioned. I analyze the spatial and racial segregation of the colonial city into an upper and lower city. By virtue of her special status as not firmly belonging in either half, Suzanne circulates freely between the two. Psychoanalytic research into identity formation suggests that identity is constituted in the play of spatial stabilization and destabilization. Suzanne becomes a flâneuse and appropriates the street for herself; this act is fraught with anxiety and public censure, but she repeats it nonetheless. Her outings become focused on trips to the upper city's cinemas, where she immerses herself, blissfully at first, in Hollywood films whose endings depict heterosexual contact as a vampiric merging in a fade-out on the kissing couple. Suzanne takes control of her sexuality by refusing to give over her body to M. Jo. She also starts to use short assertive bursts of speech quite clearly copied from the film scenes. Her final decision to leave the city and to leave the plain as well is announced in the words, "Je pars, je ne peux pas faire autrement" ("I am leaving, I can't do anything else"). These words have a cinematic ring to them: Suzanne partly sees her life as an unfolding melodrama, but it is the terse, action-based script of a Western she is following, playing the male lead, the one who announces in determined tones that it is both his duty and his choice not to settle down but to embark on further adventures.

The city, even though it is tainted and ambivalent just as cinematic consumption is, provides the imaginative model for personal transformation through forward movement. In *Mr. Mackenzie* the female protagonist also listens to a theatrical voice that urges her to leave, to "leave without looking back," but by contrast that voice is a female voice expressing a warning rather than encouragement. The voice of the unseen female singer seems to convey maudlin nostalgia and fear of the unknown rather than a promise for change through movement, and this is where the attitudes of Rhys and Duras differ markedly. Whereas Rhys envisions the city as a prison house from which there is no escape, Duras sees the city as a theater of experimentation, an educational stage the female protagonist passes through.

29

Liminoid Urban Spaces and Palimpsestic Selves in Margaret Drabble

In the fiction of the contemporary British writer Margaret Drabble, the city functions as a place of educational opportunity for women. Typically, her protagonists travel from the margins to the center to escape a confining family in a northern suburb or small town. Clara Maugham in *Jerusalem the Golden* (1967) is a good example of Drabble's belief in the stimulating properties of city culture: she comes to London on a scholarship, and the city affords her intellectual freedom and brings her into contact with people from all levels of society, thus allowing her to test various affiliations and observe varied professionally successful women against which to orient her own quest. The greatest difference we notice between Drabble's female characters and those of Rhys and Duras is that they work hard at a professional skill—they get stipends, awards, or degrees in subjects that must, however, still be considered part of the traditionally female areas of education and caretaking: they become literature and language teachers like Clara; or later like Alix Bowen in *The Radiant Way* (1987); or art historians like Esther Breuer in the same novel; or social workers like Evelyn Stennet in *The Middle Ground* (1980) and Alix in *A Natural Curiosity* (1989); they also become archaeologists like Frances Wingate in *The Realms of Gold* (1975); psychiatrists (Sigmund Freud likened his work to archaeology) like Liz Headleand, one of three central female characters in the most recent set of novels—*Radiant Way, Natural Curiosity,* and *The Gates of Ivory* (1992); or they become journalists for a women's magazine (a kind of archaeology of the daily life of women) like Kate Armstrong in *Middle Ground*. Many of Drabble's plots have an archaeological bent to them: in *Gates of Ivory,* Liz reconstructs the fate of her vanished friend, in *Middle Ground,* Kate makes a documentary about the lives of her high school classmates, in *Natural Curiosity,* Alix investigates the roots of a murderer's trauma—to name but a few.

Drabble's unfailing belief in the legibility of city life as a whole and the individual life as produced by this whole within its testifies to her humanistic values. She maintains that piecing together clues about an individual is a healing activity, that nonfunctional members must be reintegrated through some form of social work performed for them by her female professionals. This may seem reminiscent of the attitude of nineteenth-century male writers who used female subjectivity as the arena in which both conflicts of male subjectivity were debated and male quests for agency were redeemed,[32] but Drabble's protagonists practice their ethic of care on both male and female victims of the urban struggle for survival, and they do it not only in their roles as women friends or mothers, but also as professionals. Nonetheless, it is disturbing that over the past twenty years, Drabble does not see a wider range of professional options for women gradually opening up in the city. The majority of her characters remain teachers or healers of the psyche. Of course, these professions are well suited to the hortatory mission of Drabble's narratives. Drabble firmly espouses a Rousseauian doctrine of human perfectibility, but, unlike Rousseau, she locates this educational and transformational process in the protean city. I use Victor Turner's concepts of liminal and liminoid spaces in social ritual to describe the regenerative and transgressive properties of Drabble's city spaces: houses, squares, pubs, greens, sewers, "the companionable gutter," as Drabble lyrically names it in *Jerusalem*.

From the eighties onwards, I note a pessimistic trend in Drabble's urban fiction, which is due to her critique of Thatcherism: urban policies that emphasize gentrification and big-business growth that leads to inner-city redevelopment—the building of monolithic housing blocks and access roads, the shrinking of liminoid space accessible to all, wealthy and poor alike. Hence the conversion of public into private space and, in good Rousseauian fashion, private space for exclusive use by one person or group is termed the root of social ills. Drabble increasingly portrays inner-city blight, an apocalyptic wasteland in which the criminal, the old, and minorities are left stranded. The middle class from which most of Drabble's central characters hail, leave London altogether or retreat inside their houses and apartments. She takes care though, to characterize this interiorization as temporary, a fallow period enforced by political circumstance in which the female characters regain strength for their social task. The imperative for social betterment through education and reform remains unchanged; Drabble is not in favor of labor strikes, aggressive graffiti, or postmodern simulation as means of social protest. She sees them as leading to social breakdown. Her female characters always toil diligently at their healing professions even in the face of an urban hell, because they can still recover a vision of the city as the "heavenly city."

The aging and medicalized female body becomes conflated with the sick city. The body is violently fragmented and provokes horror, as the female murder victim's cut-off head does in *Radiant Way*. But the analytic and compassionate gaze of female healer figures restores its unity-in-time, even if it is powerless to remember the physical object.

Because their own experience of/in the city has changed and continues to change over time and because they have an active memory of the city's history as well as their own life history, Drabble's women are sensitive to the palimpsestic composition of both. Drabble allows them an overview of the changing city, shifting from the subversive view from

31

below, from the city sewer in the earlier texts to the distancing and controlling bird's-eye view in *Middle Ground,* and finally to a panoramic view from the perspective of the flâneuse rediscovering and repossessing her city by looking at London and the Thames from a bridge in *Gates of Ivory.* This new flexible and inclusive vision indicates a renewed faith in the city as a powerful catalyst for social innovation and individual redemption. I analyze how Drabble parallels that movement in opening up the narrative to include multiple perspectives and plots simultaneously.

In following the progress of three interconnected female lives over time, Drabble supplies us with a genealogy of female identity as it is defined and reoriented in the British city over the last two decades. In analyzing the bonds of friendship that women form with each other in Drabble's novels, I outline the ways in which they are able to sidestep confining hierarchies and Darwinian struggles for the survival of the fittest. I think this interpretation to a discussion of psychoanalytic research into female identity formation, which indicates that women's concepts of identity depend less on subject-object splitting and more on self-in-relationship and the collective. Drabble's female characters are fully cognizant of the destructive or destabilizing potential of the city, but they counter it with introspection to refocus their ambitions, and they share "women's talk": fluid, inclusive, adaptable to change. The river replaces the sewer as the author's privileged urban symbol: as it flows and adapts to provide a habitat to the river birds, so will the city and its inhabitants last through their present urban crisis.

Surveillance and Embodied Resistance in Monika Maron

Like Drabble, the East German writer Monika Maron undertakes a sweeping critique of her government's policies of compartmentalization and restriction as they affect urban life in the late seventies and the eighties, leading to the popular uprising that helped undo the German Democratic Republic (GDR) and the Honecker regime in 1989. Her female characters are a journalist, a historian, and a writer—all chroniclers of the political relevance of daily events in the present or the past. First, I analyze how disciplinary practices in the public sphere, the workplace, and the street produce a Foucauldian subject. Then, I analyze how subversive insights into the functioning of Foucauldian surveillance machinery are won through female mobility paired with observation. In *Flugasche* (1981), Maron's first novel, the journalist Josefa Nadler travels on assignment between the capital Berlin and the fictional southern industrial city of B. (standing for the real Bitterfeld), with its sad claim to notoriety as "the most polluted city in Europe." Even this limited but repeated shuttling between the two B's—two urban destinations of such different aspect—produces critical consciousness. Josefa decides to write the truth about B. and opts for political engagement. After her engagement in city politics fails, she is disciplined and excluded from membership in the Socialist party. Maron criticizes both the naive faith of the citizen in her society and society's correct functioning for the benefit of all. Josefa reacts too unimaginatively to the state's power by setting her moral standards and her good intentions against it. She withdraws into childlike dependency and refuses to function socially. Rosalind, the historian who is the main protagonist of Maron's subsequent city novels, starts out in Josefa's place—only it is she (or rather her rebellious body) who determines her own exclusion. Her legs refuse to function, so that she is forced to sit quietly at home and contemplate her deadening situation at work in the historical archives, her depleted personal life, her stunted poetic and emotional sensibilities.

In *Stille Zeile 6* (1991) Rosalind once again begins by choosing the contemplative life, but seeks out dialogue with a retired party functionary, thus once again addressing her complaints to those whom she holds responsible for her deprivations. This time her strategy of opposition is more focused and her criticisms more embittered, whereas her male interlocutor is weakened by age and disability. Rosalind triumphs in an Oedipal struggle by "killing the Father," removing the party's insidious hold on her, and extracting retribution for another. I analyze what factors sustain this rebellion in the face of comprehensive surveillance mechanisms. One factor is the latent but recoverable potential of the city's palimpsestic history. Another is the search for female alter ego figures who mirror and complement the subversive desires of the self. Whereas Josefa imagines flying over the city and escaping from it, Rosalind seeks out subversive liminoid pockets in its most basic structure: streets and rivers can be reconnected in the imagination because their counterparts or continuations still exist on the other side of the Wall. The forbidden Western half of the city functions as a historical and actual memento of the constructedness of the heavily fortified and seemingly so-entrenched one in the East. Of course, the whole city can only be visited in the imagination through acts of historical reconstruction, but that is after all, Rosalind's profession. In a sense, Maron shows her exercising her profession for her own benefit, not that of the state—thinking her way out of the impasses and obstacles deliberately created by a police state to contain and suppress individual initiative. Maron symbolizes the administrative apparatus as a defective body, describing its public buildings as devouring mouths when seen frontally, but as internally blocked and nonfunctional bodies when observed from the back or from the underside.

In establishing private links to other women, Rosalind further mobilizes her defense network. Together, these women create a subversive interior reality in which they rediscover what matters to them personally, teach each other new skills, and affirm the value of painting and music as alternative expressive languages. To overcome the hold of the inner censor, Maron uses fantasy and surrealist imagery. She also conceives of the endangered self resisting surveillance and incarceration by multiplying itself into several selves. In *The Defector,* Maron supports Rosalind's growing critical consciousness with alter ego figures—Martha the poet and Claire the unruly body, both of whom create disturbances of the public order.

As the Drabble's texts, the wounds that social control mechanisms inflict are rendered visible on the female body. Maron's texts abound with paralyzed, decaying, and scarred bodies. She invokes literary symbols of demonic automatization—the *golem* and Frankenstein. Against state intervention into the body, she sets a submerged secret language erupting out of the body's interior in elliptic spurts. Introspection and interiorization strengthen the locus of subversive speech, which like the old city plan is only covered over, not erased. Maron locates it in *Heimlichkeit* (secrecy; literally, the essence of home), and before it can make itself heard in public, it has to establish a felt sense of being at home in the self. In her most recent novel, Maron chooses the *Antigone* as a model for civic disobedience. Rosalind ultimately defends not only her own life against a tyrant, but also that of a brother figure. Maron's protagonists all use the city as a battleground with depersonalizing socialist institutions. It allows them to recover a sense of interconnectedness because underlying the walls, barricades, channels, boxes, and holes built as labyrinthine traps for the individual moving about on its surface are traces of the buried city—a different and antecedent order where other laws held sway. A return to the subterranean city therefore entails once again an archaeological project, setting free desires that lay dormant, bonding with those who have been released from a mechanistically conceived productivity in the socialist collective. In the end, she cannot free herself completely from the past in which she herself was instrumentalized as part of the socialist collective: This indebtedness is symbolized by the unwanted gift that returns to Rosalind at the conclusion of *Stille Zeile 6:* The biography of the socialist leader that she had typed for him as merely mechanical labor now comes back to her in the form of a bequest. Like Suzanne in *The Seawall,* Rosalind will have to recontextualize this object—to integrate it into her life somehow until it has lost its harmful power. She chooses to bury it under papers in her bookshelves, but Maron implies that she will open it and reread it at a later point. In any case, the female subject need not completely separate herself from what is now extraneous to her, she maintains distance to the object, but does not repudiate it entirely because it has formed part of her past.

From Dissent to a Dialogics of Self-in-Society in Contemporary Political Theory

Women are perhaps more alert to the alienating consequences of postmodern discourse about the body than men because as a group they have been targeted longer by disciplinary practices. Innovation can come from local coalitions among women who form specific interest groups to effect local change. Luce Irigaray theorizes agency in nonhegemonic terms. She develops an argument for self-in-dialogue with society that relies on an ethic of nurturance and mutual respect rather than an exploitive economics of market value and commodity fetishism. Her dialogic theories about agency allow us to break free from our specular fixation and investment in surfaces. Irigaray rethinks the relationship between nature and culture as well as man and woman as nonhierarchical and irreducible to a single category. This more inclusive restructured concept allows us to envision agency as transformative and ethically necessary for humans in postmodernity and beyond, but it does not necessarily call for the creation of a distinct or closed community of like-minded citizens. The drift towards hegemony is latent in all attempts at community building.

Irigaray's concept of debate is informed by her belief in dialogue and plurivocality. I contrast her view of identity and social innovation with that of the American political scientist William Connolly. His concept of identity betrays a nostalgia for a unitary, essential self, and he sees debate as mortal combat between opposing factions. The modern city is the paradigmatic ground for such encounters. In my analysis of the urban fiction of Rhys and Duras, Drabble and Maron, I show how these writers move from contestation to dialogue with the social scripts for women in public life.

Maron's characters are rooted in the Antigone, one of the earliest archetypes of female agency and civil disobedience in a hierarchical society. The French feminist critic Luce Irigaray uses the *Antigone* as a model for the courageous contestation of restrictive social laws, for opening them up to debate. Antigone's act of charity towards her brother's body arises out of a culture of difference. She invokes divine law anterior to, and outlasting, the edict issued by Creon as the new law of the city. Divine law, however, is not natural law: Its precepts are transmitted and practiced in society—to uphold these precepts is cultural work. When Antigone appeals to divine law, therefore, she performs a cultural act, not

35

a return to an essential nature. She justifies her deed to Creon by speaking publicly and assertively:

> I dared.
> It was not God's proclamation. That final Justice
> That rules the world below makes no such laws.
>
> Your edict, King, was strong,
> But all your strength is weakness itself against
> The immortal unrecorded laws of God.
> They are not merely now: they were, and shall be,
> Operative for ever, beyond man utterly.
>
> I knew I must die, even without your decree: I am only
>   mortal. . . .
>
> .   .   .   .
>
> This death of mine is of no importance; but if I had left my
>   brother
> Lying in death unburied, I should have suffered.
> Now I do not.[33]

Antigone appeals to the people of the city, she justifies her act in dialogue without abandoning her subjectivity, contrary to Creon who sees his rule threatened by dialogue because he wants to rule alone and feels insecure in his claim. He speaks to his son Haimon, his designated successor, but who is also Antigone's fiancé. When he speaks, he betrays his deafness to public dialogue:

> If I permit my own family to rebel,
> How shall I earn the world's obedience?
> Show me the man who keeps his house in hand,
> He's fit for public authority.
>
> .   .   .   .
>
> Whoever is chosen to govern should be obeyed—
> Must be obeyed, in all things, great and small,
> Just and unjust! O Haimon,
> The man who knows to obey, and that man only,
> Knows how to give commands when the time comes.
>
> .   .   .   .
>
> [Creon:] Then she is not a criminal?
> [Haimon:] The city would deny it, to a man.
> C: And the City proposes to teach me how to rule?
> H: Ah. Who is it that's talking like a boy now?
> C: My voice is the one giving orders in this city.

36

> H: It is no city if it takes orders from one voice.
> C: The State is the King!
> H: Yes, if the State is a desert.[34]

The very essence of the Greek city is its plurality of voices, its constitution through public dialogue.[35] Public authority should be exercised by all, the king should request others' advice in a crisis pertaining to the polis, but he posits himself as an absolute ruler, transforming the city into a desert, where human life is at risk. Antigone's punishment for speaking out is to be buried alive underground in a remote place; Creon orders her forcible removal from the public sphere to foreclose the possibility of further contestation through dialogue.

In a recent essay, "Droits et devoirs civiles pour les deux sexes" (Rights and Civic Duties for the Two Sexes), Luce Irigaray reclaims Antigone as a model for civic identity. She links her to a maternal law that concerns itself with cosmic order and the preservation of nature as integral aspects of public life: "Respecter la généalogie maternelle suppose de prendre soin des corps vivants engendrés par la mère, de les inhumer s'ils sont morts, de ne pas préférer l'aîné au benjamin (soit Étéocle à Polynice), ni le fils à la fille." ["To respect maternal genealogy supposes taking care of the living bodies engendered by the mother, to bury them when they die, not to prefer the older to the younger son (be it Eteocles to Polynices), nor the son to the daughter."][36] She opposes cyclicality and interdependence between natural and human order to the concept of an agonistic struggle for survival or dominance (over nature, of one sex over the other). It is important to stress, though, that Antigone practices rites of a different *culture* from Creon's—she is not living out purely *natural* demands. For Irigaray, Antigone represents a culture of difference, of female subjectivity in dialogue with the other; this culture is not an essential given, the female self acquires it gradually through work. Its task is to create a consciousness of female specificity, to conceive of it as processual and radiating out into multiple social relations: to the mother, to other women, to men, to the universal as she envisions it in social reality. In emphasizing contiguity between the female self and the other, which is partially the same, Irigaray escapes the hierarchical relationship of the part and the whole as it is expressed by metaphor: the subject thinks itself as both specific and part of a larger present entity instead of covering over a split between itself and the absent entity that it represents to itself as a love object through metaphorization, through symbolic activity.

Unlike her teacher Jacques Lacan, Irigaray does not see identity as constituting itself around a lack, a loss of feeling at home in the universal.[37] Irigaray submits this double thinking as a task for each gender with the aim of mutual respect so that they may then work in unison for social preservation and innovation:

> Each woman will therefore be for herself the woman in becoming [la femme en devenir], model for herself as woman and for the man whom she needs, just as he needs her to ensure the passage from nature to culture. In other words, to be born woman demands a culture, particular to this sex and to this gender, which it is important for the woman to achieve without, however, renouncing he natural identity. She must not submit herself to a model of identity imposed by anyone else: not by her parents, her lover, her child, the State, a religion, nor by culture in general. . . . She must, on the contrary, gather herself within herself in order to achieve the perfection of her gender for herself, for the man whom she loves, for her children, but equally for civil society, the world of culture, and a definition of the universal corresponding to reality.[38]

The model for giving birth to the Irigarayan subject is a nurturing dialogue coupled with introspection, as it can be found in successful analysis.[39] In order to test the models of female identity held out by the various social entities, the woman-in-becoming must have experienced a positive relationship to a fully grown female self: Irigaray privileges the maternal dyad as "the matrix which can generate change" followed by its linguistic expression in "language or discourse as process of enunciation, a dynamic interchange between interlocutors which can transfigure flesh and blood. This is also the prerequisite for dialogue between the sexes, so that each can offer a house or home to the other."[40] The relationship of the self to the polis would then be based on a dialogics of self-in-society, not on the submission of the subject to an inflexible and distancing law as Creon wishes to impose it on Antigone.

The example of Creon elucidates the principles on which "masculinity" establishes its tenuous hold to power: Creon is afraid of not being masculine at all if he does not suppress alterity with severity. He asks, for instance: "Who is the man here, / She or I, if this crime goes unpunished?"[41]; and "If we must lose, / let's lose to a man at least! Is a woman stronger than we?"[42] He reproaches his son publicly in front of the chorus of elders: "This boy, it seems, has sold out to a woman." Haimon replies: "If you are a woman, my concern is only for you."[43]—to hear himself linked even hypothetically to what he rejects as weak throws Creon into a murderous rage. Creon's identity depends on the other being inferior and fearful of his authority, and he is obsessively concerned with his subjects selling out their loyalty for money. He takes money as a new standard for the exchanges between men. According to Creon, transactions between men center around appropriation and devaluation—in another play, he travels to Colonus to seize and take away Oedipus' daughters and to revile the blinded and aged Oedipus, whom he still sees as his rival despite his being in exile and supported only by women. Irigaray denounces this reliance on possession and rivalry as individually and socially nugatory:

> Nous vivons dans une société de l'entre-hommes fonctionnant selon le respect exclusif de la généalogie des fils et des pères et la compétition des frères entre eux. Cela veut dire que nos sociétés ont replié la généalogie des femmes dans celle des hommes. . . . l'homme, dans sa logique, ses discours, ses comportements, toute son économie subjective—oscille en permanence entre le *oui* et le *non* qu'il dit à toutes formes de mères dans la constitution de son identité. . . . L'homme a besoin de ces *oui-non* pour se tenir à distance de la matière qui l'a produit. Le plus souvent, il essaie de se garder dans la dénégation de cette mère ou matrice premières. . . . La femme n'est pas du tout dans le même type d'identité subjective que l'homme. En effet, elle n'a pas à se distancier de sa mère comme lui. . . . Elle doit être ou devenir femme comme sa mère et, en même temps, être capable de se différencier d'elle. Mais sa mère est même qu'elle. Elle ne peut être réduite ni manipulé comme objet ainsi que le fait le petit garçon ou l'homme.[44]

> [We live in a society constituted between men, functioning according to the exclusive respect shown to the genealogy of sons and fathers and the competition of brothers with each other. This means that our societies have folded the genealogy of women into that of men. . . . Man in his logic, his speech, his behaviour, his whole subjective economy—wavers permanently between the *yes* and the *no* he tells all kinds of mothers in the establishing of his identity. . . . Man needs these *yes-nos* to keep himself at a distance from the matter which produced him. Most often, he tries to keep himself in the denial of that first mother or [anterior] matrix. . . . The woman is not at all invested in the same subjective identity as the man. And really, she need not distance herself from her mother as he does. . . . She needs to be or become woman like her mother and at the same time, be able to differentiate herself from her. But her mother is the same as her. She cannot be reduced or manipulated as an *object* as the little boy does it or the man.]

The woman's relationship to her mother is based on a kind of parity on similarity; she does not have to supplant her mother to become fully adult:

> Son économie est celle de l'entre-sujets plus que des rapports sujet-objet. . . . Il faut que la femme puisse se dire en mots, en images et

symboles dans cette relation inter-subjective avec sa mère, puis les autres femmes, pour entrer dans une relation non destructrice aux hommes. . . . Pour se constituer comme identité sexuelle, une relation généalogique avec son propre genre et le respect des deux genres sont nécessaires.[45]

[Her economy is intersubjective rather than based on subject-object relations. . . . The woman must be able to express herself in words, in images, in symbols in that intersubjective relationship with her mother, then with other women, so that she may enter into a non-destructive relationship with men. . . . To constitute oneself as a sexual subject, a genealogical relationship with one's own gender as well as the respect of both genders are necessary.]

In her writing of the early eighties, Irigaray asserts a process-oriented logic of becoming, a different scientific model for ordering the universe, which stresses fluidity and variability. Scholars especially in America have mistaken her postulate for a renewed mysticism of the feminine founded on female biology and body fluids, but what Irigaray is really talking about is a more flexible worldview analogous to recent research into the mechanics of fluids. Irigaray posits a new female subjectivity that does not regard its body and consciousness as "all," or as a closed system; she privileges permeability, a critical stance that questions itself and puts the position from which it speaks more at risk.[46]

In Irigaray's writing since the mid-eighties, the essentialist streak has become less and less foregrounded in the establishing of a feminist consciousness; instead, she emphasizes a kind of dialogic obstetrics between women that grounds itself primarily in a sense of the woman as subject in society, and only secondarily on a female natural identity. Irigaray's earlier insistence on female body fluids, multiple sites of sexual pleasure, and so on,[47] can now be read less literally and more metaphorically as an imaging, a locational politics of difference—of a different, processual economy of energy. She expresses this sense of female specificity very lucidly in *Le Temps*. The female economy of hormonal energy can serve as a metaphor for social innovation because it relies on gradual change, a gradual, spiral buildup and release of energy without a dramatic collapse. We may now see Irigaray's appeal to natural rhythms in the context of a speeded-up and destructive cycle of production and consumption in postmodern society.

The British literary critic Iain Chambers summarizes the disorienting feeling of hyperreality that pervades contemporary city life:

The metropolis no longer orders space but time. The physical ambient is traversed, sliced and cut up, by individuals circulating and maintaining contact via the tepid heat of semi-conductors, cathode ray tubes, tape heads, answering machines, pick-ups. We plug in, our hands press the buttons, touch the keys, and our distracted bodies close the circuits. Here sense is connected to speed: messages are threatened by instant obsolescence and meaning becomes movement. In this apparently rootless and boundless landscape, where the signifier refuses to be slowed down and classified, we experience the semiotic blur and limitless cross-referencing of the ever-present and ever-ambiguous sign. This semiotic vista furnishes a language that, through clothes, styles, fashion, magazines, advertising, music, film, video, television and telecommunications, provides much of the architecture of our daily lives and yet is without apparent purpose. It is a language that exists beyond the obvious sense or isolated "reading" of the individual sign; it involves a syntax that apparently carries its referents within itself.[48]

Irigaray counters such postmodern highly mechanized and dispersed intersubjectivity with a different kind of personalized, embodied intersubjectivity. Again and again the idea of *oikos,* a spiritual home for the subject is brought into play, as Margaret Whitford explains: "The ideal dialogue would be one in which neither pole or interlocutor was frozen, immobile, fixed to one position, frozen in a predicate . . . , but in which each was able to respond to the other, to provide a symbolic house for the other, to move readily between subject and object positions without being immobilized in either."[49] Irigaray privileges a consciousness in which spiritual substance exists and "is experienced otherwise than as a good that is exterior to the self. . . . [where] the interior or the interiority of the body is cultivated and is not reduced to the obscurity of the natural."[50] Irigaray does not deny the desire for the universal, but she makes it the task of both sexes to pursue an ethical being-in-the-world, incompatible with commodification: "Money as mediation represents the loss or the alienation of singularity in an abstract universal of the natural without adequate spiritualization of the latter and with no return to self possible."[51]

Irigaray emphasizes a sense of time as flow (historical connectedness as well as orientation towards the future) in her return to the city as the site of (re)humanized cultural activity. It is in this spirit that I return to the city as all four writers are concerned with the historical time frame. Other thinkers critical of contemporary urban life emphasize its simulation of a constant present, the disjuncture of the individual, and his or her rapidly changing environment. The political scientist William Connolly in his recent book *Identity/Difference* holds out a particularly bleak view for the individual who "goes to market" in today's urban economy:

The identity available to the late-modern self remains bound up with historically received standards of self-responsibility, self-discipline, and freedom. . . . But while these standards of identity and responsibility remain intact, the institutions in which they are situated have become more highly and pervasively organized. One must now program one's life meticulously to meet a more detailed array of institutional standards of normality and entitlement. If one fails to measure up to one (or more) of these disciplines, one runs a high risk of entrapment in one of the categories of otherness derived from it. . . . One can either treat one's life as a project, negotiating a path through a finely grained network of institutionally imposed disciplines or requirements, or one can struggle against those disciplines by refusing to treat one's life as a project. To follow the first route is to be indebted to the institutions in which one is enclosed: one's office space, self-esteem, income, merit, mobility, power, family and personal identity now depend on microconformity to pervasive norms that come with the territory. And this remains so whether those standards are established democratically or imposed from above. To select or be selected by the second path, on the other hand, is to be shuffled out of the good life available and to increase one's susceptibility to one of the categories that license institutional discipline.[52]

Connolly's implied notion of an ideal self is one that would be free of institutional constraints, have unrestricted access to the good life, and be guaranteed a less contingent hold on the possessions or status attained through work. The acceleration of the exchange and the proliferation of new standards spoil the individual's drive towards joyful participation in this economy. Connolly desires more permanence and greater harmony between individual and institutional requirements. But as a solution he presents entirely opting out of the present economy as his only alternative. This thinking seems to me to be characterized by oppositional pairs (abject compliance versus rebellion, having all or nothing). Perhaps one could learn to treat one's life as a different project. Why should (male) identity depend so heavily on symbols of ownership. Might another standard be found valid? Connolly depicts a masculinist universe in which we struggle agonistically against impersonal rivals, political power networks that we can no longer control and that manipulate us. His concept of identity is based on debate as contestation, unlike Irigaray's, which is based on dialogue. For him identity is preferably separational and founds itself on a series of what Irigaray calls "yes-nos"—exclusions of what he does not want to be, but finds itself more and more trapped in an enclosing organized system.

Of course, in a sense Connolly's attitude betrays nostalgia for an untrammeled self anterior to society. This confuses the entire issue of agency. The late modern individual has to accept that there was never a "deep self" at its origin: "Not only psychoanalysis and Marxism, but also, more recently, structural linguistics and structural anthropology indicate that we are determined by structures which precede and exceed the individual, and into which the individual is obliged to insert him or herself in order to be a social individual at all."[53] Connolly still subscribes to a core identity that gains distinctness through friction against sets of differences. He then argues that because these differences are necessary to his experiencing of self within society, he is compelled to hold them in grudging respect:

> My identity is what I am and how I am recognized rather than what I choose, want, or consent to. It is the dense self from which choosing, wanting, and consenting proceed. Without that density, these acts could not occur; with it, they are recognized to be mine. Our identity, in a similar way, is what we are and the basis from which we proceed.
>
> An identity is established in relation to a series of differences that have become socially recognized. These differences are essential to its being. If they did not coexist as differences, it would not exist in its distinctness and solidity. Entrenched in this indispensable relation is a second set of tendencies, themselves in need of exploration, to congeal established identities into fixed forms, thought and lived as if their structure expressed the true order of things. . . . The maintenance of one identity . . . involves the conversion of some differences into otherness, into evil. . . . [Identity] converts difference into otherness in order to secure its own self-certainty.
>
> Identity is thus a slippery, insecure experience, dependent on its ability to define difference and vulnerable to the tendency of entities it would so define to counter, resist, overturn or subvert definitions applied to them. Identity stands in a complex, political relation to the differences it seeks to fix. This complexity is intimated by variations in the degree to which differences from self-identity are treated as complementary identities, contending identities, negative identities, or nonidentities.[54]

Connolly clearly privileges hermetical bodies that are secure in their distinctness, he does not like that they can only feel themselves to be solid through social interaction with contending bodies. He advocates a more tolerant attitude towards these other entities as a way out of an apocalyptic struggle of international interests. He never questions whether his account of socialization is shared by all, he assumes that it is true.

Irigaray however privileges analogy, not paradox, as a rhetorical model for identity. The woman is a specific entity but also the same as her mother, she takes care of the world as her ancestors once did because it was confided to them. For Irigaray, in the beginning there was a gift. Connolly would say in the beginning there was an act of possession. For Connolly, identity is only felt in the realm of the social, the Lacanian symbolic (i.e., "what we are") only becomes expressed in our actions as a subject. For Irigaray, there is a distinction between identity and subjectivity, they are produced by an interplay of the imaginary and the symbolic, both of which are, at least in part, socially shaped. Whitford explicates the interrelation of imaginary and symbolic as follows:

> Identity is imaginary, but it takes a symbolic (representational) form. . . . in practice the two overlap, because one never finds one without the other. . . . That break with the imaginary, in which one is capable of thinking about one's own imaginary, instead of being thought by it, is unlikely to take a social form as long as there is no real other. . . . What we have is an economy of the Same, exchange between men—the same, male imaginary with nothing to act as the "break," except women . . . [real women who refuse to be exchange objects in the male economy]. . . . For men to make a break with their imaginary, another term would be needed—women as symbolic term. . . . And they will only be able to do this when [the woman has established her own intersubjective economy as valid, by speaking her relationship to her mother] it becomes possible to distinguish between the mother and the woman, when the relation between mother and daughter is symbolized.[55]

Connolly, on the other hand, never affords the different entity that symbolic validity as truly other, difference is only perceived within the framework of contestation. He envisions a paradoxical ideal of strife and interdependence:

> To strive to convert an antagonism of identity into an agonism of difference, in which each opposes the other (and the other's presumptive beliefs) while respecting the adversary at another level as one whose contingent orientations also rest on shaky epistemic grounds. An antagonism in which each aims initially at conquest or conversion of the other can now . . . become an agonism in which each treats the other as crucial to itself in the strife and interdependence of identity/difference. A "pathos of distance" (to borrow a phrase from Neitzsche) begins to unfold whereby each maintains a

44

certain respect for the adversary, partly because the relationship exposes contingency in the being of both.[56]

Connolly's interactive antagonism is, in fact, interdependence in name only. It is completely unclear from his system why different voices should respect each other.

Irigaray provides a solution for the adversarial stalemate in which Connolly is entrapped: partnership. Intersubjectivity without agonistic distance does not have as its ineluctable consequence the absorption of difference. Rather, as Margaret Drabble demands, we must form late modernity's "shapeless diversity" to create the polis as a localized network, which both supports us and leaves openings for the new to enter.[57] Iain Chambers understands postmodernity as a time in which difference has been acknowledged without being posited as problematic or destructive:

> The ingression of other voices and histories leads to the preceding sense of politics being displaced. There is no *one* place which now has the exclusive prerogative on speech. With respect to its traditional sense, politics now confronts an excess of sense. It is this excess that, simultaneously investing distinct realities and histories while maintaining their differences, provides us with the possibility of a shared set of interfaces and involvement, and a *political* sense of the commonplace.[58]

A growing awareness of the contingency of our own point of view and political goals need not result in disaffection from the political process. The simultaneous and differing claims of the many constituencies who assemble on urban ground cannot be reduced to a single voice. Women as agents are less likely to attempt such a reduction because they already base their sense of being-in-society on a more flexible conception of self as distinct and extending itself through being-in-relationship. In growing up female, they become aware of the constructedness of gender, which in turn makes them more suspicious of the constructedness of other identificatory categories in society, such as ethnicity and race. They acknowledge alterity more readily than those who have until now thought of themselves as firmly placed at the center and who mourn the loss of that security.

It is the embodied presence of women's histories in the city that constitutes it as the paradigmatic site of sociality. What is crucial in their self-awareness is the intervention of memory; in remembering their own struggle with the marginality femininity imposes, they can empathize with the struggle for self-fulfillment other groups face in the urban arena. They can be leaders in social innovation by building coalitions with others around local as well as global goals. This, however, remains an essentially utopian scenario. Although women are more aware of the constructedness of gender, this does not prevent them from being ensnared in its performance.

One must recognize and respect the fractured nature of all coalitions, avoiding the tendency towards a forced consensus in the drive towards solidarity. One cannot simply assume that well-intentioned white feminists speak for third-world women. The Chilean-born cultural critic Celeste Olalquiaga, in her recent *Megalopolis: Contemporary Cultural Sensibilities,* mentions the possibility of change from below, even in the relentlessly consumer-oriented and superannuating culture of the postindustrial global village.[59] For example, the cultural recycling of first-world consumer culture in the third world often carries parodic overtones that allow for innovation and transformation of cultural values. Olalquiaga thus disagrees with Jameson on the transformative potential within the cultural sphere. Jameson believes that disenchantment and social criticism all too readily fall prey to market forces and become commodified and politically mainstreamed. As Olalquiaga points out, however, commodification is a curiously dynamic process: goods that become obsolete are easily retrievable and are often broken down and idiosyncratically reconfigured in the third world. This form of pastiche can become a kind of cultural critique. Jameson is, nonetheless, correct in asserting that even subversion can become a commodity. This danger can be circumvented through the creation of more locally oriented and varied coalitions, ones that recognize difference. Negotiation hinges on sustained dialogue rather than contestation, the latter always carrying connotations of class privilege and hierarchy.

In fact, acts of submission and acts of subversion are not readily distinguishable in the works of twentieth-century women writers. In Rhys, the protagonist remains too trapped in the simultaneous pursuit of, and rebellion against, middle-class values to enter into dialogue with other women. Rhys's social critique always takes on a desperate and monologic quality. In apparent contrast, Duras highlights dialogic exchange between mother and daughter, sister and brother. However, this exchange is predicated on contestation, separation, and intergenerational hostility. Drabble's community of women friends manages to sustain dialogue over a lifetime, but it is overly dependent on personal friendship based on similarity and therefore oblivious to women of different class or race. Maron's female protagonists establish dialogue between different ages, classes, and genders. Although they take a more activist political stance than many of the previous protagonists, their acts of resistance are exclusively focused on toppling a repressive and monolithic socialist regime. In the postmodern Western capitalist sphere, resistance needs to be more canny in the face of a more elusive and diffuse source of repression.

One must bear in mind, however, that postmodernism can be read as a refinement of authoritarianism, no less constraining to the individual and the group. Female agency resists commodifying and paralyzing social practices.

All of the writers treated in this study delineate the physical and mental peregrinations into the city and within its precincts. Such movement is not without its risks for female identity: once they enter into the prototypical realm of commodity display, these protagonists are in danger of assimilation. After all, in postmodernity, all meaning becomes defined and attenuated by communication on the electronic interface. For these women writers, however, the actual and imaginative traversing of the urban communicative interstices transforms the flatness of apperception into the depth of a critical consciousness. This consciousness is truly put to work in the shuttling back and forth between the metropolis and less urbanized areas. For the women in these novels, such trips represent not only an acknowledgment of, and coming to terms with, personal history, but also an inchoate movement towards social innovation and regeneration.

1

Somatic Rebellion
in Jean Rhys

Virtually all the women characters in Jean Rhys's novels are dispossessed and deracinated. They are impoverished middle-class women without professional skills who find themselves resorting to marketing their bodies to older middle- or upper-middle-class men. They all inevitably travel a downward spiral into despair, penury, and isolation: this series of events is concomitant with the process of commodification. By reenacting this downward mobility in each of her novels, Rhys provides a powerful critique of the potential attenuation of women into exchange objects. Each character performs rebellious acts, but these remain equivocal and fleeting gestures. In a time of social transformation between the two world wars, the female body registers class anxieties about social status. It becomes a symbol of dispossession and contagion, and it can only protest its vilification by speaking somatically. The hysterical body acts out an aggressive critique of commodification practices. Its ostracism reflects the alienation and cultural pessimism dear to the modernist sensibility, yet we find in the protagonist's struggle for self-expression the beginnings of a search for critical consciousness and agency.

The short novels I analyze are all written after World War I, which signaled the contraction and decline of the British Empire and brought about a rupture in consciousness for its participants, jolting the British middle-class out of its complacency. Although wartime in Rhys's novels is remembered as a time of bonding across barriers of class and nationality, the period between the two wars sees an attempt to deny the social ruptures and shifts that have taken place through an obsessive insistence on middle-class values, such as order, respectability, and strict control of the body in private as well as public spaces.

In *After Leaving Mr. Mackenzie*,[1] the thirty-six-year-old protagonist, Julia Martin, returns to London after a ten-year absence, having left it for the Continent shortly after the Armistice, which allows us to date the time to about 1928. She takes lodgings in Bloomsbury and revisits familiar city sites and neighborhoods, which elicit memories of her earlier stay in London during the war:

> That cinema on the right-hand side. . . . She remembered going in there with a little Belgian when they had shown some town in Belgium being bombarded. And the little Belgian had wept. During the war . . . My God, that was a funny time! The mad things one did—and everybody else was doing them, too. A funny time. A mad reckless time. An exultant and youthful feeling took possession of her. She crossed Oxford Street into Charing Cross Road.[2]

Julia's initial progress through the city shows that she wishes to locate herself in upper-class city zones—lodging in Bloomsbury, a highly respectable residential area of the city; later buying herself a corsage of violets from an old man in Woburn Square at the heart of Bloomsbury; then proceeding straight down major thoroughfares like Tottenham Court Road and Charing Cross Road towards Westminster and Whitehall, the city's seats of commercial and governmental power. Rhys suggests through Julia's movement in the city that her character is struggling to appear ladylike. A subversion of the categories of class and nation in the architectural heart of London, which might at an earlier time have been equated with the essence of Englishness, did take place as a result of World War I (the Great War)—the Belgian refugee witnesses the destruction of his home country watching a newsreel at the cinema. He is infantilized—a little man, he weeps; and the memory of sharing his breakdown and grief leaves the female protagonist feeling youthful and exultant. It seems particularly appropriate that the homeless Julia remembers bonding with another displaced person, for Julia is a victim in the other Great War, the war of the sexes. The experience in the trenches had created shell-shocked male veterans, who exhibited such symptoms as loss of bodily control, weeping, and anxiety similar to what had been coded a female disease, hysteria—to which middle-class women were especially prone.[3] Hysteria is a somatic language, and I argue that Rhys substitutes a hysterical response as more expressive than verbalization at crucial moments of female rebellion against commodification.

Before analyzing some examples of somatic language, it is helpful to remind ourselves of the other great change the war had brought along. The unprecedented numbers of young men who died or returned traumatized ushered in a period in which gender roles were open to revision. As Mary Lou Emery describes in her 1990 book on Rhys, by the time in which her narratives are set, women had entered the public sphere in ever-increasing numbers, thereby challenging ideological attempts to relegate them back into the private sphere of the home and the concomitant roles of wife and mother:

> "Hordes" of women's bodies seemed to flow into the streets during the early part of the century. They stormed the gates of colleges, the professions, and of politics, but they also simply worked, as typists, clerks, shop "girls," sales "ladies," mannequins, artists' models, actresses and prostitutes. Like Rhys's geographically and spatially displaced heroines, they appeared without escort in business offices, matinee audiences, cafes and bars. They trespassed on territory traditionally reserved for men, or at least for male control, and threatened to disprove, visibly, the lingering nineteenth-century ideology of separate spheres.[4]

Although there is a nostalgia for "home" in Rhys's female protagonists, they do move about, however uncomfortably, in public space, and they do hold down jobs, however tenuously. They are no longer wife or mother: in the case of Julia—"Madame Martin"—she has left her husband, gotten a divorce, and her baby has died. In the case of Anna Morgan, the protagonist of *Voyage*, she leaves a middle-class existence as a colonialist's daughter in the West Indies to come to England and take up the precarious professional life of a touring actress, gradually slipping into prostitution. Sasha Jansen of *Good Morning, Midnight* has been left by her husband, has a baby who died, has worked as an English teacher for other expatriates in Paris, and as a freelance short story writer. At the periphery of their perception of other women exists another type of nontraditional woman, the full-fledged female professional. It is interesting to note that the central female characters, who are torn between embracing a cult of femininity and restraint, at the same time rebel against it by drinking, bringing men up to their rooms, affecting disorderly dress, and so on, view these "masculine" women with a mixture of awe and dislike.

In *Mr. Mackenzie*, for instance, Julia encounters three different professional women at different times in the narrative. First, in Paris, an artist for whom she sits as a model; second, a woman with a large attaché case on the underground in London; and last, Miss Wyatt, a nurse who looks after Julia's mother and keeps her sister Norah company. "Wyatt" (as she is referred to familiarly by Norah) is coded as a lesbian, and Julia reacts to her presence with terrified homophobia. Here is truly a "third woman," one who has acquired a professional skill, even if it is a stereo-typically female occupation, who has also taken over the "good" daughter Norah's affection, thus usurping what Julia feels to be her own place as Norah's sister and her invalid mother's daughter:

> The door . . . was opened by a middle-aged woman. Her brown hair was cut very short, drawn away from a high, narrow forehead, and brushed to lie close to her very small skull. Her nose was thin and arched. She had small, pale-brown eyes and a determined ex-pression. She wore a coat and skirt of grey flannel, a shirt blouse, and a tie. She said, without smiling, "Good afternoon, Julia. Come along in." . . . An open tin of Navy Cut tobacco and a book of cigarette-papers lay on the table near Miss Wyatt. She rolled herself a cigarette very quickly and neatly. Her gestures were like the ges-tures of a man. Her hands were small and thin but short-fingered and without delicacy. She said: "Have a cigarette, Julia? There's a box of Marcovitches on the table behind you. I got them for Norah—not that she smokes much." Julia wanted to say: "Please make one for me. I'd like that." But when she met Miss Wyatt's eyes she turned without speaking, took a cigarette from the box behind her, and lit it. "I always make my own," Miss Wyatt said. "I have to; it's cheaper. . . . " Miss Wyatt was obviously on the point of going out. She wore a macintosh. . . . "The doctor says she hardly suffers at all," Miss Wyatt answered in a non-committal voice. . . . [After the mother's death] Miss Wyatt had her hand on Norah's shoulder. Julia trailed after them into the sitting-room, which looked very bright and cheerful. . . . Miss Wyatt was patting her [Julia] on the shoulder. "Cheer up, Julia," she said.[5]

Wyatt looks like a man with her short hair, grey flannel costume with a tie, lack of make-up or other feminine frills. Her short fingers roll ciga-rettes like a man, she speaks decisively and makes no verbal or gestural attempts to pacify or be deferential. Julia interprets this paradox of a woman speaking unemotional male speech as hostility directed towards herself. She is unable to meet Wyatt's gaze and not feel cowed—like an obedient child she does exactly what Wyatt asked her to do. The un-spoken option: "Please make one for me. I'd like that." would perhaps cast Julia in the feminized role to this butch woman—and therefore remains unspoken. Or, once voiced, it might establish community be-tween the two women and contaminate Julia's status as a highly femi-nized exchange object among men. Through her choice of plain garb and plain, factual speech, Wyatt rejects the performance of a dependent, child-like femininity as masquerade, and so calls into question Julia's whole *raison d'être*. Julia's self-presentation hinges on a "respectable" appearance, which she falsely believes would protect her from commodification. Her obsessive concern with dress and appearance also betokens an insecurity about her new position as a woman in public space. For Julia, successful masquerade means survival in the Darwinian struggle of the fittest, which is brought to the forefront in the urban settings of London and Paris: "She told herself that if only she had had the sense to keep a few things, this return need not have been quite so ignominious, quite so desolate. People thought twice before they were rude to anybody wearing a good fur coat; it was protective colouring, as it were."[6]

As *Good Morning, Midnight* bears out, the fur coat the impoverished Sasha Jensen still owns misleads a young gigolo into picking her up because he infers from her dress that she must be rich:

> I want to shout at him "I haven't got any money, I tell you. I know what you're judging by. You're judging by my coat. You oughtn't to judge by my coat. You ought to judge by what I have on under my coat, by my handbag, by my expression, by anything you like. . . . Well, there you are—no use arguing. I can see he has it firmly fixed in his head that I'm a rich bitch and that if he goes on long enough I can be persuaded to part.[7]

Ironically, the "respectable" coat does not protect Sasha from commodification, it merely inverts her position in the seduction-for-money scenario. She becomes a potential benefactor instead of being in the role of the supplicant. At other times in Rhys's narratives, the protagonists wear coats that are too short, too tight, or too short at the back. Their obsessive concern with appearance is especially focused on their back(side)s (the back cannot be surveyed from the front, even in a mirror one's body has to contort itself to permit a full look at the back) which, in adding depth, disturb the economy of the frontal, surface-oriented male gaze these female characters have internalized.[8] Furthermore, the backside as a secondary sexual characteristic is associated with shameful uncontrolled sexuality, anality. From medieval times on, baring too much of one's backside, for instance, betokens disrespect or contempt for others.[9]

Julia Martin is very concerned about having clothes that are too tight or too short, as the following two examples show:

> The ghost [of herself in London ten years ago] was thin and eager. It wore a long, very tight check shirt, a short dark-blue coat, and a bunch of violets bought from the old man in Woburn Square. It drifted up to her and passed her in the fog. And she had the feeling that, like the old man, it looked at her coldly, without recognizing her.[10]

> At three o'clock she was back at her hotel, carrying the boxes
> containing the clothes she had bought at a second-hand shop in the
> Rue Rocher—a dark grey coat and hat; and a very cheap dress, too
> short for the prevailing fashion. She at once dressed herself in her
> new clothes, but the effect was not so pleasing as she had hoped.
> She fidgeted before the glass for a while, viewing herself from
> different angles.[11]

In choosing clothes that are ill-fitting, Julia unintentionally appears more
fleshy, hence she corresponds closer to the physical characteristics of the
prostitute, fatness and indolence, that Gilman traces in the medical literature of the late nineteenth-century.[12] He states:

> Parent-Duchatelet's descriptions range from the detailed to the an-
> ecdotal. His discussion of the embonpoint of the prostitute begins
> his litany of external signs. Prostitutes have a "peculiar plumpness"
> which is attributed to "the great number of hot baths which the
> major part of these women take"—or perhaps to their lassitude,
> since they rise at ten or eleven in the morning, "leading an animal
> life." They are fat as prisoners are fat, from simple confinement. As
> an English commentator noted, "the grossest and stoutest of these
> women are to be found amongst the lowest and most disgusting
> classes of prostitutes. These are the Hottentots on the scale of the
> sexualized female.[13]

These attempts at categorization and exclusion demonstrate a desire to
contain the working class through criminalizing them and labeling anatomical differences as deviant. Under the medical gaze, the categories of
class, gender, racial other, and nonhuman blend seamlessly into one another. This normalizing practice has pernicious effects on the ability of
the objectified Other to make herself heard. Her very presence and self-
presentation provokes the beleaguered middle-class woman to hostility.
A woman who dresses like Julia is not a lady, because her too-tight dress
emphasizes her body, and yet she is somewhat of a paradox, "an extraordinary creature"[14] as Norah calls her, because the colors she wears do
connote respectability—dark blue, dark grey; black velvet in the case of
Anna Morgan, another puzzling "creature." The very use of the term
creature bespeaks an attempt to dehumanize the woman who is "not a
lady" by ranking her with animals and artifice—it takes make-up skills to
create a semblance of beauty, youth, and refinement—all of which are, of
course, qualities to which a "real lady" should aspire as well.

The middle-class ideal of the "lady" betrays a paradox in Rhys's social
critique. Having thoroughly internalized that ideal, her protagonists
would still like to rebel against it. In the return of the truant sister Julia to

her home in England, Rhys demonstrates the virtual impossibility of this ideal for women of straitened circumstances. It is not long before the masks fall as Julia and her sister Norah compete for ladylike status:

[Norah] thought: "She doesn't even look like a lady now. What can she have been doing with herself?" Norah herself was labelled for all to see. She was labelled "Middle class, no money." . . . "And who's better dressed—you or I?" said Norah. A fierce expression came into her eyes. . . . "You're an extraordinary creature," said Norah. Something in her voice enraged Julia.[15]

Another example of the relentless pursuit of ladylike qualities is provided in *Voyage,* when Ethel Matthews—a middle-aged manicurist who hopes to better her income by making the pretty Anna Morgan move in with her as her apprentice—discloses her social aspirations. Unlike Miss Wyatt, the threatening *other* woman located beyond the ladylike/unladylike binarism that structures the female world Rhys describes, Rhys does not permit Ethel to keep an honorific in front of her name—she is working class, but also works at being regarded as a "lady": "That's what I can remember best—Ethel talking and the clock ticking. And her voice when she was telling me about Madame Fernande [a madam] or about her father, who had a chemist's shop, and that she was really a lady. A lady—some words have a long, thin neck that you'd like to strangle. And her different voice when she said, 'A manicure, dear.' "[16] Ethel Matthews is a professional masseuse, she wears a "white overall with the sleeves rolled up. Her hair was tidy. She looked much nicer than I [Anna] remembered her." She uses words like "dainty," "lovely room," and "nice," as in "a nice set of manicure things," and she decorates her sitting room in glazed chintz, which at that time used to be a standard fabric for the English country house.[17] All this is to suggest that Ethel Matthews leads a leisured life when she is at home. In fact, the leisured look she creates is not so much for her own benefit as for her male clients, to whom the decor is to intimate respectability and upper-middle-class relaxation. As Anna soon discovers, the veneer of ladylike respectability for which Ethel strives is a flimsy disguise for the potential sordidness of her professional enterprise: the men come there expecting to get sex, not merely a massage or a manicure.

In a scene reminiscent of a Hogarth print satirizing London sexual mores, Rhys lets Anna witness the collapse of the pretense. Ethel tries to control the carnivalesque chaos a client causes in her room with ladylike speech, but this appears as merely ridiculous:

The man had been there for about twenty minutes when I heard the crack of wood breaking and he started to swear at the top of his voice. Ethel knocked again. "Am I to come in?" I said at the door. "Yes," she said, "come in." I went in. The massage couch had collapsed at one end and the basin was upset. There was water all over the floor. The man had a blanket wrapped round him. He was hopping around on one leg, holding the other foot, and swearing. *He looked very thin and small.* He had grey hair; I didn't notice his face. "There's been an accident," Ethel said. "One of the legs of the couch has given way. . . . I'm ever so sorry. Does your foot hurt?" . . . While I was mopping up the water he sat on the piano-stool playing with one finger. *But his foot kept jerking up and down, as a thing does when it has been hurt. Long after you have stopped thinking about it, it keeps jerking up and down. As soon as I got out of the room I began to laugh, and then I couldn't stop.* It's like that when you haven't laughed for a long time.[18]

Not only is Ethel exposed as not ladylike, the man is symbolically castrated and exposes himself as not a gentleman by swearing continuously and moving about like a monkey. The pretense that has propped up the exploitive male-female commercial relationship is literally knocked out from under it, and both participants lose face. In addition, the man's wounded foot speaks its own language; Anna empathizes with his pain that she feels like a phantom limb and that reminds her of her own lack, her own narcissistic wound sustained in childhood as part of her acculturation process to the ideal of growing up into a lady. Instead of speaking, she laughs hysterically, and this irruption of the Platonic *chora* into *semiotike*— the ordered, but entirely hypocritical universe of social language—is far more unsettling as a social critique than speech could be.

Of course, on the metatextual level, Rhys the author is the one who transforms the somatic speech of her alter ego female character[19] into coherent descriptive narrative, thereby gaining linguistic control of the whole breakdown scenario. Next, Rhys sketches in the possibility of subversive female bonding—if Ethel and Anna could laugh at the incident together, they could at least momentarily transcend class barriers and render the real holder of economic power, the male customer, powerless over them. In any case, Anna who enters the scene as an external observer sees him as faceless, that is, without individuality, a type; old (the grey hair), "very thin and small." Rather reminiscent of the "little Belgian" referred to earlier the man is infantilized—after all, he is undressed and wrapped in a blanket. This spectacle of humiliation elicits a feeling of triumph in the female observer, but all it really does is to invert the status of male commodifier and female commodified body; it does not do away with the hierarchy. Rhys seems to suggest that the gender and class hierarchies could indeed be collapsed, if only momentarily, were the two women to join in laughter on an equal level: "Well, . . . it was damned funny. It was a hymn he was playing, did you hear?" . . . Cheer up!" I said. "It was really rather funny." I knew she was getting ready to go for me, but I couldn't stop laughing. . . . [Ethel speaks] 'Who are you laughing at? Look here, I'll tell you something. You can clear out. You're no good; I don't want you here.' "[20] Like Julia's, Ethel's self-concept rests wholly on projecting respectability, especially as her profession is on the borderline between prostitution and a medical skill. She cannot join in Anna's laughter, instead she feels personally attacked by it. It is a skillful stylistic choice on Rhys's part to have Ethel invoke the gaze "look here . . ." as a statement opener, whereas Anna had invoked the economy of listening "did you hear?" as a tag question. Being looked at, is once again commodifying, and unequal wins out over a shared hearing that might have opened out the women's field of perception—listening to a third voice vacillating between swearing and hymn playing might have deconstructed that male individual's position of social power.

It is useful at this point to refer to the sociologist Erving Goffman's insights into role-playing and attempts at creating role distance, because that is precisely what Anna manages to do when she refuses to act out her assigned role of the respectfully silent and submissive servant girl. Goffman states:

> The individual must be seen as someone who organizes his expres-
> sive situational behavior <u>in relation</u> to situated activity roles, but
> that in doing this he uses whatever means are at hand to introduce a
> margin of freedom and maneuverability, of <u>pointed disidentifica-</u>
> <u>tion</u> between himself and the self virtually available for him in the
> situation. . . . Thus, the person who mutters, jokes, or responds
> with sarcasm to what is happening in the situation is nevertheless
> going along with the prevailing definition of the situation—with
> whatever bad spirit.[21]

By laughing out loud, Anna carries her "pointed disidentification" so far that it amounts to a refusal of the virtual role self; furthermore, she challenges Ethel's role as a professional who is in control and whose status as the one who gives orders and can expect compliance is therefore not recognized. Even though she realizes that Ethel will soon reassert dominance, Anna refuses to step back into the submissive role. This rebellious act is mainly driven by a hysterical symptom, unstoppable laughter, and there is no place within the social system of this narrative from which such subversive laughter could safely be uttered. The only place for it is at the level of metanarrative, in the author's and the female reader's presumed identification—they may recognize themselves as per- haps both having been in a similar position to Anna; but they are at the time of writing down situated safely beyond the victimization described within it.

The third professional woman Rhys describes in her narrative is a female artist for whom Julia Martin sits. Unlike the failed attempts at communication between Julia and Wyatt (or Anna and Ethel), Julia does speak to this woman and tries to explain her lifestory. If this attempt met with her listener's approval, it would enhance Julia's self-esteem by making her feel that she "owned" her narrative, even if it had been one of loss and commodification up to that point:

> And then I came along to Paris by myself. And then after a while I met this woman, and I started sitting for her. She gave me so much a week, and I used to go there nearly every day for as long as she wanted me.
>
> . . . And she thought that everything outside was stupid and that annoyed me. She was a bit fanatical, you know. She had something of an artist in her—I mean really. So, of course she was fanatical. And then she was a woman. About thirty-five years old. And so she simply wouldn't believe that anything was true which was outside herself or anything but what she herself thought and felt. She just thought I was stupid because it was outside her scheme of things that anybody like me should not be stupid. . . . I wish I could tell you, how much I liked it, just having tea with her like that. . . . And so one day, when we were sitting smoking, and having tea, I started to tell her . . . why I left England. . . . I wanted to go away with just the same feeling a boy has when he wants to run away to sea—at least, that I imagine a boy has. Only, in my adventure, men were mixed up, because of course, they had to be. You understand, don't you? Do you understand that a girl might have that feeling?
>
> I wanted to get away. I wanted it like—like iron. Besides, I wasn't frightened of anything. So I did get away. I married to get away. . . .
>
> And all the time I talked I was looking at a rum picture she had on the wall—a reproduction of a picture by a man called Modigliani. . . . This picture is of a woman lying on a couch, a woman with a lovely, lovely body. . . . And a face like a mask, a long, dark face, and very big eyes. The eyes were blank, like a mask, but when you had looked at it a bit was as if you were looking at a real woman, a live woman. At least, that's how it was with me.
>
> Well, all the time I was talking I had the feeling I was explaining things not only to Ruth—that was her name—but I was explaining them to myself too, and to the woman in the picture. It

was as if I were before a judge, and I were explaining that everything I had done had always been the only possible thing to do. . . .

I wanted her to understand. . . . It was a beastly feeling I got—that I didn't quite believe myself, either. I thought: "After all, is this true? Did I ever do this?" I felt as if the woman in the picture were laughing at me and saying: I am more real than you. But at the same time I *am* you. I am all that matters of you."[22]

Mary Lou Emery has already provided an excellent analysis of this scene, focusing on the symbolic meaning of the Modigliani portrait as a representation of the silenced mistress.[23]

The relationship between the female model and the female artist merits close analysis, because Rhys's characterization of female artistic creativity seems problematic and may be read as reflecting her own problems with validating her writing as a professional activity, and thus empowering herself as a new category of woman beyond the ladylike/unladylike dichotomy, that had marked her upbringing.[24] Julia Martin feels ambivalent towards the artist who has hired her to sit, criticizing her as "a bit fanatical," but at the same time wanting her approval, "I wish I could tell you how much I liked it, just having tea with her like that." She is the same age Julia is at the time she tells this story, so we might interpret her as an alter ego figure. Julia condemns the very single-mindedness of the artist's vision while admitting that, as a woman, she had to be that way. An unspoken expectation of Julia's is that because her employer is female, she will care to hear her experiences and respond with nurturing[25]: "I wanted her to understand. . . ." When her listener's response is not sufficiently emotional, Julia feels rejected and withdraws. As was the case with Miss Wyatt's factual and direct statements, Julia is unused to what we might term unempathetic male speech issuing from female mouths, "I told everything. I went on and on. . . . And when I had finished I looked at her. She said: 'You seem to have had a hectic time.' But I knew when she spoke that she didn't believe a word."[26] We can observe a clash of speaking styles here, Julia speaking hysterically, going "on and on" somewhat like Anna laughing unstoppably, whereas the listener responds briefly and euphemistically. It might well be possible that in choosing to respond that way she wishes to let Julia preserve face by not emphasizing the terribleness of her woes and by focusing on the present rather than dwelling on the injuries of the past: "You seem to have *had* [italics mine] a hectic time [but it's over now]." In short, Rhys characterizes the female artist as not sufficiently feminine and motherly, hence as masculinized and hostile to other women.

The artist-model relationship further bars communication on an equal level and underscores the gender-stereotyped behavior of the interlocutors. The model is paid to be the silent object of the painterly gaze. This dynamic does not change significantly when the gender of the artist is female, but Julia expects that it would. She misreads the artist's polite but stereotypical offer of tea as an invitation to reveal her troubled history and aspirations in a confessional narrative. Social rituals like chatting and making tea for a guest are coded as typically female, whereas smoking is transgressive female behavior, making value judgements is an accepted male social behavior: ". . . she thought that everything outside herself was stupid." Within the artist-female model framework, we experience a confusion of gender roles—the female artist exhibits traits of both genders, and this is felt by her female interlocutor to be both threatening and potentially liberating when she confesses: "I wanted to go away with just the same feeling a boy has when he wants to run away to sea—at least, that I imagine a boy has. . . . Do you understand that a girl might have that feeling?" Mirroring herself at least fleetingly in the female artist as a social oddity, Julia embraces her unconventional flight from England and the highly normative social behavior expected there as a rebellion that makes sense for her and, more important, she remembers it as a willed act: "I wanted it—like iron." Wanting something that strongly is, once again, a scarily unfeminine form of self-expression, and because Julia has internalized so much of the social prescriptions for appropriate gender and class role playing, she feels insecure "as if I were before a judge; . . . I didn't quite believe myself either." Ultimately, Julia condemns her own story as unreal, "And I was there like a ghost," but the cathartic value of grappling with a coherent autobiographical narrative that would allow her to take charge of her present situation remains in her mind and is never forgotten, even though it is not fulfilled. Instead she is compelled to repeat her story to another listener, Mr. Horsfield, and Englishman who feels like a trustworthy outsider to her because of his damaging war experience, and she makes another appeal for help and sympathy, which he only partially reciprocates.

In speaking, Julia uses parataxis, which provides sequential statements, "and then," "and . . . ," "and so," "and all the time . . . ," but that gives her communication a curious flatness, rather like the frontal glance of surveillance into the mirror, which all of Rhys's female characters practice incessantly and automatically. Hypotaxis creates depth in statements that, we might surmise, is perhaps something the author wishes to avoid, as that depth is achieved only through the imposition of syntactical hierarchies. Instead, Rhys privileges incomplete narratives and snatches of song or poetry[27] as more expressive of emotional states. She makes no attempt to fill up the holes at the center of these imperfectly remembered or recited pieces, thus drawing the reader's attention to the fact that all narrative originates around a gap, a sense of incompletion and loss. But, as Freudian and subsequently Lacanian psychoanalysts have shown, an awareness of the rupture, the gap, is necessary to differentiate self from the maternal *chora,* the presemiotic state of indifferentiation.

I want to turn now to Rhys's autobiographical account of her coming to writing, because in her reconstruction of that process, writing occurs seemingly haphazardly as a side effect of trying to cover up a gap. It is also striking that she refuses to describe writing as a willed act; in her account it happens almost automatically, in a dreamlike unconscious way. The precepts for ladylike passivity that Rhys had internalized as a daughter of middle-class white colonialists prescribe this attitude: a lady must be an amateur, never a professional—therefore her work must not be seen as self-willed or hard.[28] Rhys claims, therefore, that she bought exercise books and quill pens purely for decorative purposes: "I must get some flowers or a plant or something, I thought. I can't bear that table."[29] It is worth quoting the passage in full to demonstrate the extent of the internalized social imperative to be ladylike:

> The room she got me was not in Chelsea but in Fulham. "World's End" was on the buses. The first morning I woke up there it seemed to me the furniture was so like that in the room I had just left that moving hardly made any difference. But the table, which had been in the middle and covered with a cloth, was now pushed directly under the window and *was bare and very ugly. I had put my brush and comb on it, and a box of powder, but they looked small and unimportant. I must get some flowers or a plant or something, I thought. I can't bear that table.*
>
> . . . After lunch I was walking along looking into shop windows. There were still some last dead leaves hanging on the trees. They looked like birds, I thought. I passed a stationer's shop where quill pens were displayed in the window, a lot of them, red, blue, green, yellow. Some of them would be all right in a glass, *to cheer up my table, I thought.* I went into the shop and bought about a dozen. Then I noticed some black exercise books on the counter. They were not at all like exercise books are now. They were twice the thickness, the stiff black covers were shiny, the spine and the edges were red, and the pages were ruled. I bought several of those, *I didn't know why, just because I liked the look of them.* I got a box of J nibs, the sort I liked, an ordinary penholder, a bottle of ink and a cheap inkstand. *Now that old table won't look so bare, I thought.*
>
> It was after supper that night . . . that it happened. My fingers tingled, and the palms of my hands. I pulled a chair up to the table, opened an exercise book, and wrote *This is my Diary.* But it wasn't a

61

diary. . . . I wrote on until late into the night, till I was so tired that I couldn't go on, and I fell into bed and slept.

Next morning I remembered at once, and my only thought was to go on with the writing. . . . I knew then that it was finished and that there was no more to say. *I put the exercise books at the bottom of my suitcase and piled my underclothes on them.* After that whenever I moved I took the exercise books but I never looked at them again for seven years.[30]

It is revealing of Rhys's pretended feminization that she attempts to decorate her interior space, just as a lady would be expected to with her country house. In order to distinguish her room from the impersonal style of the bed-sitter, she at first displays her cosmetics, designating the bare tabletop as a vanity table, but in the apocalyptic setting at "World's End" this is not enough of a bulwark against nothingness: "they looked small and unimportant." Outside, it is midwinter, but there are visual reminders of summer—the dead leaves that strike Rhys as birds. The ability to transform something seen (and frozen, dead) into a metaphor (birds are alive and suggest escape, flight, movement) is, of course, a writerly skill, but Rhys submerges her realization of her artistic creativity in deceptive repetitions of the qualifier "I thought," foreshadowing her hiding her writing under her underwear in her suitcase. Parallel to the discourse of ladylike disclaimers, another discourse operates: She does assert her own likes, ranging from "I can't bear that table" to "J nibs, the sort I liked" to "I said, 'Don't call me dear, I don't like it.' " later on, after writing has emboldened her. She even asserts herself verbally to the landlady: "But you must get out now, I'm very busy." Although there is the impulse to cover up, to cosmeticize the writing activity, another and conflicting desire attests itself, that of to establish writing as her prerogative, as her work—"I'm very busy"—in the face of criticism by the landlady and the lodger below her.

In writing a text that is personal, and yet not "a diary," Rhys translates her experiences from disabling memories into narratives of larger patterns of female commodification, over which she as writer can finally wield control. As Anthony Giddens put it in his 1991 *Modernity and Self-Identity: Self and Society in the Modern Age,* "the self, like the broader institutional contexts in which it exists, has to be reflexively made."[31] As Judith Kegan Gardiner points out, the self is a construct we produce in a process very similar to that of writerly fabrication:

According to self psychologists, "The self is not a thing or an entity, it is a concept; a symbolic abstraction from the developmental process. The self refers to the uniqueness that separates the experiences of an individual from those of all others while at the same time conferring a sense of cohesion and continuity on the disparate experiences of that individual throughout . . . life.

. . . The self as pretext can then be seen as shared reality, founded on linguisticality and desire for continuity, rather than primarily on experiences of integrity, intentionality, or agency.

. . . This "pretextual account of self" relies primarily on a particular telling of self and is therefore allied with narrative.[32]

In inventing female characters who are versions of earlier selves, Rhys manages to share a "telling of self," but also preserves an alterity for her present self, a distance from the scenarios of victimization she evokes. Gardiner defines Rhys's approach to narrating female self as an empathetic one that she wants the reader to imitate. She states:

The concept of empathy, a concept often associated with women, yet one denoting that bridging of differences between self and other, including gender differences, that makes fictional representation possible.

. . . empathy is a value-neutral tool of observation. ". . . we define it as 'vicarious introspection' or, more simply, as one person's (attempt to) experience the inner life of another while simultaneously retaining the stance of an objective observer." (Kohut)[33]

To gauge Rhys's stance towards her own experience adequately, it is important to emphasize the aspect of distance, not only the "suffering with" that is part of the concept of empathy. Even though Rhys describes her female characters as trapped in commodifying circumstances, she does not merge or ask her reader to merge with the characters—instead she points to the political and class structures behind them. Through varying and repeating the exploitive scenarios she creates a sense of outrage and places the onus of implementing social change on her readers. As Gardiner formulates it:

Not only writers, but also readers, I contend, may open spaces for "subversive thought" (Cixous). . . . Women writers like Rhys . . . who, in partial and exploratory ways that should not be dismissed simply because they are so, expose social injustices and encourage social and cultural transformations. . . . A politics of empathy points to strategies for engagement across difference, accessible to men as well as to women and hopeful of bridging the gaps between reading and writing, teaching and criticism, and representation and action.[34]

Elsewhere she states that Rhys's concept of identity does not seek to imitate the male model of autonomous identity, ". . . this identity is not

63

bourgeois male autonomy but a concept representing a process, part of which, one's sense of self, may involve a longing for coherence even as it represents itself as divided."[35] This strikes me as the central paradox of Rhys's writing—the divided self is so foregrounded that one tends to overlook the moments in the narrative that express a "longing for coherence." Giddens concurs with Gardiner in describing the fabrication of the self in processual and dialogic terms when he says, "The reflexive project of the self, which consists in the sustaining of coherent, yet continuously revised, biographical narratives, takes place in the context of multiple choice as filtered through abstract systems. . . . the notion of lifestyle takes on a particular significance. . . . there are standardising influences too—most notably, in the form of commodification, since capitalistic production and distribution form core components of modernity's institutions."[36] Rhys enacts a dialogue with earlier fictional selves to attain a stronger sense who she is now at the time of telling. She repeats commodification scenarios in which she is no longer the passive sufferer but the active narrator, wielding a compensatory control over her female characters. The author herself would argue that she needs to illustrate female commodification in all its bleakness to jolt the reader into awareness. The utopian moment occurs in the reader's response to the social critique and the portrayal of individual failure. Rhys held strong opinions about the hortatory purposes of her fiction:

> Rhys said that she lied but that her fiction told truth, especially the truths that life is unfair and social conventions mad. Fiction could redress this unfairness, not through the poetic justice of inventing a better world, but instead through the representation of an unfair world which, unlike the social reality we normally perceive, obtrudes its unfairness upon us. . . . Confessional release strives for knowledge and therefore for control.[37]

The result of having the unfairness forced upon us as readers is unsettling and may easily lead to blaming the author for not creating more self-affirming options for her characters.

For instance, Deborah Kelly Kloepfer posits a counternarrative of maternal bonding as the opportunity the characters lack, and implies that if only Rhys would allow them that experience, they could resist the commodifying practices of their society:

> Jean Rhys's characters are . . . abused, abandoned, powerless and passive. . . . All the men she [Julia] encounters exploit her both sexually and linguistically, holding power over her body and her language. . . . Julia's attempts to translate her (female) experience into a male system are doomed to failure, and yet Julia, having as

yet no access to the voice and body of the mother, has no other system or disposition to call into play.[38]

I see this theory as problematic because social critique can be more effective to pointing the way to utopia than any actual delineated model of such an ideal community, which is almost always blithely posited but still unattained by practice. Moreover, Kloepfer's critique mythologizes the mother figure as not implicated in the commodifying practices, as a refuge from them, when (as we shall see in a moment from Rhys's autobiographical recollections) it is primarily she who first teaches them to her female child. Furthermore, the mother is not an all-powerful oppositional figure because she is also a woman and, hence, holds only limited social power. A nostalgia for mother and the home as sites of the formation and nurturing of a transgressive female self must remain unfulfilled because Rhys does not share that belief.

I follow Emery's line of argument in this when she claims, ". . . it is important to understand the specific difference of this estrangement [Rhys feels from her society], that as outsiders among already eccentric texts [the experimental texts of modernism which portray antiheroes and fragmented selves as desirable] Rhys's novels portray an absence rather than a loss of identity and the homelessness of one who never had a home."[39]

Added to that absence is the weight of colonialist discourse, which renders a recuperation of an untainted self impossible. As Gayatri Spivak argues in an article on *Wide Sargasso Sea*, "No perspective critical of imperialism can turn the Other into a self, because the project of imperialism has always already historically refracted what might have been the absolutely Other into a domesticated Other that consolidates the imperialist self."[40] The ideology of an aggressively telic imperialism separated out women and blacks by identifying them with their bodies. As Iris Young demonstrates, although it denigrated them, they were also necessary to its understanding of its own mission as unitary, decisive, and militaristic: "The idea of a unified nation which developed in Europe in the nineteenth century, [George] Mosse argues, depended precisely on opposing manly virtue to the heterogeneity and uncertainty of the body, and associating despised groups with the body, setting them outside the homogeneity of the nation."[41] What we are confronted with in the case of Rhys, then, is an experience of displacement and disorientation on multiple levels—as a member of the ruling colonialist minority on Dominica, she is placed in a doubly precarious position: she is distanced from England, which she is nonetheless taught to consider her true home and the source of civilized comforts, such as books, liberty bodices, and knife-cleaning machines;[42] and she is exhorted to maintain racial and social distance from the black majority on the island while experiencing them as close in everyday interaction. After all, they are her family's caretakers—cook, nursemaid, gardener, field-worker. In addition, her maternal grandfather had been a disliked slaveowner but had also fathered children with a Creole, which created both hostility and a wish for rapprochement between the little white girl growing up and her black caretakers. Once Rhys went "home" to England, she discovered that the English considered her as inferior because she hailed from the colonies. Gardiner explains this ambiguous status very well to show how all these perceptions influenced Rhys's sense of herself as deficient and a misfit:

> The paranoid assessment that people were attacking her has social roots: she recounts instances of hostility directed towards her by blacks in the West Indies because her family had been slave owners and by whites in England who taunted her as though she were black. . . . Thus on both sides of the Atlantic she felt in the position of a member of a racial minority living among a resentful majority, a situation whose rage fuels much minority literature.[43]

In addition to the destabilizing effect of colonialist politics on Rhys as an individual, I perceive the double imperatives of class and gender, namely, to act like a lady and to act feminine, as disabling. It is precisely to an exploration of these aspects of female socialization that Rhys devotes most of her writerly attention.

Judith Butler has provided an incisive critique of French essentialist critics like Julia Kristeva, Hélène Cixous, and to a lesser extent Luce Irigaray, who look for an emancipatory site for female subjectivity located either in the maternal dyad or in the female body with its body fluids and plural sexual zones. Just as there is no essential self predating and outside society, Butler argues, there is no polymorphous female sexuality "outside" and anterior to the social norms that circumscribe our behavior as gendered subjects.[44] She draws our attention to the enactment of gender as social performance, and this is particularly significant for Rhys's women who struggle unhappily to execute performances of femininity. If gender is performative, so is identity—the one shapes the other:

> Foucault proposes an ontology of accidental attributes that exposes the postulation of identity as a culturally restricted principle of order and hierarchy, a regulatory fiction. . . . The appearance of an abiding substance or gendered self, what the psychiatrist Robert Stoller refers to as a "gender core," is thus produced by the regulation of attributes along culturally established lines of coherence. . . . In this sense, gender is not a noun, but neither is it a set of free-floating attributes, for we have seen that the substantive effect of

gender is performatively produced and compelled by the regulatory practices of gender coherence. Hence, within the inherited discourse of the metaphysics of substance, gender proves to be performative—that is, constituting the identity it is purported to be. In this sense, gender is always a doing, though not a doing by a subject who might be said to preexist the deed.[45]

The performance analogy has its limitations—as Sandra Bartky objects—because an actor is valued for his art, his creativity in embodying a role, and his greater personal flexibility, in that re-creation is both allowed and rewarded:

> The actor, for example, depends on his audience but is in no way inferior to it; he is not demeaned by his dependency. . . . the self-determination we think of as requisite to an artistic career is lacking here: Femininity as spectacle is something in which virtually every woman is required to participate. . . . the precise nature of the criteria by which women are judged, not only the inescapability of judgement itself, reflects gross imbalances in the social power of the sexes that do not mark the relationship of artists and their audiences.[46]

A good illustration of the actor's independence from his role is provided in an anecdote Rhys tells about a performance her siblings put on in celebration of her sixth birthday: her eldest brother simply decides in the middle of the performance that the role is beneath him and walks off the stage without getting penalized by the audience.[47] This stands in sharp contrast to the strict enforcement of bodily control and insistence on "proper performance" to which the girl child is subjected, a memory important enough for Rhys that she places it as emblematic of her sense of self at the opening of her autobiography:

> "Smile please," the man said. "Not quite so serious."
> He'd dodged out from behind the dark cloth. He had a yellow black face and pimples on his chin.
> I looked down at my white dress, the one I had got for my birthday, and my legs and the white socks coming half way up my legs, and the black shiny shoes with the strap over the instep.
> "Now," the man said.
> "Keep still," my mother said.
> I tried but my arm shot up of its own accord.
> "Oh what a pity, she moved."
> "You must keep still," my mother said, frowning.[48]

What becomes clear from this memory is that even at the age of six, Rhys was expected to perform femininely by posing, smiling, and keeping still—none of which she describes as coming to her naturally. The Creole photographer, whom the child fears as other and whom she demeans in typically imperialist fashion as ugly and impure, is complicit with the white upper-class lady in upholding the bodily regime of passivity, which, ironically, happens to be exactly what props up his own exploitation by the colonialist elite. The mother does not act as a supportive nurturer to her daughter, instead she is the stern disciplinarian.

As the scene of the birthday celebration makes clear, femininity is also silent/silenced—the mother does not explain or comment on her son's transgression, the sister who performs the role of Little Red Riding Hood (the classic innocent female victim) is silenced by her brother's refusal to act out his part, and finally, the little girl in whose honor this performance is given remains silenced and traumatized, blaming herself obscurely for her brother's loss of interest in the play. Because this memory is so bizarre, and details how early narcissistic wounds can be inflicted—and with what lasting effects on the female victim—I am quoting it in full:

> It is at Bona Vista that I have my first clear connected memory. It was my birthday, the sixth. . . . there I was crowned [with a flower wreath], bursting with pride and importance, safe, protected, sitting in a large armchair, my father on one side, my mother on the other, my shiny shoes a long way off the ground. . . .
>
> Suddenly my eldest brother, who was playing the part of the honest woodcutter, if there is such a character, said in a bored voice, "I'm not going on with this nonsense," and walked off the stage. My second brother, always good-natured, jumped from outside through the open window, growling fiercely. He was the wolf and was dressed for the part in a long white sheet. However, Red Riding Hood was silent, confused by the woodcutter's abrupt exit, and it was plain that the play couldn't go on. . . . There was a large pale blue book by the side of my chair. It was a birthday present from my father's mother. . . . When the play collapsed, my mother picked the book up, opened it and put it on my lap. Perhaps she feared I was about to cry. I looked at a picture of a little girl in a pink dress. By her side was a huge spider and underneath meaningless print, for I couldn't read them, not even short words. That's all I remember.
>
> It was very shortly after that we left for Roseau. Bona Vista had to be sold but we never went back.[49]

The birthday celebration itself has a sense of masquerade about it—the birthday girl wears a floral crown and a new white dress, visually coded as either a bride or a sacrificial victim. Instead of the promised initiation ceremony into the world of important grown-ups, what takes place is a sort of expulsion from paradise—the "family romance," as Freud calls it, is abruptly shown up to be a fiction because the omnipotent parents do not explain what happened or reassure their girls. The mother especially just wants to keep her youngest daughter quiet and proffers a picture book in lieu of verbal communication. The randomly opened book reveals a menacing, but indecipherable picture of a female in distress; she looks sufficiently like the birthday girl for her to become identified with her: instead of the neutral white, which is gender indeterminate (in fact, the wolf [brother] wears a white sheet), the girl in the picture wears a *pink* dress, that sexually codes her as "female," and "by her side was a huge spider and underneath meaningless print." The threat of being devoured by the wolf, which Red Riding Hood suffers in the fairy tale, is not lifted—the wolf attacks, and Red Riding Hood freezes. Instead of the comforting ending to the fairy tale in which order is restored, a picture of further distress in store for the now feminized girl child is superimposed: the wolf is transformed into a huge spider sitting by her side, just as the mother, who magically produces the picture, sits by the narrator's side. Rhys betrays a phobia about the devouring mother who, like some spiders, devours her young, and its consequence is a sense of physical endangerment coupled with further loss: "Bona Vista had to be sold but we never went back."

After this threatening episode, Rhys depicts herself as having internalized the mother's disapproving glance, ". . . from my head to my black stockings, which fell untidily round my ankles, I hated myself."[50] Sandra Bartky describes the source of this sort of internalized surveillance as "patriarchal culture," which I would qualify by emphasizing—as Rhys does in her autobiography—that in the bourgeois home this surveillance is exercised initially by the mother, not necessarily by a male. It is the mother, not the father, who oversees bodily control regimes having to do with cleanliness, tidiness, food-intake, and so on:

> In the regime of institutionalized heterosexuality woman must make herself "object and prey" for the man. . . . In contemporary patriarchal culture, a panoptical male connoisseur resides within the consciousness of most women: They stand perpetually before his gaze and under his judgment. Woman lives her body as seen by another, by an anonymous patriarchal Other. . . . To succeed in the provision of a beautiful or sexy body gains a woman attention and some admiration but little real respect and rarely any social power. A woman's effort to master feminine body discipline will lack importance just because she does it: Her activity partakes of the general depreciation of everything female. In spite of unrelenting pressure to "make the

69

most of what they have," women are ridiculed and dismissed for the triviality of their interest in such "trivial" things as clothes and make-up. Further, the narrow identification of woman with sexuality and the body in a society that has for centuries displayed profound suspicion toward both does little to raise her status. Even the most adored female bodies complain routinely of their situation in ways that reveal an implicit understanding that there is something demeaning in the kind of attention they receive.[51]

The "panoptical male connoisseur" eventually supplants the mother as a control figure: Rhys remembers meeting an Englishman at her uncle's wedding on another island who for her quickly comes to represent the superior standards of the "homeland:"

> Staying in Castries for the wedding was a young man, Mr. Kennaway. When he watches me I can see that he doesn't think I am pretty. Oh God, let me be pretty when I grow up. Let me be, let me be. That's what's in his eyes: "Not a pretty little girl." He is English. The night before the wedding my aunt plaited my hair into many tight little plaits, so it should be wavy next morning. And it was. With my bridesmaid's dress, my wavy hair, and holding my bouquet, I looked at Mr. Kennaway when we met. But his eyes were just the same: "Not a pretty little girl."[52]

What is striking in this passage is the sudden shift in tenses, which suggests that the memory still holds power over the narrator in the present. She has become, as Bartky puts it, a "self-policing subject,"[53] who attempts to attract the possibly quite uninterested male observer by submitting her body and her hair to cosmetic rituals that will render them more feminine looking: Bartky succinctly expresses this in stating: "Whatever else she may become, she is importantly a body designed to please or to excite. . . . Since the standards of female bodily acceptability are impossible fully to realize, requiring as they do a virtual transcendence of nature, a woman may live much of her life with a pervasive feeling of bodily deficiency. Hence a tighter control of the body has gained a new kind of hold over the mind."[54] Nothing expresses this internalized surveillance more disturbingly than the following quotation from *Smile Please:*

> I was nine years of age. Catching sight of myself in the long looking glass, I felt despair. I had grown up into a thin girl, tall for my age. My straight hair was pulled severely from my face and tied with a black ribbon. I was fair with a pale skin and huge staring eyes of no particular color. My brothers and sisters all had brown eyes and hair; why was I singled out to be the only fair one, to be called

Gwendolen, which means white in Welsh I was told? I was wearing an ugly brown Holland dress, the convent uniform.[55]

It seems particularly ironic that the attributes of "whiteness" and pale skin, which were highly prized and associated with a ladylike appearance since the time of Chaucer at least, should become markers of difference as lack in the colonial context. The narrator experiences her body as insubstantial, not fitting into the norms of height and weight, and of an insistent ghostlike transparency (the "huge staring eyes of no particular color"). In contrast, it is interesting to note in another colonial text that the body of a white male can be seen by female observers as equally unattractive, but that this perception is not internalized by him, and therefore less damaging to the self.[56]

Rhys's rejection of her whiteness went so far as wanting to be black, a kind of protective mimicry in reverse, because the blacks are treated like children and are "seen" as objects of concern by the white minority: "[Rhys's mother] loved babies, any babies. Once I heard her say that black babies were prettier than white ones. Was this the reason why I prayed so ardently to be black and would run to the looking glass in the morning to see if the miracle had happened? And though it never had, I tried again. Dear God, let me be black."[57] As the expendable middle daughter in a family in which sons counted more,[58] Rhys felt invisible, and she wished to counteract that experience of social death by wanting a black body and by checking the mirror to see if the metamorphosis had occurred. Her desire for this transformation is essentially naive: she envisions herself as joining a community but is unaware that it, too, is an object of manipulation and oppression. As far as her will to power is concerned, the path she takes is a circular and self-defeating one.

In a way, her experience of being socially dead paralleled that of the zombie in Vodoun belief, which was also part of Dominican island culture, and to which she was exposed by her nurses. The zombie's significance, according to Wade Davis, an ethnobotanist who has extensively researched the folklore and the actual phenomenon, is that he or she "is socially dead": "Zombies do not speak, cannot fend for themselves, do not even know their names. Their fate is enslavement. . . . because of the colonial history, the concept of enslavement implies that the peasant fears, and the zombie suffers, a fate that is literally worse than death—the loss of physical liberty that is slavery and the sacrifice of personal autonomy implied by the loss of identity."[59] In desiring to leave the white community and join the black, Rhys subjects herself to an emptying out of identity. It is a guileless and disingenuous gesture. The zombie in the black community is, in fact, an insensate pariah and therefore represents the most tragic figure of alienation.

A survey of Rhys's fiction bears this out: Anna Morgan, for instance, experiences herself as outside her body, split between actor and observer, while being powerless to change the action, "I heard my voice going on and on, answering his questions. . . ."[60] Or, when she looks at herself in the mirror, "It was as if I were looking at somebody else. I stared at myself for a long time, listening for the door to open."[61] When Anna's English stepmother explains menstruation to her, she starts to feel claustrophobic, as if she were being entombed in her own body, a symptom typical of the fear of becoming a zombie, ". . . I began to feel awfully miserable, as if everything were shutting up around me and I couldn't breathe. I wanted to die."[62] Like the young Jean Rhys, Anna does not want to be white or grow up into an English lady; she feels trapped in her body and attempts to rid herself of it through deliberately making herself ill, just as she later tries to rid her body of the unwanted pregnancy. Once more, the metaphor for her loss of identity is "being buried alive," and Anna takes this punishment on herself because she feels herself to be an outcast in a no-man's-land between the two races. In effect, she produces a body through her illness that bodies forth this intermediate status visibly, "I got awfully thin and ugly and yellow as a guinea, my father said":[63]

> But I knew that of course she [Francine, the black cook who is her confidante] disliked me too because I was white; and that I would never be able to explain to her that I hated being white. Being white and getting like Hester and all the things you get—old and sad and everything. I kept thinking, "No. . . . No. . . . No. . . ."
>
> I felt I was more alone than anybody had ever been in the world before and I kept thinking, "No . . . No . . . No . . ." just like that. . . .
>
> I thought, "Well, all right. This time I'll die." So I took my hat off and went and stood in the sun. . . .
>
> . . . The pain was like knives. And then I was cold, and when I had been very sick I went home.[64]

Anna "punishes" her body in a misguided attempt to strike out against the middle-class white role that is being forced upon her as she grows up. She does not verbalize her disenchantment with that role because she does not think she could make herself understood. Her refusal is internalized and turned against herself.

Menstruation is for her the cut-off point for the experience of being part of the black community on the island, because from then on, Anna must adopt more fully the ideals of womanhood and ladylike behavior proscribed by white English society: " 'I don't know what'll become of you if you go on like that,' Hester said. 'Let me tell you that you'll have a very unhappy life if you go on like that. [Anna had said that she hated Hester's lapdog.] People won't like you. People in England will dislike you very much if you say things like that."[65] Because nothing is explained to her about her body and she is not welcomed into the adult female role, Anna can only understand what is happening to her body as a sign of defilement and shame that portends her social death.

The adult Anna drifts though her life like a ghost, depleted of energy: "Sometimes not being able to get over the feeling that it was a dream. The light and the sky and the shadows and the houses and the people—all parts of the dream, all fitting in and all against me."[66] The down-and-out Julia Martin compares living in England to being buried alive, and, of course, that is precisely what zombies undergo, only to be resurrected to start another, but not better life in another place. "I listened to them both laughing and their voices going up and down. 'She'll be all right,' he said. 'Ready to start all over again in no time, I've no doubt.' " as the doctor says of Anna after her botched abortion.[67] When Julia is walking in the streets of London, she experiences the dark streets like an inevitable gravelike doom:

> Julia felt bewildered when she got into the street. She turned and walked without any clear idea of the direction she was taking. Each house she passed was exactly like the last. Each house bulged forward a little. . . .
>
> It was the darkness that got you. It was heavy darkness, greasy and compelling. It made walls round you, and shut you in so that you felt you could not breathe. You wanted to beat at the darkness and shriek to be let out. And after a while you got used to it.[68]

In all these instances, the female protagonist is alienated from her surroundings and cannot voice, only dumbly experience her loss of connection and self.

If we compare this fictionalized account of zombification to an account of the actual experience, the similarities become evident. In 1980, Clairvius Narcisse, a zombie, returned to the Haitian village where he had lived before his sixteen-year ordeal of wandering about without a memory and was recognized by his family. This case was exceptionally well documented and finally led to the discovery of the factual basis of the whole zombification process.[69] Davis explains:

> The widespread belief in physical zombies is based, therefore, on those rare instances in which the victim receives the correct dose of a toxic preparation, revives in the coffin, and is taken from the grave by the *bokor* [sorcerer]. The victim, affected by the drug and

traumatized by the set and setting of the total experience is report-
edly bound and led before a cross to be baptized with a new name.
After the baptism, or sometimes the next day, he or she is made to
eat a paste containing a strong dose of a potent psychoactive
drug . . . which induces a state of disorientation and amnesia. During the course of that intoxication, the zombie is socialized into a
new existence.[70]

Emery has commented on the uncanny feeling readers get of having read
Rhys's narratives somewhere before, which we can also understand as a
textual effect produced through its zombified female protagonists:

> We know the character has been here before, someplace outside
> and before the text, in this case not in a fictional precursor, but in
> a kind of ghost text that haunts the one we're reading. . . . The
> ghost text floats outside but also through the novel, making the
> characters appear only to disappear, and the plot, like Julia's life,
> an insubstantial series of "disconnected episodes." . . . The ghost
> text channels instead a modernist exploration of specifically female
> postwar disillusionment.[71]

The ghost text, I would argue, is produced on the one hand by the
familiar tradition of female commodification, on the other by the context
of Vodoun beliefs about identity and social transgression. Emery very
rightly points out that feminist critics of Rhys must take into account
specifically Caribbean concepts of identity rather than positing postmodern constructs of subjectivity as the guideline to which Rhys's characters
fail to measure up, but she merely defines those alternate concepts as
multiplicitous selves and an embracing of the carnivalesque as a moment
of resistance to European colonial oppression:

> The notion of a unified autonomous self conflicts with the protago-
> nist's quest, a quest for place within a collective history and pluralist
> culture. European and North American psychological theories of
> identity and ego development impose inappropriate or only partially
> appropriate values on texts that emerge from a Caribbean context.
> Even Lacanian psychoanalysis, with its acknowledgement of the de-
> centered subject, remains focused on the individual's internalized
> oppositions and differences within European patriarchal society, ig-
> noring broader cultural differences and collective histories.[72]

In the light of Davis's account of Haitian society, Emery's assertion of the
redemptive Caribbean context emerges as wishful thinking. The inherent
danger of envisioning the Caribbean as the place for the Other is that it
becomes remythologized. Anna cannot return to a black community

because she was never integrated into it in the first place. Second, this community is not truly an alternative because some of its rituals are recapitulations of slavery, putting it into the thrall of the colonialists.

Although it is true that Vodoun religion combines elements of many different African tribes who were sold into slavery to the islands of the Caribbean,[73] the Vodoun concept of identity not only mirrors displacement and the tenuousness of identity, it is also grounded in the body and structured to include a strong notion of individual willpower and subjectivity. In the West this concept arises out of the individual's ability to maintain a narrative of self and is not necessarily tied to the body, but in Vodoun belief the self is housed in the *ti bon ange,* a guardian spirit that surrounds the body and forms a visible part of it. Opposed to the Lacanian concept according to which self is constituted linguistically by a separation, a rupture between itself and the Other,[74] the Vodoun self consists of four elements that have to be in balance with each other: the *z'étoile,* an individual's hopes for his future life, projected into the sky as a star; the *n'âme,* the physical body; and the *gros bon ange* and the *ti bon ange* that together constitute the soul.

> The two aspects of the Vodoun soul, the *ti bon ange* and the *gros bon ange,* are best explained with a metaphor commonly used by the Haitians themselves. Sometimes when one stands in the late afternoon light the body casts a double shadow, a dark core and then a lighter penumbra, faint like the halo that sometimes surrounds the full moon. This ephemeral fringe is the *ti bon ange,* the "little good angel," while the image at the center is the *gros bon ange,* the "big good angel." The latter is the life force that all sentient beings share; it enters the individual at conception and functions only to keep the body alive. At clinical death, it returns immediately to God and once again becomes part of the great reservoir of energy that supports all life. But if the *gros bon ange* is undifferentiated energy, the *ti bon ange* is that part of the soul directly associated with the individual. As the *gros bon ange* provides each person with the power to act, it is the *ti bon ange* that molds the individual sentiments within each act. It is one's aura, and the source of all personality, character and willpower.[75]

Davis goes on to say that the *ti bon ange* is captured and separated from the person's body during zombification, and that the resurrected zombie's body is often beaten so that the *gros bon ange* will leave the body and only return when the zombie is given a new existence through baptism:

> It is the loss of the *ti bon ange,* that part of the soul which manifests willpower, personality, and individual identity, which breaks the

equilibrium of an individual and leaves in his or her wake the zombie. . . . Another means of stealing the *ti bon ange* is to spread toxic powders in the form of a cross on the threshold of the victim's doorway. . . . The *zombie cadavre* that has its *gros bon ange* and *n'âme* can function; however, separated from the *ti bon ange* the body is but an empty vessel. . . . It is this notion of alien, malevolent forces taking control of the individual that is so terrifying to the Vodounist. In Haiti, the fear is not of being *harmed* by zombies as much as *becoming* one. The *zombie cadavre* is a body without a complete soul, matter without morality.[76]

The paradigm of the zombie acknowledges the precariousness of identity, its susceptibility to outside forces. Zombies have no language to express what is happening to them. They are alienated from their former selves and disoriented in the space around them.

This also indicates, then, that thresholds and crossroads are magically powerful places at which harm can befall an individual, or, more positively, at which the *loa* (the gods) can enter to "mount" an individual, take over his or her body.[77] The city as the paradigmatic settlement that is built at the crossroads then becomes the logical locus for zombification. It is in the city that one encounters other *zombis cadavres,* such as the emaciated old man with whom Julia dances at a club:

The other male dancer was elderly, nearer seventy than sixty, thin, dressed in a very loosely fitting grey suit. His face was cadaverous, his nose long and drooping. He smiled continually as he danced, displaying very yellow teeth. . . . Julia was looking at the old man dancing with an absorbed expression. . . . As he leaned over the table his face was all bones and hollows in the light of the lamp striking upwards, like a skeleton's face. . . . Julia was being hugged very tightly by her partner, who hung a little over her shoulder, pervading her, as it were, and smiling. . . . Her body looked abandoned when she danced, but not voluptuously so. It was the abandonment of fatigue. . . . She seemed to be moving stiffly and rather jerkily. . . . Julia was sitting alone at the table. [Mr. Horsfield] raised his eyebrows and said in an ironical way: "Well?" She laughed so hysterically that he was taken aback, and glanced round rather nervously.[78]

Rhys skillfully blends the zombie motif with the European dance-of-death motif, after having been taken over by the zombie—Julia can only react like a galvanized corpse, laughing hysterically. Such hysterical laughter arises out of a threatening of the borders between bodies, her body has been claimed by an evil figure like the Vodoun *loa,* Baron Samedi, the god of the graveyard.[79] In itself, this ghoulish scenario only stands as a heightened metaphor for Julia's own commodification: her body is taken over by men for their pleasure, she abandons her body to them. She registers protest through somatic language, but, although it always reaches its addressee, this resistance is all too easily branded as deviant and subjected to even tighter restraints.

Julia's last new customer, Mr. Horsfield, provokes another attack of hysteria when he touches Julia's body on the dark staircase going up to her room. The stairs are a transitional zone in the house, they mediate between inside and outside. The are also described as being at the center of the rooming house, and would thus be occupying the place of the *poteau mitan*, the centerpost in Vodoun ritual gatherings. Given this context, it is only logical that Julia would interpret the strange touch as a taking over of her body by an evil spirit:

> He groped and touched her hand, then her arm, and the fur collar of her coat. Then he ran his fingers downwards again, as a blind man might have done. He felt a strange pleasure in touching her like that—wordlessly, in the dark. She said in a loud voice: "Oh God, who touched me?" . . . "Who touched me?" she screamed. "Who's that? Who touched my hand? What's that?"
>
> "Julia!" he said.
>
> But she went on screaming loudly: "Who's that? Who's that? Who touched my hand?"[80]

The attack occurs in the dark, and resembles in its secrecy and inexplicability the raising of the entombed zombie by the *bokor*, the evil witchdoctor, who then administers a potion that, according to Davis, produces very similar effects to the ones Julia suffers: "Alone, its intoxication has been characterized as an induced state of psychotic delirium marked by disorientation, acute confusion, and complete amnesia. . . . It is in the course of that intoxication that the zombie is baptized with a new name and led away to be socialized into a new existence."[81] Rhys masterfully suggests the zombie's drugged state before Julia is indeed sent packing by the landlady, excluded from even the flimsy form of human togetherness a rooming house provides: " 'Who was it touched me?' said Julia. Her eyes were very wide open, the pupils dwindled to pin-points."[82]

It is implied by the landlady's reaction that the new name with which Julia is baptized is that of whore, and the new life is merely another shift in location from London to Paris, from one commodifying urban center to another. Another crucial characteristic of the zombie is that Julia does not know her name. Being known by one's name implies social recognition, and of course that is what is being withheld from a zombie. When Horsfield addresses the zombified Julia by her name, she cannot recognize herself in his call. An equivalent scene takes place between Julia and her dying mother, who also appears to have been zombified:

> Her mother's eyes opened suddenly and stared upwards. Julia put her face closer and said in a frightened, hopeful voice: "I'm Julia, do you know? It's Julia."
> The sick woman looked steadily at her daughter. Then it was like seeing a spark go out and the eyes were again bloodshot, animal eyes. Nothing was there. She mumbled something in a thick voice, then turned her head away and began to cry, loudly and disconsolately, like a child.[83]

There is no mutual recognition between commodified women, only mute suffering and inarticulate expressions of pain. The dying maternal body does not remember, but still feels pain, and this prospect is what awaits the daughter.

The disturbing political significance of the diseased body in Rhys's fiction is analyzed very well by Emery: "Perceived as potential carriers of 'social' disease, they [the female characters] themselves become ill. . . . Illness and disease become tropes and actualities in Rhys's fiction that enable an exploration of otherness. . . . The morality of health and the rightness of the well-fed no longer holds as illness opens the way for new perceptions and socially critical visions."[84] The stigmatized female characters themselves only rarely verbalize that criticism directly, more often it is presented as muted and at a distance, as when Julia talks back to her chauvinist uncle, taking sides with Dostoevsky as a social critic who speaks for her from the place of the diseased body:

> When luncheon was over, Uncle Griffiths sat in the arm-chair and went on talking, eagerly, as if the sound of his own voice laying down the law to his audience of females reassured him. He talked and talked. He talked about life, about literature, about Dostoevsky. He said: "Why see the world through the eyes of an epileptic?" Julia spoke mechanically, as one's foot shoots out when a certain nerve in the knee is struck: "But he might see things very clearly, mightn't he? At moments."[85]

Over and over, images of the injured body, both male and female, intrude upon speech. Incompletely regimented, they signify more directly and unequivocally than verbal expression what ails the postwar community. The anthropologist Mary Douglas draws our attention to the political significance of obsessive concern with the body's boundaries, such as orifices and skin: "When rituals express anxiety about the body's orifices the sociologist counterpart of this anxiety is a care to protect the political and cultural unity of a minority group. . . . The threatened boundaries of their body politic would be well mirrored in their care for the integrity, unity and purity of the physical body.[86] Examples of this concern can be seen in the obsessive attention Rhys's women pay to their skin, "There's something you can buy that makes your neck fat. Venus Carnis. 'No fascination without curves. Ladies, realize your charms.' But it costs three guineas and where can I get three guineas?"; or to presenting a smooth and contained body surface and silhouette, "He laughed and then he said, 'You've got a hairpin sticking out on this side, spoiling your otherwise perfect appearance.' " . . . "But she stayed there staring at me, so I went outside and finished putting on my gloves standing on the doorstep. (A lady always puts on her gloves before going into the street.)"[87]

Such an "epidermalizing" of the female body suggests a pervasive communal fear of contamination by waste matter, a wish to stave off death by clinging to physical perfection and cleanliness.[88] All of this can be understood in the context of the traumatizing carnage soldiers experienced on the battlefields of the World War I. There is a striking insistence in the texts that women's clothes must be *whole,* not torn, wrinkled, or gaping open—if they are not perfectly composed, swift social sanctions follow, because symbolically speaking, the fictive "wholeness" of the social fabric in postwar Britain would be rent. The alliance of the working girl and the "torn kimono" is highly significant in this respect. Kimonos are worn by Japanese women, and the cliché of the geisha girl—as a male fantasy of possessing an exotic love-slave as well as a threat to more stolid British xenophobic housekeeping—haunts the British lower-middle-class households Rhys describes in *Voyage:*

> [Anna and Maudie, the chorus girls,] had good rooms. The landlady had said, "No, I don't let to professionals." . . . after Maudie had talked for a while, making her voice sound as ladylike as possible, she had said, "Well, I might make an exception for this time." Then the second day we were there she made a row because we both got up late and Maudie came downstairs in her nightgown and a torn kimono. "Showing yourself at my sitting-room window 'alf naked like that,' the landlady said. 'And at three o'clock in the afternoon too. Getting my house a bad name.' "[89]

This example shows how fragile the border between the professional woman and the prostitute is: A professional can dispose of her own time, getting up late because her job keeps her up late, she can wear "exotic" clothes if they are to her taste, but in making these choices she becomes marked, deliberately or not, as an anomaly, as socially impure. The reverse of this disgust for the exotic female is a kind of erotic fascination with her: another landlady collects bibelots of geishas and odalisques, and thus domesticates the exotic difference she sees as both desirable and endangering: "The mantelshelf was crowded with china ornaments—several dogs of various breeds, a pig, a swan, a geisha with a kimono and sash in colours and a little naked woman lying on her stomach with a feather in her hair."[90] The geisha and the odalisque are both emblems of Orientalist fantasies about female sexuality, and they are coded as impure by being placed next to animals like pigs and dogs. This kind of "othering" effectively places the professional woman in postwar Europe on the same level as the native woman in colonial society, and Rhys thereby underscores her impression that both societies are structured hierarchically along similar principles of suppression.

Just as the bed-sitters in which the professional woman lives are always too cold and dismal, the workplace of the black woman servant is conversely described as infernal: "But the kitchen was horrible. There was no chimney and it was always full of charcoal smoke. Francine was there, washing up. Her eyes were red with the smoke and the watering. Her face was quite wet. She wiped her eyes with the side of her hand and looked sideways at me. Then she said something in patois and went on washing up."[91] Francine's role in the colonialist family is to wash, cook, take care of bodily fluids (it is she who explains first to Anna about menstruation), just as the kept woman's role is to minister to men's sexual needs, but otherwise not to intrude on their private space. Douglas observes that same structure in the Indian caste system, and this explains why the female professional's body is so feared by those above her in the class structure:

> The lowest castes [in Hindu India] are the most impure and it is they whose humble services enable the higher castes to be free of bodily impurities. They wash clothes, cut hair, dress corpses and so on. The whole system represents a body in which by the division of labour the head does the thinking and praying and the most de-spised parts carry away waste matter. . . . Thus for any ego within the system the threatening non-structure against which barriers must be erected lies below. The sad wit of pollution as it comments on bodily functions symbolizes descent in the caste structure by contact with faeces, blood and corpses.[92]

If the "threatening non-structure lies below" this fear of contaminating chaos even gets transferred onto the female body as such: the lower body is a zone that needs to be carefully controlled, and yet always seems to be unruly, exhibit disorder. The following example from *Mr. Mackenzie* may illustrate this point: "Her coat was very old. She had grown fatter in the last few months and it was now too tight and too short for her. She imagined that it gave her a ridiculous appearance, especially behind. Indeed her rare impulses towards activity vanished when she thought of

80

her coat."[93] However, there is also subversive potential in that body zone. In her autobiography as well as in *Voyage,* Rhys mentions a ritual that is followed when the black woman Francine and the white colonialist daughter talk:

> Years later I made great friends with a Negro girl called Francine. I've written about her before. Francine's stories were quite different, full of jokes and laughter, descriptions of beautiful dresses and good things to eat. But the start was always a ceremony. Francine would say "Tim-tim." I had to answer "Boissêche," then she'd say, *"Tablier Madame est derrière dos"* (Madam's apron is back to front). She always insisted on this ceremony before starting a story and it wasn't until much later, when I was reading a book about obeah, that I discovered that Boissêche is one of the gods. I grew very fond of Francine and admired her; when she disappeared without a word to me I was hurt. . . . I still think of Francine and now I can imagine other reasons for her complete disappearance from the house and from my life.[94]

Once the mistress's apron is turned around, carnival logic rules, what is a constraining code of layering and covering up in everyday social life now is turned back to front, what was hidden underneath is now exposed.[95] If masquerade is embraced intentionally and playfully between women, it becomes liberating, enables female bonding and the formulation of a counternarrative "full of jokes and laughter."

There is a curious indeterminate stage between playful masquerade as enabling and masquerade as restrictive bodily regimen, which is reached by the professional prostitute. Laurie in *Voyage* does not merely give her body up to men for pay, she follows masquerade strategies to change her appearance at will, and she thus obtains more money from a larger pool of customers:

> "I bank half of everything I get," she said. . . . Her bedroom was small and very tidy. There were no photographs and no pictures. There was a huge bed and a long plait of hair on the dressing-table.
> "I kept that," she said. "I pin it on sometimes when I wear nightgowns. Of course, in pyjamas I keep my own short hair. Why don't you cut your hair? You ought; it would suit you. Heaps of girls in Paris have their hair cut, and I bet they will here too sooner or later. And false eyelashes, my dear, sticking out yards—you should see them. They know what's what, I tell you."[96]

Laurie manipulates her appearance to create gender ambiguity, she can be either the Victorian girlchild with long hair in a nightgown or the more modern twenties' style *gamine* in masculine pyjamas and short hair. The

81

exaggerated production of femininity as a spectacle—false eyelashes "sticking out yards"—calls forth a certain exuberance. The one who wields these tools with calculation believes herself to be in control of the men and does indeed achieve a blank space of her own, free of the saccharine photographs or pictures that cover the walls of all the bed-sitters Rhys describes like a blight. Rhys exposes Laurie's belief in her independence as false consciousness, but she seems at the same time admiring of the working girl's ruthlessness and matter-of-fact attitude. Perhaps "they know what's what" after all because they market themselves successfully and, provided they follow bourgeois rules of thrift and persistent work, gain some measure of economic independence, even if they do not escape commodification.

The cinema provides an urban location for women to fantasize themselves into a different existence, even if the opportunities for female role-play shown on the screen are profoundly ambivalent. Postwar British moviegoers in Rhys's texts get to see female criminals like Three-Fingered Kate perform acts of theft from the dwindling ranks of the monied aristocracy, or they witness the erotic display of *Hot Stuff from Paris*.[97] Anna in *Voyage* is emboldened by watching the antics of Kate, she focuses on her agency. Her companion Ethel, the manicurist with upper-class pretensions, on the other hand, feels threatened by the send-up of the social hierarchy in the crime story. She disparages the outlaw Kate for being a foreigner: "Did you notice her hair? I mean, did you notice the curls she had on at the back? . . . 'Well,' she said, 'that girl who did Three-Finger Kate was a foreigner. . . . Couldn't they have got an English girl to do it? . . . And she stuck red curls on her black hair and she didn't care a scrap. . . . An English girl wouldn't have done that.' "[98] Ethel inadvertently destroys the filmic illusion for Anna, and this is ultimately liberating for her. If Kate can impersonate a particular identity by sticking fake curls on her head, then so can any woman. Kate shows up gender to be a constructed performance, not an inherent set of physical determinants. It follows that performance is not sacrosanct or immutable, as a first step it can be parodied and discredited. Judith Butler expresses the unsettling potential of such parodic representation of gender when she says:

> In what senses, then, is gender an act? As in other ritual social dramas, the action of gender requires a performance that is repeated. . . . Gender is an identity tenuously constituted in time, instituted in an exterior space through a *stylized repetition of acts*. The effect of gender is produced through the stylization of the body and, hence, must be understood as the mundane way in which bodily gestures, movements, and styles of various kinds constitute the illusion of an abiding gendered self. This formulation moves the

conception of gender off the ground of a substantial model of identity to one that requires a conception of gender as a constituted *social temporality.*

. . . The possibilities of gender transformation are to be found precisely in the arbitrary relation between such acts, in the possibility of a failure to repeat, a deformity, or a parodic repetition that exposes the phantasmatic effect of abiding identity as a politically tenuous construction. . . . parodic displacement, indeed, parodic laughter, depends on a context and a reception in which subversive confusions can be fostered. What performance where will invert the inner/outer distinction and compel a radical rethinking of the psychological presuppositions of gender identity and sexuality? . . . and what kind of gender performance will enact and reveal the performativity of gender itself in a way that destabilizes the naturalized categories of identity and desire.[99]

Kate reveals gender *and* class to be a masquerade, and it is for this subversive discovery rather than the theft of the necklace that she gets "five years hard." The female outlaw on the screen is an oddity, but one with whom that other oddity, the young urban self-supporting single woman, can identify. Parody is momentarily empowering in Rhys's narratives, but it gets punished if it is directed at men, for instance when Germaine, a French prostitute, mimics her male friend's social gaffe:

"You think you're perfect, don't you?" Germaine said. "well, you're not perfect. Whenever you drink champagne you belch. I was ashamed of you the other night. You go like this." She imitated him. The waiter, who was on the other side of the room, heard; and he looked across at us with a shocked expression, pursing his mouth up. "Did you see that face?" Germaine said. "Well, that's the way you look sometimes, Vincent. Scorn and loathing of the female—a very common expression in this country."[100]

Parody can only be directed at the established members of society from outside, hence it must be the foreign woman who gives it expression. Her foreignness puts her in a precarious position vis-à-vis the hierarchy, as an outsider she is easily dismissed.

Another urban location that offers a space for difference to be articulated is the record shop. When Julia returns to Paris after her failure to recover a sense of home in her visit to London, she goes to a Pathéphone Salon and listens to records: "A woman's voice, harsh and rather shrewish, began to sing in her ear. . . . She felt the hardness of the receiver pressed up against her ear. The voice sang the chorus of a sentimental and popular song. 'Pars, sans te retourner, pars.' An unlucky song."[101] The woman's disembodied voice communicates an injunction to disobey the female social standard of the "ethic of care," to leave and move forward without turning around, looking (at the) back, but this attitude is an impossible one for the embodied woman who is paralyzed, frozen in her tracks, by constantly monitoring her appearance from the back. Nonetheless, once that suggestion is planted in Julia's mind, she attempts to act on it: " 'Well, she thought suddenly, no use getting into a state.' . . . her plan of spending the evening in Montparnasse had retreated into the back of her mind. She only wanted to walk somewhere straight ahead. She turned her back on the Place St. Michel and began to walk towards the Châtelet [which is located in a straight line across the river]."[102] This forward progress is impeded, however, when a man starts to follow her, as had happened in the first part of the narrative. We get a sense of circular movement and entrapment, largely because female speech is dismissed by men when it is protesting its own commodification and tries to transcend it.

Ultimately, violent *gestures* of rebellion remain at least momentarily more effective than *verbal* protest—Anna pressing her cigarette down on Walter's hand;[103] or Julia slapping Mr. Mackenzie in the face publically,[104] or pushing a hotel door into a man's face to dissuade him from following her.[105] The hysterical body expresses female rebellion, as Elaine Showalter has documented: "Staying within the roles offered women no protection against hysteria either. For a feminist analysis, we have to turn the question around. Instead of asking if rebellion was mental pathology, we must ask whether mental pathology was suppressed rebellion. . . . Was hysteria— the 'daughter's disease'—a mode of protest for women deprived of other social or intellectual outlets or expressive options?"[106] In this context, we might also be able to read the women's inability to speak in full sentences or to speak decisively, as a refusal to adopt the Lacanian Law of the Father: "In patriarchal socialization, the power to formulate sentences coincides developmentally with a recognition of the power of the father."[107] For instance, Rhys's female speaker often hesitates: "She faced him and said: 'let me tell you, you are—you are. . . .' The word came to her. 'You are *ignoble.*' "[108] This resistance is perceived by the male interlocutor as irritating because it disrupts the telic order of the social universe. But as resistance it merely has a hampering effect, holding up the flow of things, it is not truly subversive, as the following attempt at intimate communication between Julia and Mr. Horsfield, surely the most sympathetic male listener Rhys invents in her fiction, indicates:

> Then her face assumed such a vague expression that Mr. Horsfield thought: "Well, go on, get on with it. If it's going to be the story of your life, get on with it."

> . . . She spoke as if she were trying to recall a book she had read or a story she had heard and Mr. Horsfield felt irritated by her vagueness, "because," he thought, "your life is your life, and you must be pretty definite about it. Or if it's a story you are making up, you ought to at least have it pat."[109]

The problem of *who owns the narrative*—". . . your life is your life, and you must be pretty definite about it"—is precisely what is at stake here. The commodified woman does not feel she owns her narrative and can only tell it at a remove, just as she experiences her body at a distance, through the commodifying male gaze.

It is Rhys's merit that she drives it home unrelentingly to what an overwhelming extent women in her society are conditioned to define themselves through compliant behavior and the reactions of those around them, men in particular. The cinema becomes for her characters liberating because of its relentless stereotyping: repeated moviegoing brings about a heightened and increasingly critical awareness of inflexible gender roles. This critical awareness, however, is still bound up by the passive spectatorship that cinema encourages: it is essentially reactive. Rhys's female characters are still too dependent on mirroring themselves in the reactions of those around them to operate as autonomous agents. In his analysis of modernity, Anthony Giddens formulates very simply and compellingly what allows an individual to feel that she owns her self: "The existential question of self-identity is bound up with the fragile nature of the biography which the individual 'supplies' about herself. A person's identity is not to be found in behaviour, nor—important though this is—in the reactions of others, but in the capacity *to keep a particular narrative going.*"[110] Rhys sees the city as the site where female imprisonment in commodifying practices is made public, and, in an easily overlooked aside at the beginning of *Voyage,* she goes so far as to equate the city with the woman's gaol:

> He asked how long I had been in England, and I told him, "Two years," and then we talked about the tour. The company was going on to Brighton, then Eastbourne, and then we finished in London.
> "London?" Mr. Jones said, lifting his eyebrows.
> "Well, Holloway. Holloway's London, isn't it?"
> "Of course it is," Mr. Jeffries said.[111]

Returning to this assertion, that Holloway *is* London,[112] after having explored the systematic abjection of women in Britain and France between the wars, we see that Rhys forces her readers to answer that question: yes, it is, but it is *made* to be, and this implies the moral imperative to unmake the city as prison house, to construe a vision of the city, and by extension society, as empowering and offering up better choices to those who come to it. We shall witness a more politicized and informed systemic critique in the period of alienation following World War II when we consider *The Seawall*, an early novel of Marguerite Duras. Her female protagonist makes great progress towards agency through increased physical mobility coupled with experimentation and mimicry. She begins to treat her status as an exchange object as a game in which she controls her own *mise en jeu* with the help of recontextualizing practices, verbal punning and parodic reenactment of male roles. Duras concludes the narrative with Suzanne's decision to remove herself from the commodity exchange, but does not show her integration in a new community based on nonexploitive principles. That becomes possible only after the feminist movement of the late sixties established a public awareness of women as a group force who can accelerate social change.

CHAPTER

2

Jamming the Exchange Machinery in Duras's *Un Barrage contre le Pacifique*

In *The Seawall*, Duras critiques a colonialist market economy that is based on suppression and exploitation. Her systemic critique is far more comprehensive and articulated than that of Rhys. Duras points to capitalist economic practices as alienating and immoral, but unlike Rhys, she understands that the alienation characters experience is an intentional systemic effect of capitalism. Duras wants to abolish this form of social organization altogether, whereas Rhys pleaded for a humane reform of the system. Rhys remains too implicated in middle-class values to envision a political alternative, whereas Duras espouses a leftist agenda for social change.

Unlike Rhys's commodified women in London and Paris, white single women are a sought-after rarity in colonial Indochina. This allows them to conceive differently of their value. In a border zone on the periphery of empire, Duras's protagonist Suzanne learns to manipulate her own status as an exchange object as a game. Far from being restricted to somatic speech, she learns to use verbal parody as a way of transcending and finally even opting out of the market economy altogether. Suzanne begins to make choices and negotiate spaces with far greater confidence than Rhys's zombified characters. Whereas Rhys's characters are displaced from their homeland and feel alienated from their surroundings, Duras's female protagonists are taught a memory of their origins and articulated values like tenacity and intelligence that foster a certain

87

pride in who they are. In a process of trial and error, Suzanne experiments with, and takes control of, her sexuality. She eventually refuses to market herself to any man and leaves the colonial commodity exchange. This resistance is verbalized and politicized, but it is still an individual act. By contrast, women writers like Drabble and Maron who write after the feminist movement are able to conceive of local coalition building between women and collective resistance to oppressive political practices.

The opening of Marguerite Duras's autobiographical coming-of-age novel *The Seawall*[1] is marked by an agonistic opposition between a small isolated family group and an uncaring outside world and its denizens, "ceux qui vivent ailleurs, . . . ceux qui sont du monde."[2] Appropriately, the family is located in a border zone: their shack is by the road that connects two fictional colonial cities in Indochina, Ram and Kam. Furthermore, it is built on land that itself belongs to a shifting zone between land and sea. The only appeal for connection the family can direct at the larger society it experiences as a remote and unified body is through trade: they buy a horse that is supposed to act as a link between their outpost and the people of the colonial cities. The idea of a forcible extraction of profit is a basic tenet of the colonialist enterprise, and the family wants to participate in it in a desperate effort. To this end they mimic the colonialists' language of productivity and profit. This terminology can be used to reveal and conceal, just as mimicry protects an animal from its natural predators by blending its appearance with its surroundings while letting it follow its own activities.

Duras exploits the ambiguities of colonialist rhetoric to expose its underpinnings. In playing upon the double meanings of words like *cheval* (sawhorse) and *transports* (emotional intoxication), for instance, Duras emphasizes the constructedness and precarious artificiality of the family's colonialist enterprise. She reveals the family's hopes of an improved existence as fraudulent. Through the use of sarcasm and laconic statements, she also puts her reader into a similarly disempowered position towards the narrative as is the family's situation in relation to the colonialist structure. She achieves this by giving out so limited an amount of information at the beginning that the reader is forced into an identification with the family, because they at least are more clearly defined than the remote and undifferentiated "world out there."

On the level of language, Duras skillfully mimics the collapse of hope by introducing shifts through repetition and variation: there is a slippage from the initial assertion "une bonne idée" to "une idée, ça prouvait qu'ils pouvaient encore avoir des idées," just as there is a falling-off from "c'était quelque chose" to "pas grand-chose" to "misérable."

Cheval (horse/sawhorse) is both a means of transportation and a means of support, a prop that holds up a larger object. In other words, it moves and is animate or it is fixed and a man-made object. After some hopes of success are raised by the purchase of the horse/prop, they are quickly undercut by two laconic statements: "Cela dura huit jours. Le cheval était trop vieux . . . , puis il creva."[3]

The repetition of the family's desire "to squeeze out something"[4] is framed by qualifiers, for instance "même si," or variations on the absence of growth "leur coin de plaine saturé de sel," "d'un désert, où rien ne pousse." As a result of this kind of linguistic propping, the family's excitement soon reveals itself as a short outburst, a fit that will not produce a change of condition. It rings ironically true then, when an impersonal voice philosophizes: "C'était ça les transports." *Transport/transports* means both transportation and fit of passion, exaltation, but Duras refuses to romanticize the subversive potential of such altered states.[5]

The family defensively stakes its identity, its value as participants in the colonial enterprise on this prop, from which we can extrapolate Duras's critique of a sense of identity propped on a kind of exploitive consumption of goods. It is through possession of goods that the family wants to raise its status and be integrated into the vaguely designated group of "ceux qui sont du monde." In French the word *monde* carries with it the connotation of high society; the family's goal is to belong to the top echelon of colonialist society after being released from its paralyzed state at the bottom of white society; they are, in fact, white-trash farmers without marketable goods. The main reason for this is that the mother of the family has obtained a bad piece of land on loan from the colonial administrators.

It is not just biblical hyperbole when the metaphor of the salt soaked plain is invoked—the border zone between sea and fertile higher ground is flooded regularly, its crops destroyed. Duras aligns herself with the Marxian analysis of alienated labor—whereas agricultural workers maintain some control of the production process and have the fruits of their labor to sell, postagricultural workers have nothing but their physical labor, hence their bodies to market.[6] In this situation, the nubile body of the daughter Suzanne becomes a potential commodity that might buy social prestige and connection.

From the outset Duras evokes images of dessication and stasis that form the backdrop against which the two trajectories of growth and change, the two coming-of-age stories of Joseph and Suzanne, develop. There are old, dried up bodies of failed colonialists like Ma who are too frail to bring forth lasting change. A scene in which the family mocks their miserable existence with laughter shows how Ma's body is suddenly and convulsively traversed by unstoppable laughter, just as if her land were being flooded and her crops ruined. The aged female body is only a frail barrier against destruction and nothingness:

> Tais-toi, dit la mère, je vais avoir une crise.
> Elle était très rouge. Elle était vieille, elle avait eu tant de malheurs, et si peu l'occasion d'en rire, que le rire en effet, s'emparant d'elle, l'ébranlait dangereusement. La force de son rire ne semblait pas venir d'elle et gênait, faisait douter de sa raison.[7]

> ["Shut up," said Ma. "I'm going to have an attack."
> She was very red. She was old, she had had so much misfortune and so little occasion to laugh about it that the laughter, in truth, took hold of her, shook her dangerously. The strength of her laughter did not seem to come from her but from outside. It was worrying, it made her look slightly insane.][8]

Because the daughter is able to observe her mother's hysterical symptoms, she learns to evaluate them as ineffective means of resistance. She realizes that the mother's laughter is both freeing and debilitating and that more effective resistance will have to be rationally articulated.

Opposed to the frail maternal body is the grotesquely bloated body of the successful male colonialist, Père Bart, the canteen keeper at Ram. Even though his body is substantial compared to Ma's, he is almost immobilized by his vampiric feeding on the alcohol that has made his fortune:

> Il ne se déplaçait que pour accueillir ses clients. Il ne faisait rien d'autre. Il allait vers eux avec une lenteur de monstre marin sorti de son élément, sans presque soulever ses pieds du sol tant le gênait son ventre inoubliable, véritable barrique d'absinthe. Il ne faisait pas que la boire. Il vivait d'en faire la contrebande, et en était riche. On venait lui en chercher de très loin, depuis les plantations du Nord.[9]

> [He never moved except to greet a customer. He did nothing else, and when he displaced himself it was with the slowness of a marine monster removed from its native element, almost without lifting his feet from the floor, so weighty was his unforgettable paunch, that barrel of absinthe. He drank nothing but that, and scarcely did anything else. He lived, and had become rich, by selling it illegally. People came to him from great distances, as far off as the plantations of the North.][10]

The phlegmatic body becomes a metaphor for colonialist commerce, whereas the emaciated one stands for the social dislocation it produces.

Although his body is self-contained and impermeable, hers is vulnerable to outside forces. What both bodies have in common, however, is that neither can sustain active movement or a change of state. The only transformation that is conceivable for those bodies is their collapse in death.

Suzanne's nubile body, on the contrary, has its full potential as a commodity in the colonialist economy, and initially this realization dawns on Suzanne, bringing alone a feeling of mobility and empowerment. She understands suddenly that her body is a commodity to be seen and to be circulated in the world—"to make its way in the world": "Elle, elle était là, bonne à être vue, il n'y avait que la porte à ouvrir. Ce n'était pas fait pour être caché mais au contraire pour être vu et faire son chemin de par le monde."[11] ["She, she was there, worth seeing, she only needed to open the door. Her body was not made to be hidden but quite the opposite to be seen and to make its way in the world."][12] I am not arguing that the commodified and displayed female body could act per se as a subversive agent in the colonialist enterprise, but rather that Suzanne's awareness of possessing something worthy of being seen, that is, recognized, is empowering for her. It allows her to inhabit her body with pride and to conceive of moving out from the incestuous and constraining family constellation into an imagined larger network of social relations. Duras marks here a moment of self-recognition that is as crucial as Lacan's mirror stage for the infant: Suzanne becomes conscious of how she appears to others and this sense of her visual value is linked for her to activity, to making one's way in the world.

For entering the social market with the body as a commodity, there are a variety of traditional modes of exchange. Each family member tries to enter a socioeconomic contract of exchange, all of which end up being exploitive, just as the larger colonialist framework of the relationship between France and Indochina is essentially exploitive.

It may be helpful at this point to remind ourselves of what anthropologists say about modes of exchange as social ritual. Pierre Bourdieu draws a useful distinction between the practices of swapping, lending and gift-giving. For him, gifting includes an element of surprise and risk, of personal choice that is excluded from the other two rituals:

> The temporal structure of gift exchange, which objectivism ignores, is what makes possible the coexistence of two opposing truths, which defines the full truth of the gift. In every society it may be observed that, if it is not to constitute an insult, the counter-gift must be *deferred* and *different,* because the immediate return of an exactly identical object clearly amounts to a refusal (i.e., the return of the same object). Thus gift exchange must be opposed on the one hand to *swapping,* which, like the theoretical model of the cycle of reciproc-

ity, telescopes gift and counter-gift into the same instant, and on the other hand, to *lending,* in which the return of the loan is explicitly guaranteed by a juridicial act and is thus *already accomplished* at the very moment of the drawing up of a contract capable of ensuring that the acts it prescribes are predictable and calculable.[13]

The French colonialists exploit the labor and the natural resources of the colony and process them into commodities. Contracts are used exploitively to maintain the status quo, and power rests in the ability to manipulate these contracts. Ma has paid over her life's earnings in the colony for the right to farm a plot of land for a given time. Ma is more under the sway of the colonialist dream because she insists that her land can be wrested away from the sea and because she believes her house has some significant market value, when she boasts at the canteen: "Ne les écoutez pas, c'est une bonne maison, solide. Si je la vendais j'en tirerais un bon prix. . . . Trente mille francs."[14] ["Don't listen to them. It is a good house, solid and strong. If I sold it, I would make a good profit. I could get thirty thousand francs for it."][15] The obsessive repetition of verbs that signify violent acts of taking possession ("en extraire quelque chose," "en tirer un bon prix") indicates Ma's attachment to heroic labor and its reward, a large amount of money. Poor as they are, an imaginary lump sum of money that could become theirs has attained fetishistic value, but it also typifies the colonialists' dream, the economic purpose behind their civilizing mission. As Bourdieu explains it, lending presupposes a temporal structure, but the loan is guaranteed by equity, so there is no open-ended obligation. In Ma's case, the lenders insist on the validity of the contract even though they have given her barren land, something that will not produce a cash crop and thus will not permit Ma to accumulate any capital to pay off her debt and accede to ownership. They retain all the profit and the social power it buys.

Swapping, on the other hand, presupposes equal value, a kind of interdependency. It is a prearranged transaction in which people trade services or items that are reciprocally useful to them, and that they presumably need right away. The status of the gift in *Barrage* is problematical. For instance, Suzanne attracts a rich admirer, M. Jo, who proffers various gifts to get in her good graces: nail polish, a dress, a record player, and eventually a diamond. He wants to exercise financial power and the power of humiliation over her in revenge for the affective hold she exercises over him. " 'Devinez ce que je vous apporte,' disait-il avec malice."[16] When he pleads with Suzanne to open the bathroom door and let him see her naked, she is gradually won over by his pleading—she is willing to bestow the sight of her body as a precious gift to him. At the very moment when she is about to give herself up to his gaze, he introduces the idea of a reward, the record player: "le dernier modèle de La Voix De Son Maître et des disques en plus, les dernièresnouveautés de Paris."[17] So, he is offering a machine in exchange for a body, a novelty item, one of a long line of identical and therefore replaceable objects, a mechanical patriarchal voice to which she might then listen with rapt and abject attention like the dog on the phonograph label. This counteroffer cheapens her own value as an exchange object, but rather than refuse her proposed prostitution, Suzanne becomes a rebellious female agent, more than a mere pawn. She takes the initiative by insulting M. Jo and flaunting her body at him simultaneously, tentatively copying a vulgar expression from her brother, who will become her role model in her quest for agency and mobility: "Vous êtes une ordure," dit-elle faiblement. Joseph a raison, une ordure. Je vais lui cracher à la figure. Elle ouvrit et le crachat lui resta dans la bouche. Ce nétait pas la peine. . . .—Voilà, dit-elle et je vous emmerde avec mon corps nu. Joseph disait: 'Et je l'emmerde avec ma B.12". . . . M. Jo . . . était rouge et respirait mal comme s'il venait d'être frappé et qu'il allait tomber."[18]

I see this verbal outburst as an important step in Suzanne's dawning of self-awareness—she realizes she has value as a human being and that her sexual attractiveness makes her marketable. She then decides to take over her own marketing from Ma and Joseph, and ultimately she refuses to be an exchange object in the colonialist economy altogether. Once the record player arrives, Suzanne redeems its original status as a gift by giving it to her brother. As Micheline Tison-Braun remarks: "Suzanne voudrait rendre Joseph heureux, lui donner un phono neuf, une auto, lui trouver une femme platinée. Le don est sa forme d'amour."[19] Gifting has to do with love as it is a form of erotic commerce,[20] but more important, with creating prestige structures because each gift eventually demands a countergift. So, if Suzanne recognizes the importance of her brother by giving him a highly desired object, she also considers herself worthy of a reciprocal kind of consideration by him. As the French anthropologist Marcel Mauss stated his seminal discussion on gifting, published the same year as *Barrage:* "There is a succession of rights and duties to consume and reciprocate, corresponding to rights and duties to offer and accept. . . . everything—food, women, children, property, talismans, land, labour services, priestly functions, and ranks—is there for passing on, and for balancing accounts."[21]

Contemporary anthropologists Sherry Ortner and Harriet White-head rather than subscribing to traditional methods of anthropological analysis that were centered on the symbols alone, additionally direct our attention to "social actors" who create symbols. Ortner/Whitehead in-clude in their field of observation the social structures that subtend them—they term these prestige systems, practices that apportion prestige

93

and thereby position male and female actors along a vertical scale that determines the value of what it means to be male or to be female in a given society. They state:

> The concept of "actor" is central to the sociology of symbols and meanings in a way that it is not central to more conventional social anthropology, partly for the simple reason that meaning does not inhere in symbols but must be invested in symbols and meanings and interpreted from symbols by acting social beings; thus social actors must be part of the analysis.
>
> We suggest that the structures of greatest import for the cultural construction of gender in any given society are the structures of prestige. . . . More specifically, we find that the cultural construction of sex and gender tends everywhere to be stamped by the prestige considerations of socially dominant *male* actors. In effect, the way in which prestige is allocated, regulated, and expressed establishes a lens through which the sexes and their social relations are culturally viewed.[22]

Bourdieu explains the connection between the parent and the daughter/ son of marriageable age whom the parent "gives away" and the acquisition of prestige: "To demand a large payment for one's daughter, or to pay a large sum to marry off one's son, is in either case to assert one's prestige, and thereby to acquire prestige: each side intends to prove its own 'worth' "[23] Ma, therefore, in demanding a high bride-price for her daughter makes a claim for social inclusion at a much higher level of prestige than her pitiful economic circumstances would seem to justify. This claim emanates purely out of her pride, her consciousness of herself as a subject. It is this kind of heroic leap of consciousness above circumstance that will enable the daughter to grow into self-determined identity and agency.

Suzanne becomes aware that she is the first member of her family to fulfill their dream of making a profit, making something of value come across the desert to their shack: "C'était grâce à elle qu'il était maintenant là, sur la table. . . . Et elle trouvait qu'elle méritait ce phonographe. . . . Pour elle, il lui suffisait de l'avoir, par ses seuls moyens, extrait de M. Jo."[24] ["It was thanks to her that it was now there on the table. . . . And she thought that she deserved that record player. . . . For her it was enough to have gotten it out of M. Jo all by herself."][25] Paradoxically, this action marks Suzanne as a successful actor in the colonialist prestige system—she has extracted payment for a commodity she has not had to trade according to the original terms requested, just like the bankers who took Ma's money without trading her something of value. So, in a sense it is a spirit of revenge that activates Suzanne, shakes her loose from the family's hold, and allows her to become an agent.

We can measure the anomalous nature of her acquisition of a valuable object and her gifting it more fully if we remind ourselves of the customary division of gender roles in simple societies. Jane Collier and Michelle Rosaldo differentiate between the prestige of men and women that arises out of food distribution: "Although women's gathering or gardening and men's hunting both contribute needed foods to the diet, women are required to feed families, whereas men distribute their meat through the group according to rules favoring members of the senior generation. These rules, associated with bride service, permit *all* adult men to appear as the forgers of social relationships."[26] Suzanne, in a sense, takes over her own bride service—she gathers in M. Jo, she shares out his gifts—which gains her prestige within the family, and, in addition, she attempts to trade herself outside the family and thus becomes a "forger of social relationships." The family employs additional rituals to establish kinship and create obligation—covered by the anthropological term *comensality,* defined as the sharing of food and drink to create a bond between unrelated members of a group. The family meet M. Jo in the canteen where they drink with him, then they invite him for a meal at their house. They also use storytelling as a means of establishing community when they recite the catalogue of their attempts to farm the land, build on it and prosper. It is significant that they do so in a humorous self-deprecatory manner to evoke the stranger's sympathy and make him feel more successful than they are. They also admire M. Jo's car, which symbolizes his spending power. But the gulf between his status and theirs is too great: he owns a car special-ordered from Paris, they own a wreck. He orders champagne and wears diamond rings, whereas Ma's only ornament is a rubber washer for her braid. The family starts to laugh at their own misfortune and at the tremendous disparity between themselves and him, which reverses the power balance. Suddenly they appear more powerful, because they can laugh at their fate, whereas M. Jo feels victimized by his riches and can only speak in maudlin tones of his situation. Nonetheless, a common bond is created: they are each unhappy with their present state:

> "La richesse ne fait pas le bonheur," dit nostalgiquement M. Jo, "Comme vous avez l'air de le croire." La mère proclamait: "Il n'y a que la richesse pour faire le bonheur. Il n'y a que les imbéciles qu'elle ne fasse pas le bonheur."[27]

> ["Riches do not make happiness," said M. Jo, nostalgically. "Although you seem to think so." "Money's the only thing necessary

for happiness," said Ma loudly. "It's only imbeciles that can't be happy with money."][28]

M. Jo is taken down from his lofty position of economic superiority by his confession of his inability to be happy with his riches, because as every member of the family asserts, they would know how to be happy if they had his money—in fact, they then set about getting it. Actually, M. Jo is made insecure by their insults and by their group coherence:

C'était arrivé en quelques secondes. M. Jo paraissait décontenancé. Il devait se demander si son succès ne se trouvait pas un peu compromis et comment parer à ce risque. . . . M. Jo essaya de rire. Il se forçait un tout petit peu. Peut-être qu'ils allaient l'oublier. Ils avaient l'air un peu sonnés.[29]

[It had happened in a few seconds. M. Jo looked mortified. He began to feel unsure of his success and wondered how to get back on safe ground. . . . Monsieur Jo tried to laugh. He managed to laugh a little. They were forgetting him. They all looked a little beside themselves.][30]

Ortner discusses the importance of centripetal processes for group identity building: "There is thus great cultural emphasis on centripetal processes, on 'pulling,' 'binding,' and 'concentrating.' . . . Kinswomen—especially daughters and sisters—are crucial to this 'pulling in' process."[31] The active role Suzanne takes in the "pulling in" of M. Jo bears this out. Suzanne manages to combine the male and female "pulling in" roles. Even more important than her sexual attractiveness in binding M. Jo's desire to her is that she is a body with a voice of its own: she contradicts M. Jo, and she introduces him to her mother and brother, taking over the traditional male role without abandoning the female role of desired object. The class factor enters into negotiations between the two families; whereas Suzanne's family is white trash, M. Jo's belongs to the moneyed French upperclass. It is an attractive goal for the lower-class family to enhance their social prestige by "pulling in" M. Jo as a son-in-law, but it would lower the status of M. Jo's family to be associated with a family so far beneath their own position. This is precisely why the marriage ultimately does not take place, but Duras is interested in rebellion against the traditional social stratification and in how far women can be successful agents in the subversion of social hierarchies. This is logical because of women's reproductive potential—they can give birth. As Ortner formulates it: "Status mobility through descent line building is an avenue potentially open to all."[32] We have to pay particular attention to the geographical location of Suzanne's family as well as to their location within the local colonialist hierarchy in order to understand why they even become possible trading partners for M. Jo. Their geographical location is far from the highly stratified society of the colonial capital, close to the ocean, which periodically erases all man-made boundary lines. Even though Ma is poor, she enjoys higher status than the Vietnamese men and women, and she employs "the corporal," a Vietnamese peasant, as her servant. Of the residents in that location Ma, her son and daughter represent the top level of that social hierarchy. However, there are irregularities: the slot of the father is empty, and there is no maternal uncle to take over his function in overseeing marriage negotiations. This vacancy necessitates that the mother fulfill that role together with the son. Joseph is an unempowered male because he seems dogged by failure—his teeth are rotting, his horse dies, his car falls apart, his catch of fish rots as does the game he hunts in the mountains. He does not fulfill the expectations set in a traditional male hunter, which are that he provide edible food for his family by braving obstacles outside the protected realm of the house and garden/field which in turn is gendered as the female domain. These structural anomalies free up Suzanne and Ma to move into traditionally male roles. The question is how successful these female characters are at occupying male roles and whether they innovate on them or alter them in some way. Initially, Ma embodies the male colonialist role perfectly when she reclaims land from the sea and puts it under cultivation. She decides to grow rice (a food staple), but her ultimate goal becomes to stop hunger on the plain, not merely to make a profit and feed her own family. She later acts as a political leader of the Vietnamese peasants by organizing them to help her on the barrier project to keep out the destructive flooding. In a sense, we might say she takes on the role of the patriarch, like the biblical Noah who marshals resources for survival and who also builds a sheltering, life-preserving barrier—the ark, an object of gigantic size, like the seawall. Ma's mission is heroic but not sanctioned by a divine (male) command, and perhaps that is why it fails. Ma's behavior is unacceptable in a colonialist hierarchy built around the patriarch. She does realize that her project is not intrinsically flawed; she knows, for instance, what materials she would have needed to make her barrier impenetrable—reinforced concrete. She just does not have access to it. I interpret Ma's failure at building the seawall as caused by social restrictions on female agency. As her next project, Ma takes on the marketing of her daughter. The family would be able to leave the plain, a dream that unites all of them. In attempting to give away the daughter to a powerful male, Ma and Joseph wish to create obligation for themselves and for the potential offspring of that marriage. Ironically, it is revealed that M. Jo has no decision-making power of his own. He is the weak son of a rich and geographically remote father, for whom he acts professionally as a low-level overseer. He has no say in giving himself away in marriage and could therefore be said to occupy a feminized position.

On the symbolic level, Joseph and Ma are asking M. Jo to organize a potlatch in celebration of/exchange for their giving away of their only valuable asset, their beautiful young daughter. Mauss claims that "In certain kinds of potlatch, one must expend all that one has, keeping nothing back."[33] He goes on to say that potlatching is a form of ritualized rivalry that allows individuals chiefly to obtain status. This is precisely how M. Jo wishes to be regarded, but he is unwilling to play by the potlatch rules. Mauss states: "The potlatch, the distribution of goods, is the basic act of 'recognition,' military, juridicial, economic, and religious in every sense of the word. One 'recognizes' the chief or his son and becomes 'grateful' to him."[34] Suzanne's family demands to be recognized, and I argue that such a demand can only be made successfully in a border zone, a transitional space in which social as well as physical boundaries are blurred or in danger of disappearing altogether. There are some convincing parallels between the exchange structure Duras sets up in *Seawall* and the potlatch ritual as the coastal Kwakiutl Indians practice it to this day. First, both groups live in border spaces far removed from the colonial capital—for the Kwakiutl this meant that they were better able to hold on to their rituals after the Canadian government tried to colonize them. As Douglas Cole points out: "The potlatching Kwakiutl, even when subjected to an increasingly authoritarian paternalism, were convinced that nothing was wrong with the potlatch and that the law was mistaken."[35] Essentially, Ma and Joseph also refuse to be ashamed of their lower status and are convinced that they ought to be treated as M. Jo's equals even though the law of social hierarchy places them far below him. By laughing at their lowly rank in society they refuse to stay in it. Next, they try to raise their rank by marrying off Suzanne; the possibility of using marriage to this end is precisely what distinguishes the Kwakiutl as a group from other Northwest Indians, as Cole explains:

> What probably made the Kwakiutl potlatch exceptional was a combination of the hazy gradation in ranks, especially among neighboring groups brought into closer relations by post-contact developments, and the ability to obtain rank by marriage, even by multiple marriages. . . . Among the Kwakiutl and Bella Coola, marriages were the major vehicle for enhancing prestige. . . . The potlatch encouraged prostitution of native women as a source of potlatch funds.[36]

Just as the Kwakiutl women trade the use of their body for potlatch funds, Suzanne uses her sexual attractiveness as bait to obtain goods from M. Jo. In doing that she observes a fine line between prostitution and preserving her virginity, as the scene at the threshold of the bathroom demonstrates.

Equally ambiguous is the courtship ritual Suzanne and the elders follow, when M. Jo "visits" her at the house, although her family leaves the two of them alone, but Ma insists that the doors be kept open and watches over her daughter from the nearby garden plot:

> Et si elle exigeait qu'ils laissent la porte du bungalow ouverte, c'était pour ne laisser à M. Jo aucune autre issue que le mariage à l'envie très forte qu'il avait de coucher avec sa fille. C'était là-dessus que cette porte restait grande ouverte."[37]

> [And if she demanded that they keep the bungalow door open, it was in order to give Monsieur Jo no alternative (literally, no other exit) but marriage to satisfy his strong craving to sleep with her daughter. It was for that reason (literally, it was on this issue) that the door stood wide open.][38]

It is perhaps significant that the moment in which Suzanne becomes most desirable to look at is when she emerges from the shower: a kind of rebirth of the self has taken place (this has biblical as well as painterly echoes—David desiring Bathsheba as he watches her bathe herself, [Sancho] Botticelli's Venus arising from the sea)—a sort of baptism of the female self is what is performed here because Suzanne is aware of having an audience on the other side of the threshold. The liminal position of the female social actor who is poised on the threshold between a private/ intimate space (the bathroom) and a quasi-public space (the family living room that is open to the outside) echoes Ma's earlier attempt at separating off a space of her own from the annihilating force of the sea. Of course, the distinction between what is outside and what is inside the female body is not as simple as it at first seems, *la mère* (the mother, Ma) is a homonym of *la mer* (the sea). Thus we might infer that although *la mer* threatens to erase boundaries and wash away individual distinctiveness, the mother's presence is felt to have the same effect on her children—by holding them in for too long, she threatens to submerge their individual capacity for agency.

Duras challenges the postindustrial worldview that splits the world neatly into gendered spheres—coding the private as female space and the public as male. A binary model that is predicated on the tension between two poles "individual distinctiveness" versus "integration into society"[39] is too rigid to accomodate Durassian concepts of space, identity, and gender. The space in/of which Ma, Suzanne, and Joseph have taken hold is controlled by the cyclical return of dispersing, centripetal natural processes (the flooding), but it is also bisected by a road leading from one colonial city to another. Along this road, colonialists travel from the coastal port to the capital, and goods are distributed. The family is excluded from active participation in this *trafic* (trafficking),[40] but they are onlookers at the spectacle of colonialist invasion and they witness the destruction it causes—native children crawl into the road or play there and get killed by cars. In addition, even greater numbers of them die from eating unripe or rotten food, are buried in the mud, and are washed out to sea. Set against this context, Suzanne's potential as a centripetal force becomes even more anomalous as well as crucial to the family's survival. But she realizes that she has the choice to refuse, to withhold, and thereby increase her centripetal power, her hold over M. Jo's desire. She learns to take control of her virginity, deciding to use it as a bargaining chip in the exchange. Duras's narrative of Suzanne's marketing of her body has some parallels with Ortner's description of the trading of women in simple societies, but differs regarding the exchange object's agency:

> What is symbolized by her virginity is not her self-control . . . but the control by her kinsmen over her behavior. . . . The daughter's virginity thus represents the kinsmen's "hold" on her, necessary for the process of building or simply maintaining descent line size and strength. It is vital that she be "held" symbolically even when sent out in marriage for strategic purposes. . . . If one side of the symbolic coin is strong control of the girl's sexual behavior, rendering her remote if not wholly inaccessible, the other side entails enhancing her attractions and her value. Hence the apparently contradictory practice of elaborately beautifying the girl while keeping her under surveillance and control. The daughter/sister is clearly being used as "bait."[41]

One of the salient differences between Ortner's model and Suzanne's position is that instead of the daughter being under strict surveillance by her family, Suzanne's suitor is in that feminized position:

> Il avait pris une chambre à la cantine de Ram et une autre chambre à Kam, couchant tantôt dans l'une tantôt dans l'autre afin sans doute de déjouer la surveillance de son père.[42] [He had taken a room at the Ram canteen, and another room in Kam, spending the nights now in one place, now in the other, doubtless to elude the vigilance of his father.][43]

Furthermore, it is M. Jo who expends labor and money on beautifying Suzanne, not her family; no doubt this contributes to her growing sense of self-determination in the marketing of her body:

> Toujours dans le salon et toujours couvé du regard par la mère, M. Jo apprenait à Suzanne l'art de se vernir les ongles. Suzanne était

assise en face de lui. Elle portait une belle robe de soie bleue qu'il lui avait apportée, parmi d'autres choses, depuis le phonographe. Sur la table, étaient disposés trois flacons de vernis à ongles de couleur différente, un pot de crème et un flacon de parfum.[44]

[Still in the sitting room and still under the brooding observation of Ma, Monsieur Jo was teaching Suzanne the art of enameling her nails. Suzanne was sitting facing him. She was wearing the beautiful blue silk dress that he had brought her, among other things, after the phonograph. Set out on the table were three bottles of different colored nail polish, a jar of cold cream, and a bottle of perfume.][45]

First, by being positioned in front of the closed door in an attempt to glimpse Suzanne's body and second by squatting facing Suzanne serving her narcissistic pursuits, M. Jo has been further debased; it is now Suzanne who has taken over the traditionally male role of the observer: she looks at him to mirror her new self in him. The arrangement of the cosmetics suggests a vanity table, with M. Jo playing the role of the mirror. He is a mere tool in Suzanne's quest for subjectivity, which starts here with an awareness of living in her body and then continues with practices that perfect the body—Duras sees the growth of female subjectivity as a movement from the outside in. Mirroring leads to mimicking—soon it is Suzanne who mimics M. Jo's words in inviting the family to go for a drive to the colonial city: "C'était d'ailleurs Suzanne qui, en général, annonçait l'heure d'aller à Ram."[46] ["Moreover, it was usually Suzanne who announced the time for going to Ram."][47] The metaphor of M. Jo's physical presence as objectified appears doubly appropriate because it was he who attempted to reduce Suzanne to the status of an object he could purchase. The miscommunication between M. Jo and the family stems from a confusion about the nature of gifts versus commodities.

In a recent anthropological study of exchange and colonialism in the Pacific, Nicholas Thomas draws up a useful grouping of qualities that gifts and commodities possess:

commodities	*gifts*
alienable	inalienable
independence	dependence
quantity (price)	quality (rank)
objects	subjects

The set of dichotomies provides a useful departure point by showing that gifts are radically different from commodities. Indebtedness may not necessarily take a universal form, and the precise character of the singularity of the gift will require further clarification, but the differences can provisionally be seen to emerge sharply from the fact that giving always has a distinct social effect: mistakes made in giving have consequences that commodity transactions almost never have.[48]

The record player is a commodity that the giver claims to be giving in the spirit of a gift but actually intends to purchase a reciprocal object—the daughter's body. This transaction is bound to fail if we analyze it in anthropological terms: the contract is one-sided because the family did not ask for that object as the price for their daughter; furthermore, the object is easily replaceable, but the family only has one daughter's body to give away. In the scene in which the "gift" is handed over, Duras skilfully plays upon the recipients' refusal to "see" the object and their unwillingness to recognize the giver by looking at him. In Durassian narrative to be looked at is to exist, to be recognized at some level, even if it involves commodification—this obtains for male and female actors alike.[49] On the arrival of the wrapped object, Suzanne forbids M. Jo to unveil it; she refuses to see it just as she would not let M. Jo see her unclothed. When the mother and brother enter the room and sit down for the meal, they turn the tables on M. Jo who is reduced to the one receiving their handout. They, too, pretend that the object is not there and that no exchange other than the one they initiate is taking place. M. Jo himself becomes for them a mere conduit for the display of consumer goods, his elegant car, expensive handmade suit, his hat, his chauffeur, his diamond rings: "Du moment qu'il avait donné le phonographe, il inexistait autant. . . . Peut-être serait-il devenu d'une transparence de vitrine vide, parfaite."[50] ["As for M. Jo, the minute he had given the phonograph he had ceased to that extent to exist. And really, deprived of his limousine, his tussore silk suit, his chauffeur, maybe he would become completely insubstantial, as empty of interest as an empty showcase."][51] M. Jo only becomes solid, identifiable as an individual, when he is surrounded, propped up, by objects. Without these props he is transparent, people look right through him as if he did not exist, which equals his social death. He can, however, function as a looking glass for the family—they look through him to a utopian future in which they imagine themselves to be rich and living in a fabulous city.

For Suzanne, the mirroring breaks the familial bonds of sameness and contiguity: through M. Jo's desire she sees herself as other than the daughter or sister. In this context, the function of voice and listening is also important: once the song arises out of the machine, it is the first catalyst for pleasurable communication. It is unlike Ma's voice, always shouting and giving orders to "the corporal," her deaf servant, about whom she complains: "Il est de plus en plus sourd, . . . il devient de plus en plus sourd."[52]

["He's harder and harder of hearing, . . . harder and harder of hearing."][53] It is unlike Joseph's voice, cursing or complaining; nor is it like M. Jo's voice alternating between dejection and self-aggrandizement, demanding to be lionized as "le bienfaiteur de la famille."[54] "Une voix s'éleva, d'abord insolite, indiscrète, presque impudique au milieu de la réserve silencieuse de tous. . . . À la fin du disque, la glace était fondue."[55] ["A voice rose, new, strange, indiscreet, almost outrageous in the midst of the general silence. . . . At the end of the record, the ice had melted."][56] This voice establishes community, a shared pleasure beyond the realm of commodification, it sings of an exotic city location and an atmosphere promising love and sensuality "loin de tous les regards jaloux" ("far from all jealous glances"). It is the invocation of a woman, Ramona, who is to make all of this pleasure possible, but at the same time it is a promise to her that she will share in it equally. The atmosphere that Duras establishes here is that of the family before its corruption in the colonialist hierarchy, an alternative to the hellish life the family led in a narrative predating this one, *L'Eden cinéma*. Ma had been the accompanist on the piano to movies played at the Eden movie house in a colonial city. It was always dark, the children only saw their mother's shadow against the screen and were left to the exploitation and possible molestation of strangers in the darkened theater. Ma had earned the money that had brought her the concession as a kind of human record player, mechanically accompanying the films, whereas the song on the record, which is machine produced, paradoxically releases a promise of better times in the city, of harmony and bliss. "That's beautiful," Ma agrees.[57]

> Lorsqu'ils partiraient ce serait cet air-là, pensait Suzanne, qu'ils siffleraient. C'était l'hymne de l'avenir, des départs, du terme de l'impatience. Ce qu'ils attendaient c'était de rejoindre cet air né du vertige des villes pour lequel il était fait, où il se chantait, des villes croulantes, fabuleuses, pleines d'amour.[58]

> [When they would leave all this, they would whistle that tune, thought Suzanne. It was the hymn of the future, of departures on journeys, of the end of long waiting. What they hoped for was to find again that tune, born of the giddy cities for which it was made, where it was sung, tumultuous cities, cities full of love.][59]

Duras expresses the dream of fulfillment in the city with images of pregnancy—Ma hopes to "hatch" ["*couver*"] her expectations of economic independence by fixing her gaze on the wealthy suitor; "du terme de l'impatience" suggests a pregnancy coming to term; and finally the word "né" helps to imbue the city utopia with a telos, making it seem feasible. She also implies that differentiation and independence are come by at the cost of destroying a kind of passive consumption of specular images: What I mean by this is that narcissistic self-reflection in others is only a first step to self-awareness, a disembodied *voice* speaking and creating a general narcissistic desire brings it to life more fully: "À la fin du disque, la glace était fondue" ("At the end of the record, the ice had melted") may also be read homonymically as "À la fin du disque, la glace était fendue" ("When the record ended, the mirror was cracked/split"). Duras sees identity being established through a violent separating off from a matrix, in which she is close to Freudian and Lacanian interpretations of identity formation. In the place of the fixed, absorbed gaze into the mirror, movement, melody, and a romanticized merging with a changing, burgeoning cityscape are desired. Suzanne's imaginary cities teeter giddily on the brink of change and dissolution, a permeable self that interacts with its surrounding space is desired, and there is a utopian wish for oneness and merging in an oceanic feeling of love. We can therefore read the cityscape as a projection of the positive aspects of maternal love and a desire to be held by a supportive matrix without being engulfed or restricted, which are the negative aspects of maternal love as Duras has shown them in the relationship between Ma and her children.[60]

The next exchange contract between M. Jo and Suzanne is stated much more explicitly than the one that produced the record player: if she will visit the city with him and stay there for three days, he will pay her by giving her a diamond worth the equivalent of the mother's bungalow. Not only is the proffered payment of higher value that the first one, it also has a personal connection to M. Jo's family: the diamond rings he brings to Suzanne are inherited from his mother ["They were my mother's," said M. Jo sentimentally, "she was crazy about them."][61]

> C'était une chose d'une réalité à part, le diamant; son importance n'était ni dans son éclat, ni dans sa beauté mais dans son prix, dans ses possibilités, inimaginables jusque-là pour elle, d'échange. C'était un objet, un intermediaire entre le passé et l'avenir. C'était une clef qui ouvrait l'avenir et scellait définitivement le passé. À travers l'eau pure du diamant l'avenir s'étalait en effet, étincelant.[62]

> [It was real and it was a thing apart, this diamond. Its importance lay not in its sparkle or in its beauty but in its price, in the possibilities, unimaginable until then to her, of its exchange value. It was an object, an intermediary between the past and the future. It was a key which would open the future and definitely seal the past. The diamond was limpid water, through which showed the sparkling future.][63]

For Suzanne, the diamond is not invested with its customary symbolic value in Western society—she does not treasure it as an engagement ring, even though she slips it on her ring finger right away. Instead, she values the link it provides to a world of ownership and economic independence. These are now in her hands, whereas her mother had to slave away for ten years to earn even a fraction of the diamond's worth. Its aspect shares some of the self-enhancing qualities of a mirror, only it is multifaceted— "limpid . . . "sparkling." The ensuing *fort/da* game that is played with the ring between Suzanne, M. Jo, and Joseph is initiated, sustained, and resolved by Suzanne, in that, like Freud's little boy with the yarn spool, she plays with possessing, relinquishing, and once again possessing the ring. As a result of this fairly complex social transaction between herself and the two men, Suzanne acquires the ring free of any of the (un)original conditions M. Jo had put upon the giving of it: "She took it, did not put it on her finger but shut her hand over it, and, without saying goodbye to M. Jo, she ran towards the bungalow."[64] As in the case of the first "gift," the context in which it is given and refused, then given once again, emphasizes the exchange processes of which the object is part much more than the object itself. Contemporary anthropology supports the notion of the contingent nature of gifts, as Thomas explains: "insistence upon the fact that objects pass through social transformations effects a deconstruction of the essentialist notion that the identity of material things is fixed in their structure and form . . . the mutability of things in recontextualization."[65] For instance, I have shown that the record player acquires new prestige when Suzanne recontextualizes it by giving it to her brother; this also holds true for the diamond ring when it is first offered as a bribe for Suzanne to sleep with M. Jo and then offered once again as a reward almost for her insistence on her nonmarketable self-worth. In addition, it is necessary to remind ourselves that exchange processes bring two different cultures into contact with each other—in this narrative they bring two different social classes into contact, but they also redraw the lines between the French governing colonialists and the French underclass who has fulfilled the ruling elite's worst fear by becoming allies with the Vietnamese peasant class—they have gone native without having become submissive.

The family's rebellious attitude towards the falsely patriarchal gift-giving foreshadows a more comprehensive critique of class hierarchy, gender hierarchy, and racial intolerance that Duras extends to encompass two strongly tabooed subjects: sister-brother incest and socially forbidden interracial contact between the white virginal girl and the older man of another race in her later versions of the *Barrage* narrative—*L'Amant* (1984) and her most recent even more detailed autobiographical version of that same narrative *L'Amant de la Chine du nord* (1991). The latest version emphasizes that, despite his apparent wealth and initial freedom to do as he pleases, the French girl's Chinese lover is not an autonomous agent once considerations of marriage come into play; he ultimately remains the Chinese patriarch's submissive "son," forever obligated in the system of filiality. He is not free to choose across racial and class boundaries whomever he wishes for his mate, instead he submits to an arranged marriage with a Chinese woman of the same class. The Chinese man occupies the position of an elder and far richer brother in relative social status to the girl's family; this parallel in turn reinforces the taboo-breaking incestuousness of their relationship.

Thomas reads objects as mediators for managing alterity between cultures:

> Objects have been central in these transcultural histories; they have often marked alterity and particular strategies for dealing with it—through appropriation and incorporation or distancing and recontextualizing. Some things mark the (partial) acquisition of the capacities or attributes of the other; others express indeterminacy and a bridge between apparently incompatible systems; others now stand for totalities formerly unrepresented, which are discovered, as explicit forms, through the process of contact.[66]

Analogously, I argue that objects like the two I have discussed represent an urban, postindustrial society to their recipients, whose lives up to that point were circumscribed by poverty in a malfunctioning agricultural society. Both objects are two-tiered complex luxury items produced with the help of fairly sophisticated technological processes: faceting and polishing the stone, then setting it in a ring; grooving the prized record and setting it on the player to make it play. We have seen that Suzanne and Joseph use strategies of distancing and recontextualizing the objects, whereas their mother mediates alterity for herself through appropriation and incorporation. An excellent example of this is her taking the ring from Suzanne and then hiding it, first in her bedroom, then later attaching it to her body.[67] As in the earlier example of the canteen keeper, Père Bart, these strategies work only so far—to the point where the body becomes grotesquely distorted and leads to the individual's death. I read the two objects primarily as bridge objects that make life in another world, an urban utopia, imaginable for their recipients. It is also true that they represent a surplus of love or pleasure, they speak of a Barthian *jouissance* in the midst of a stagnant existence marked by Sisyphean toil that goes unrewarded. It initially falls to Joseph, as the only male in the family, to voice this belief in a radically different life ahead. Once again, as during their first encounter with M. Jo at the canteen in Ram, the family transcends their assigned lot through subversive laughter:

> "Si on veut, on est riches," affirma Joseph, "si on veut on est aussi riches que les autres, merde, suffit de vouloir, puis on le devient."

106

> Ils riaient. Joseph tapait à grands coups de poing sur la table.
> La mère se laissait faire.
> Joseph c'était le cinéma.
> . . . Lorsque ça lui arrivait, rarement il est vrai, c'était peut-
> être encore mieux que le cinéma.[68]

> ["If we want it we can be as rich as the next one. Hell, all we got
> to do is want it, and we're rich." They laughed. Joseph banged his
> fist upon the table. Ma let herself go. Joseph was as good as the
> movies. . . . Joseph sometimes worked himself up like this. And
> when it happened—rarely, it is true—it was almost better than the
> movies.][69]

By emphasizing the transforming role of individual willpower, Joseph
sketches out an alternative to Ma's fatalism: no matter how many times
she has lost out in her struggle with the colonial authorities, she never
questions their right to power and always believes that her luck will be
better next time. When she fails again she complains "c'était la déveine"
("it was bad luck") but is unable to distance herself from the colonial
hierarchy of exploitation in which one is either actively exploiting the
native labor source or passively being exploited. This is why Ma's only
conceivable project is to sell the diamond in order to pay off the interest
on her bank debts. She falsely hopes this will ingratiate her with the
authorities who would then give her a higher mortgage and allow her to
buy herself into owning the concession. As the series of exchanges
around the diamond have shown, ownership in an exploitive economy is
not permanent, nor does it entail lasting rights. The colonial enterprise
depends on the constant *conversion* of raw materials into commodities and
their *circulation* from the center to the periphery of the colony and from
there back to the homecountry, where the profit that accrues is also
invested, usually in purchasing land or building a country house.[70] An
example of the specific conversion of profit back into land purchases in
the homecountry, which the architectural historian Anthony King documents extensively for the British empire[71] can be seen in Duras's narrative
when another colonialist suitor, Joseph Barner, appears and tells Suzanne
how he invests his profits:

> "Ma mère," dit Barner, "n'aime pas les bijoux, elle est très simple.
> Tous les ans je lui achète un petit terrain dans le sud anglais, et c'est
> ce qui lui fait le plus plaisir."—"Moi, je préférerais les diams," dit
> Suzanne. "Les terrains c'est souvent de la merde." "Oh! fit Barner,
> oh! quel est ce langage?"—"C'est du français," dit Suzanne.[72]

> ["My mother," said John Barner, "does not like rings. She has very
> simple tastes. Every year I buy her a piece of land in southern

107

England, and that's what gives her the most pleasure." "Me, I prefer sparklers," said Suzanne. "More often than not land is just muck" [in the French text, "shit"]. "Oh!" said Barner. "Oh! What kind of language is this?" "French," said Suzanne.][73].

Duras subsequently condemns the colonial enterprise in sexualized language; she calls it, for instance, "un bordel magique où la race blanche pouvait se donner, dans une paix sans mélange, le spectacle sacré de sa propre présence."[74] ["a magic brothel, where the white race could enjoy, in undiluted peace, the sacred spectacle of its own existence."[75] The metaphor of the brothel is perhaps a particularly appropriate choice to characterize colonialism, as its operation is based on the exploitation of bodies and profit is accumulated by circulating clients' and prostitutes' bodies through the brothel space in quick succession. As Ortner and Whitehead remind us, people will eroticize forms of society, ranging from freedom movements to totalitarian states: "The point is not just that sexuality is socially shaped, and in the course of this, inevitably curbed, but that the forms of society are themselves eroticized. The psychic energy that has been rallied and rerallied behind egalitarian social movements and utopian ideals suggests strong possibilities at the other end of the spectrum as well."[76] The colonialist enterprise as Duras critiques it is heavily invested with autoerotic impulses that are obtained via the spatial, economic, and racial segregation of the other.

Commodity fetishism is also characteristic of this society, and it is described in sexualized terms. For instance, when the family goes to the city to market the diamond, they stay at the misleadingly named Hotel Central—misleading in so far as it is not geographically in the center of the city. It also functions as a brothel, however, thus it may stand in for the operations of power in the city and therefore adequately symbolizes its center. Carmen, the madam's daughter, has a protuberant jaw with prominent teeth, but classically beautiful legs, and these legs guarantee a stream of faithful return clientele. By fetishistically focusing on her legs, the colonialists forget the threat of her devouring jaw, just as in Freudian terms the male fetishist vacillates between knowing and not wanting to know that the female sex represents lack—the specter of castration.

> Mais ce qui faisait que Carmen était Carmen, ce qui faisait sa personne irremplaçable, et irremplaçable le charme de sa gérance, c'était ses jambes. Carmen avait en effet des jambes d'une extraordinaire beauté. . . . Carmen passait le plus clair de ses journées à se déplacer dans le très long couloir de l'hôtel. . . . Ce qui faisait qu'un aucun des clients de l'Hôtel Central ne pouvait les ignorer complètement, l'eut-il voulu de toutes ses forces, et qu'un certain nombre de ces clients vivaient constamment en compagnie de

l'image harcelante de ces jambes. . . . on voyait aussi le genou dans son entier. Elle l'avait parfait, lisse, d'une rondeur, d'une souplesse, d'une délicatesse de bielle.[77]

[But what made Carmen Carmen, what made her irreplaceable and gave irreplaceable charm to her hotel management, was her legs. For indeed, Carmen had extraordinarily beautiful legs. . . . Carmen spent the better part of her time moving up and down the long, long corridor of the hotel. . . . None of the hotel guests could completely ignore those legs, no matter how great the wish to do so, and a certain number of the residents lived with the tormenting image constantly before them. . . . her knees were revealed in their entirety. Her knee was perfect: smooth and round, with the suppleness and delicacy of a driving-rod.][78]

This last metaphor is especially apt, because a piston transforms an alternating movement into a circular one—hence Carmen's knee symbolizes the constant mechanical motion driving the capitalist exchange processes. The distribution of rooms in the brothel on either side of a long, dimly lit corridor reinforces the train imagery—if the rooms resemble train compartments, then the madam is the conductor patrolling the train corridor to make sure travel is progressing smoothly. The clients, blinded by the vision of the fetish and otherwise kept in a dark environment, are unaware that they are mere cogs in the circular machinery of colonial exploitation; if they think of themselves as part of a movement at all, they are duped by the spatial design (both within the buildings and within the city as a whole) into believing that there is forward or upward progress.

It is at this point that urban space begins to take on weight as a metaphor. The tramway that separates the upper from the lower city amplifies this impression:

Seuls les indigènes et la pègre blanche des bas quartiers circulaient en tramways. C'était même, en fait, les circuits de ses tramways qui délimitaient strictement l'eden du haut quartier. Ils le contournaient hygiéniquement, suivant une ligne concentrique dont les stations se trouvaient toutes à deux kilomètres au moins du centre.[79]

[Only the natives and the poor white trash of the lower districts used the trolleys. The trolley circuits, in fact, strictly delimited the Eden of the upper district from the rest of the city. They encircled it hygienically, following concentric lines, of which the stops were all at a distance of two kilometers at least from the center of the city.][80]

With this imagery, the city is even more explicitly sexualized as a female body. This city-body ultimately becomes a source of erotic power and self-discovery for Suzanne. How female identity is strengthened despite being placed in such a rigidly structured city hierarchy remains to be seen. The trainline is compared to a chastity belt that protects the white sexual organ from contact/defilement by the native city population. The white sexual organ is raised to the sky, it offers itself up to consumption, in fact, all that takes place in the upper city is leisure activity and conspicuous consumption:

> Dans le haut quartier n'habitaient que les blancs qui avaient fait fortune. Pour marquer la mesure surhumaine de la démarche blanche, les rues et les trottoirs du haut quartier étaient immenses. Un espace orgiaque, inutile était offert aux pas négligents des puissants au repos. . . . Le centre du haut quartier était leur vrai sanctuaire. C'était au centre seulement qu'à l'ombre des tamariniers s'étalaient les immenses terrasses de leurs cafés. Là, le soir, ils se retrouvaient entre eux.[81]

> [In the upper section lived only the whites who had made a fortune. And, still further to mark the superhuman difference between white people and others, the sidewalks in this fashionable district were immensely wide. An orgiastic space, quite uselessly wide, was provided for the heedless steps of the powerful-in-repose. . . . The center of the Haut-Quartier was their true sanctuary. Here only, in the shade of the tamarind trees, were spread out the immense terraces of their cafés. It was on these terraces, in the evenings, that the inhabitants enjoyed themselves in their own congenial company.][82]

What the architects have created is a replica of Parisian boulevards with their cafés, they have imported Western design into the colonial context. Duras demonstrates by the example of the trolley cars, which are also imported from the homecountry, how socially harmful such grafting is:

> Anciens hors-service de la métropole, conditionés par conséquent pour les pays tempérés, ces trams avaient été rafistolés et remis en service par la mère patrie dans ses colonies. . . . au courant d'air qu'il s'était assuré en brisant avec sang-froid . . . toutes les vitres de sa cabine. De même étaient ailleurs tenus de faire les voyageurs avec les virtres de leur wagon pour en sortir vivants.[83]

> [Old cast-offs of the metropolis, built for a temperate climate, these trolleys had been patched up and put back into service by the mother-country for use in the Colonies. . . . They had ensured themselves of that current of air by calmly breaking the glass partitions of their driver's section. . . . The passengers likewise, in order to survive, had been obliged to break the car windows.][84]

110

Metaphors of containment and constraint describe the policy towards the bodies of the native population, but they offer resistance, they break the windows, for example. If we recall that Duras had described M. Jo's body as "d'une transparence de vitrine vide" ("transparent like an empty showcase"), the explosive potential of this suppression becomes even clearer. As their city design indicates, the whites have created a dangerous imbalance of power: because they are isolated from reality at the top, they live in an artificial Eden, a garden city. This is not the dream city of "Ramona," where two lovers walk "far from jealous eyes." King points out how built spaces not only reproduce a given social order, but how they themselves condition the society that lives in them—in other words, the city is no mere backdrop to the dealings of the colonialists, it actively influences how they act in the space around them. He says: "I would maintain that the built environment is more than a mere representation of social order (i.e., a reflector), or simply a mere environment in which social action takes place. Rather, physical and spatial urban form actually constitute as well as represent much of social and cultural existence: society is to a very large extent constituted through the buildings and spaces that it creates."[85] Sharon Willis had argued from a psychoanalytic perspective that subjectivity is created through the alternating play of spatial "stabilization and destabilization" (cf. n. 60), and the colonial city allows an uninitiated visitor like Suzanne to do exactly that. King cites as one of the defining characteristics of the colonial city "the linking of radically different civilizations in some form of relationship (this is perhaps the special task of the colonial city),"[86] and it is precisely the opportunity to shuttle back and forth between these two radically different societies that enables Suzanne to become a fully aware female subject.

Ma, on the other hand, only uses her stay in the city to run from the banks to various diamond merchants, where she is unable to market her commodity. She quickly exhausts herself; because these male colonial institutions are alien to her, she is unaware that she could adapt them to her needs—even if she were suffocating, she would never break a window in the trolley car like the natives, for she has internalized too much fear and respect of the authorities. As King summarizes the anthropological research into colonial cities, he mentions for the sixties a shifting from the mere observation of the Westernization of the colony to the modes of economic production:

> The most prominent function of these cities was economic; the colonial city was the "nerve centre" of colonial exploitation. Concentrated there were the institutions through which capitalism extended its control over the colonial economy—the banks, agency houses, trading companies, shipping companies. These banks . . .

were, of course, largely European owned. . . . A situation was created in which the countryside, with the exception of the enclaves of foreign capitalism—mines and plantations–became increasingly impoverished in comparison to the towns.[87]

It is striking to note that Duras already so clearly described the economics of capitalist production in colonialism at the end of the forties, when most of the sociological/anthropological literature only began to do this by the mid-sixties and only was fully developed by "the new urban sociology" in the seventies.[88] The criteria King maps out for categorizing colonial cities fit Duras's description perfectly, for instance, under the "political/economic rubric," he enumerates the following factors: "municipal spending distorted in favor of colonial elite . . . dominance of tertiary sector . . . parasitic relations with indigenous rural sector"[89] and under the "physical/spatial" category, he enumerates eight characteristic features, all of which obtain in the case of Duras's city:

—coastal or riverine site
—establishment at site of existing settlement
—gridiron pattern of town planning combined with racial segregation
—urban form dictated by "Western" models of urban design
—specific character of residential areas
—residential segregation between exogenous elite and indigenous inhabitants
—large difference in population densities between areas of colonial elite and indigenous population, impacting life style and quality of life
—tripartite division between indigenous city, civil and military zone[90]

In what follows, I want to address the fifth, sixth, and seventh factors cited above. Racial and class segregation lead to crowding in the lower city, but also to prescribed patterns of movement for the white elite within the upper (their own space) an the lower city (the space of the Other). As Suzanne discovers, the white elite moves in groups, never singly, probably because they are already in the minority. It is also significant that gender segregation exists within the otherwise so uniformly attired colonialist elite—women do not walk alone in the streets, if they are out in public at all, they travel in groups or in cars, driven by men. Suzanne's appropriation of the street as an individual flâneuse is scandalous, but out of the public humiliation of that scandal grows her internal consciousness.

At first Suzanne is excited by her exploration of the upper city, then she notices the stares and becomes aware that she is trespassing; she feels shame, but recovers and decides she needs a destination, a goal, in order to walk with greater assurance. She decides to look for her brother, finds him, realizes that he is not going to rescue her, and decides to proceed alone. Ultimately, the five cinemas become her destination, her temporary escape from oppressive gender and class barriers. In the following rather lengthy passage, Duras emphasizes the interplay of social exclusion and individual distinctiveness. She shows how female subjectivity is acquired, namely, in a gradual process of trial and error linked to physical movement through an alien urban space that is punctuated by regression into indifferentiated space, and how much it is based on transforming what John Berger terms "the look of the male observer"[91] into actively "looking back:"

> Carmen la coiffa, l'habilla, lui donna de l'argent. Elle lui conseilla de se promener dans la ville en lui recommandant toutefois de ne pas se laisser faire par le premier venu. Suzanne accepta de Carmen ses robes et son argent.[92]

> [Carmen combed Suzanne's hair, dressed her, and gave her money. She then advised her to go for some strolls in the city, telling her all the same not to fall a victim to the first man she met. Suzanne accepted Carmen's dresses and Carmen's money.][93]

The first step to female subjectivity, then, is some experience of female mentoring—Carmen makes Suzanne over into a prettier version of herself by giving Suzanne her own dresses, but she also gives her money and with that comes the independence to make decisions on how to use it. Although Carmen can only conceive of female identity in terms of taking over one's own commodification, that is, strategically seeking out a male dupe, marrying him, and spending his money while having affairs on the side, Suzanne can critique this proposal because she has learned to detest M. Jo, when Carmen now extols as the perfect candidate and because she has experienced the ambivalent example of her mother who prostituted herself to the male colonial authorities without ever deriving economic benefits from it. Instead, she sees her mother increasingly as a "monster," as "dangerous."[94] In the verbal elision between Carmen's gifts and Suzanne's acceptance of them lies her own still unspoken choice of what to accept and what to reject.

But what ultimately makes Carmen's gesture empowering is that this female giver gives true gifts without expecting a direct return. All of this stands in stark contrast to what Suzanne experienced with M. Jo.

> La première fois que Suzanne se promena dans le haut quartier, fut donc un peu sur le conseil de Carmen. Elle n'avait pas imaginé que

ce devait être un jour qui compterait dans sa vie que celui où, pour la première fois, seule, à dix-sept ans, elle irait à la découverte d'une grande ville coloniale. Elle ne savait pas qu'un ordre rigoureux y règne et que les catégories de ses habitant, y sont tellement différenciés qu'on est perdu si l'on arrive pas à se retrouver dans l'une d'elles.

. . . On la regardait. On se retournait, on souriait. Aucune jeune fille de son âge ne marchait seule dans les rues du haut quartier. Celles qu'on rencontrait passaient en bande, en robe de sport. . . . Même les femmes étaient rarement seules. Elles marchaient en groupe.

. . . Tout le monde ne disposait pas des mêmes facultés de se mouvoir. Eux avaient l'air d'aller vers un but précis, dans un décor familier et parmi des semblables. Elle, Suzanne, n'avait aucun but, aucun semblable, et ne s'était jamais trouvée sur ce théâtre.[95]

[She had never imagined that there would come a day which would be as important to her life as this one, when alone and for the first time, at the age of seventeen, she set out to explore a great Colonial city. She did not know that a rigid order reigned there and that the categories of the inhabitants were so differentiated that you were lost if you could not manage to be classified in one of them. . . . People looked at her. They turned to look, they smiled. When they turned, they smiled. . . . Even women were rarely encountered alone. They, too, walked in groups.

. . . It was not for everyone to move about with the same ease. All these people seemed to be going to a specific place; they were in a familiar setting and among people like themselves. But she—she had no place to go, there was no one like her, nor had there ever been, not on this stage.][96]

The two-dimensionality of display and conspicuous consumption in the "white city" is alienating because it stays on the surface of the body, of what is to be seen in the street. It is also worth noting that Duras reverses the customary symbolism of white/light and black/dark in her description of the city:

Les blancs aussi étaient très propres. Dès qu'ils arrivaient, ils apprenaient à se baigner tous les jours, comme on fait des petits enfants, et à s'habiller de l'uniforme colonial, du costume blanc, couleur d'immunité et d'innocence. . . . Le blanc est en effet extrêmement salissant.[97]

[As soon as the whites arrived in the Colonies, they learned to take a bath every day, learned to be clean as children do. They also learned to wear the colonial uniform, suits of spotless white, the color of immunity and innocence. . . . White is, in effect, a color very easily soiled.][98]

The double meanings of words like *propre* (clean or one's own) and *salissant* which operate simultaneously in the text, convey the contamination of belonging to the artifically constructed elite category of the "whites"; just as their Eden is really more of a hell in which interchangeable white bodies roam, their obsession with whiteness is a fetish that is supposed to hide the real sordidness of their presence in the colony. In contrast, the dark space of the cinema acquires three-dimensionality, a depth with democratic and self-affirming connotations. . . . "C'était l'oasis, la salle noire de l'après-midi, la nuit des solitaires, la nuit artificielle et démocratique, la grande nuit égalitaire du cinéma."[99] ["It was an oasis, this vast dark room in the afternoon, it was the night of lonely people, an artifical and democratic night, the great egalitarian night of the cinema."][100] Darkness abolishes social stratification, it abolishes gender and provides an escape into nostalgic indifferentiation, not unlike a reimmersion in the amniotic fluids of the protected embryonic sac. Perhaps we might go so far as to read the phrase *"la nuit des solitaires"* to mean "the night of diamond solitaires," the obliteration of the commodity economy.

But of course, cinema is about seeing, being in a theater—the cinematic space is not truly exempt from the social space; its films reflect the society that produces them. Hence the promise of a "baptism of the dark" is not fully kept; Suzanne immerses herself in the love story of two actors in another city, Venice—the city of love *par exemple*. Duras critiques the Hollywood kiss as a false projection of merging as a process of complete reciprocal absorption. For her, merging is only partial, never reciprocal, and strongly linked to death:

> On voudrait bien être à leur place. Ah! comme on le voudrait. Leurs corps s'enlacent. Leurs bouches s'approchent, avec la lenteur du cauchemar. Une fois qu'elles sont proches à se toucher, on les mutile de leurs corps. Alors, dans leurs têtes de décapités, on voit ce qu'on ne saurait voir, leurs lèvres les unes en face des autres s'entrouvrir, s'entrouvrir encore, leurs mâchoires se défaire comme dans la mort et dans un relâchement brusque et fatal des têtes, leurs lèvres se joindre comme des pouples, s'écraser, essayer dans un délire d'affamés de manger, de se faire disparaitre jusqu'à l'absorption réciproque et totale. Idéal impossible, absurde, auquel la conformation des organes ne se prête évidemment pas. Les spectateurs n'en auront vu que la tentative el l'échec leur en restera ignoré. Car l'écran s'éclaire et devient d'un blanc de linceul.[101]

[You would like to be in their place. Oh, how you would like it. Their bodies entwined, their lips approach with nightmare slowness. And when their two pairs of lips are close together, their bodies become cut off, and then you see their decapitated heads, what would be impossible to see in real life, you see their lips facing, half open, open still more, and their jaws falling apart as if in death and then, suddenly, in a brusque and fatal release, their lips join and suck like octopuses in a crushing kiss, as if trying with the delirious hunger of starvation to devour, to absorb each other and bring about a total and reciprocal disappearance and absorption. Impossible idea, absurd idea, to which quite evidently the physical organs are not adapted. The spectators would not, however, have seen anything but the attempt. The failure would remain ignored by them. For at that point the screen lit up and assumed the whiteness of a shroud.][102]

Duras ultimately allows her female protagonist to reject the false sense of closure and fulfillment of the Hollywood kiss, Suzanne is too aware of her own needs to fall for a traditional love plot; for example, she flees later on when she once again meets M. Jo and he tries to enact with her what she had seen on the cinema screen. The relationship between the two bodies on the screen is vampiric, one tries to absorb the other, and there is violence being done to them by the camera's mutilating gaze— the bodies are truncated, and the severed heads try to devour each other. This is too reminiscent of the threat of Carmen's carnivorous mouth.

In a recent article on Virginia Woolf and Duras, Deborah Gaensbauer analyzes the function of seeing in Duras's work—seeing as a form of control, voyeuristic seeing as a form of vicariously experiencing the existence of others. Duras creates a *voyeuse* in her autobiographical writing: "The impetus to write derives from the apprehension of and compulsion to express the emptiness at what should be the core of human existence, particularly the feminine experience of it."[103] Marcelle Marini has described the writing process for Duras as a kind of self-doubling when she says: "Écrire est pour elle une sorte de démultiplication ou encore d'étagement de soi: elle se voit lectrice-auditrice de son être écrivant." ["Writing is for her a kind of multiplication or even layering of herself: she sees herself as the reader-listener of her writing self."][104] Gaensbauer goes on to suggest that "the visual quest in Duras's work tends to be a ritualized act of devouring." Whose self needs to be propped up by such a quest? Gaensbauer states: "Characters with an insufficient sense of self or limited affective capacity anxiously covet what they see. Hovering over others' experiences, they trespass visually in an attempt to expand or complete their inadequate identities."[105] In this narrative, Duras permits her alter ego protagonist to trespass "out in the street," or as Luce Irigaray has formulated it:

> How can one be a "woman" and be "in the street?" That is, be out in public—and still more tellingly, do so in the mode of speech. We come back to the question of the family: Why isn't the woman, who belongs to the private sphere, always locked up in the house? As soon as a woman leaves the house, someone starts to wonder, someone asks her: How can you be a woman and be out here at the same time? And if, as a woman who is also in public, you have the audacity to say something about your desire, the result is scandal and repression. You are disturbing the peace, disrupting the order of discourse.[106]

Duras creates, as Marcelle Marini has shown, an inner dialogue between her self who writes, and her female protagonist who relives the experiences of her autobiographical self and who herself enters into an inner dialogue with her female mentors: first Ma and then Carmen—then also Joseph, whose speech she imitates and who becomes a fraternal twin.[107] Nonetheless, Marini is almost too restrained in her conclusions about the importance of layering and doubling in Duras. The multiplication of selves becomes a crucible in the formation of agency, not simply a reverberation of voices.

If we return for a moment to the idea of total absorption as a strategy for facing alterity, this comes close to the idea of incest within the family structure, whereas in colonial society at large it can only mean the dissolution of the individual in the crowd, the effacing of individual outline, of color (in dress as in race) in the white on white: "la différence première était multipliée, blanc sur blanc, entre eux et les autres."[108] ["the initial difference being multiplied, white on white, making distinctions . . . between themselves and the others."][109] If colonialist exchange is governed by commodity fetishism, that explains why people have no sense of owning themselves; their consumption is what makes them real to themselves and to others. As Gregory puts it, gifts are inalienable and have "an anthropomorphic quality"; gift economies tend to foster a sense to belonging and group pride, whereas commodity-based economies produce hierarchies and a reification of self:

> The gift economy, then, is a debt economy. The aim of a transactor in such an economy is to acquire as many gift-debtors as he possibly can and not to maximize profit, as it is in a commodity economy. What a gift transactor desires is the personal relationships that the exchange of gifts creates, and not the things themselves. . . . Thus gift exchange is a means by which the relations of domination and

control are established in a clan-based economy. It should be remembered, too, that a clan-based economy is relatively egalitarian in the sense that there does not exist one group of people who live off the surplus product of another group of people. . . . [Gift economy] flourishes in those societies where there is an unstable clan hierarchy changeable from time to time.

. . . This is to be contrasted with Marx's theory of the "fetishism" of commodities. "Fetishism" refers to the reified nature of things as commodities and is an aspect of the alienability of a commodity.[110]

As Suzanne begins to regard herself as valuable, she starts to take narcissistic pleasure in her body, and she inhabits it with a sense of ownership:

Et au-dessus de la ville terrifiante, Suzanne vit ses seins, elle vit l'érection de ses seins plus haut que tout ce qui se dressait dans la ville, dont c'était eux qui auraient raison. Elle sourit. . . . Elle, en regardant la ville, ne regardait qu'elle-même. Regardait solitairement son empire, où règneraient ses seins, sa taille, ses jambes.[111]

[And above the terrifying city, Suzanne saw her breasts, saw the erection of her breasts higher than anything that stood up in the city, and they would triumph over it. She smiled. . . . She, while looking at the city, was really only regarding herself. She was regarding in solitude her empire, over which reigned her breasts, her waist, her legs.][112]

Suzanne feels a surge of phallic power, far from feeling disempowered by her outings in the city, she now senses herself to be all-powerful. It is not really clear how her sexuality will triumph over the city, except perhaps in the sense that it is multiple (two erect breasts have the potential for engulfing, like Carmen's jaw; they are more phallic than one man-made skyscraper). In following the downward gaze along her own body, Suzanne reassembles it as a whole and takes control of it. When M. Jo next wants her to give over her body to him, she refuses, stating succinctly: "Je ne peux pas. C'est pas la peine, avec vous je ne pourrai jamais."[113] ["I can't. It's no use. With you, I never could."][114] Later on in the narrative, Suzanne even taunts another potential commodifier, Agosti, by boasting of her sexual power to him: "Je suis bien foutue," dit Suzanne—"Tu ne te l'envoies pas dire."—"La preuve," dit Suzanne en montrant le diamant."[115] [" 'I am worth looking at.'—'You don't wait to be told, do you?' said Agosti.—'The proof,' said Suzanne, pointing to the diamond."][116] We can see here how Suzanne has adopted Joseph's short bursts of speech, which make her seem very decisive and brash. She has deviated far from the standard pattern for objectified femininity. She aggressively wields that femininity in a manner that is expressive of male power, thereby parodically undermining both femininity and masculinity. Her transgressive behavior is not, furthermore, simply a rhetorical gesture: as a result, Agosti modifies his behavior.

Suzanne enhances her sense of agency by playfully trying out different marketing scenarios for herself. She begins by trying on the different dresses people give her, ranging from the old hand-me-down dress cut out of her mother's frayed one to the vivid blue prostitute's dress M. Jo buys her (and which she eventually throws out into the muck), to Carmen's dress with the big blue flowers. She then moves on to insistent verbal persuasion, as in her attempt to market the diamond to John Barner: "Faudrait lui faire un beau cadeau une fois pour toutes, après vous seriez tranquille. . . . Si vous lui donnez une belle bague, après ce serait plus la peine de rien lui donner. . . . Je dis par exemple une bague."[117] ["You ought to give her a fine present, once and for all, then afterwards you'd have peace." . . . "If, say, you gave her a beautiful ring, then afterwards you'd never have to think of giving her anything else," said Suzanne. . . . "I say, for example, a ring."[118] Suzanne is completely aware of where she is leading with this conversation: she initiates it, follows up with assertions, and ends up silencing her male interlocutor, who is shocked and at sea. In speaking to M. Jo, whom she has already duped once successfully, she makes a game out of demanding "a ring a day" were he to obtain her sexual favors:

> [La mère] "Elle vous dévalisêrait. À la fin, ce qu'il lui faudrait c'est une bague par jour, pas moins. Maintenant qu'elle y a pris goût. . . ."—"Je sais," dit M. Jo rougissant, "mais pour vous voir qu'est-ce que je ne ferais pas. . . ."—"Une bague par jour, quand même, vous ne pourriez pas." . . . "Qu'allez-vous devenir?" . . .— "Vous en faites pas, ça durera pas," dit Suzanne. . . . "Peut-être," dit Suzanne en riant, "que je m'installerai chez Carmen. Mais il faudra qu'on me paye très cher. Toujours à cause de Joseph."[119]

> ["She would absolutely ruin you. To tell the truth, what she'd like would be a ring a day! Now that she's acquired the taste. . . ."—"I know," said M. Jo, reddening, "but just to see you, what wouldn't I do!" . . . "What is going to happen to you?" . . . "Don't you worry, it won't last long," said Suzanne. . . . "Maybe," said Suzanne, laughing, "maybe I'll fix myself up with Carmen. But they'll have to pay very dear for me. Again, on account of Joseph."][120]

Or, in a culminating moment with the *third* suitor—we may note several fairy tale patterns embedded in this tale of finding herself—Suzanne confronts Agosti, who has not even proposed an exchange to her and takes it upon herself to be the first to reject him:

> "T'as pas besoin d'avoir peur," dit-elle enfin.—"Qu'est-ce que tu racontes?" Il la lâcha et la tint à bout de bras, son visage face au sien. "J'épouserai jamais un type comme toi. Je te le jure. . . ."—"Je crois que t'es aussi cinglée que Joseph. Pourquoi que tu m'épouserais pas?"—"Parce que c'est partir que je veux."[121]

> ["You don't need to be afraid," she said at last. "What kind of craziness are you talking?" he said, releasing her and holding her away from him, looking into her face. "I'll never marry a fellow like you. I swear it. . . ." "I believe you're as cracked as Joseph. Why wouldn't you marry me?" "Because what I want is to go away."][122]

In this context, it is a compliment for Suzanne to be compared to her brother, the rebel. Suzanne may be labeled as crazy, but that only puts her in the same category as her mother and brother whose unconventional attitudes prompt them to attempt defiant and sometimes heroic gestures. Suzanne becomes convinced of her own willpower—she voices this conviction assertively and frames it positively: "Suffit de vouloir," dit Suzanne, "puis à la fin, ça arrive."[123] "If you want a thing bad enough," said Suzanne, "it finally happens."[124] In the end, once Ma dies, Joseph and Agosti expect her to leave with one of them, but, in an open ending, Suzanne really embarks on her own quest journey: "Je pars," lui dit Suzanne, "je ne peux pas faire autrement."[125] ["I am leaving," Suzanne told him. "I can't do anything else."][126]

By the end of the novel, the vicious circle of (female) commodification has been interrupted, and an open-ended forward movement has come to replace it: "les choses prenaient leur sens à mesure qu'elle avançait en elles, c'était aussi le cinéma."[127] [". . . things had meaning as you advanced into them. It was like the movies."][128] The city as backdrop becomes a catalyst for personal change: after her sojourn there, Suzanne articulates a different destiny for herself, namely, that she will embark on an independent quest for self-fulfillment. She moves on and actively embraces change, and in that, she is able to remake herself. Collier and Rosaldo state: "the capacity for naming suggest[s] creative potentials presently claimed by men."[129] Duras affords her female protagonist that creativity, emphasizing processual restructuring and conversion practices in social life.[130] What chances that creativity opens up to future generations of women in society remains unelaborated. That stage of growth is explored by younger women writers informed by the communitarian experience of modern-day feminism. Margaret Drabble's protagonists use their feminist beliefs combined with their professional skills as journalists, academics, social workers, and teachers to perform a kind of therapeutic archaeology on those whom late capitalist society has criminalized or forgotten. Drabble chronicles the shifting allegiances and political convictions of three central female protagonists over time. Her emphasis on a much longer span of time—from the sixties to the nineties—accentuates the developmental and processual aspects of social change. The sustained conversation and introspection on both personal and social issues between the women friends counteract the sense of fragmentation and unreality that pervades late twentieth-century capitalist society. The corrupt practices of the Thatcher era are reflected in the reduction of the city to an urban wasteland. Within it, the aging female body becomes conflated with the ailing social body. After a period of withdrawal from social engagement, the protagonists reenter the urban social arena and renew their efforts at local coalition building and social reform.

CHAPTER

3

Female Community in
Drabble's Fiction

A recurring concern in Margaret Drabble's fiction is the complex relationship between her female protagonists and the city as an emblem of contemporary society. Drabble describes the city as a palimpsest: social reform cannot occur without the archaeological work of remembering, just as personal transformation requires first an understanding of past behavioral patterns, then a shift, a rearticulation of one's present position and future goals in light of this awareness. The process of remembering and reshaping becomes shared work in a group of close women friends, whose lives are interconnected over the span of their adult lives. Communication and openness to diverging views are crucial in the formation and continuation of a communal agenda. Agency for Drabble's protagonists is primarily redemptive. Their perception of the social terrain is, however, often hampered by its inherent middle-class bias, which leads them to alternately romanticize and demonize the growing underclass created by globally linked capitalist conglomerates and government alliances. Nonetheless, the author's conception of change as a gradual, conscious, and incremental process rather than as radical departure betokens a more realistic understanding of intersubjective transformation.

In an early novel, *Jerusalem the Golden*,[1] as its hopeful title indicates, the city will provide a fertile medium for personal growth and creativity, its own heterogeneity and mutability sparking the birth of female autonomy. In *The Middle Ground*,[2] one of Drabble's more recent novels, however, the city turns into a space in which a Darwinian struggle for the survival of the fittest is enacted with ever-increasing violence, resulting in the systematical disempowerment and marginalization of weaker social groups—women, children, the middle-aged, the elderly, the dispossessed. Nonetheless, the hostile London of *Middle Ground* still contains pockets of subversive possibility, ambiguous spaces that mediate between outside and inside, such as pubs, theaters, or even the protagonist's house, which is connected to a chip shop—a gathering place for the poor and seedy, but a gathering place nonetheless.

To understand better the importance of such spaces for both forming and reinvigorating the identity of Drabble's female heroes, Victor Turner's distinction between the liminal and liminoid is particularly useful. The liminal characterizes a recurring prescribed social ritual occurring at natural break points in society, whereas the liminoid denotes a more individualized, playful way of reclassifying social experience; it truly bears the seeds of radical social change. Turner notes: "The passage from one social status to another is often accompanied by a parallel passage in space, a geographical movement from one place to another."[3] This rings true for Clara Maugham in *Jerusalem*, whose quest for an adult identity of her own making takes her on a journey from her bleak hometown of Northam to Paris, the resplendent "City of Lights." As her name implies, Clara seeks light, both lightness of spirit and enlightenment, and the city forms a nurturing matrix for her pursuit. Clara finds freedom and social mobility in both Paris and London. In investigating Drabble's city spaces, we must focus our attention to include the liminoid, the realm of the inchoate. Turner goes on to say: "There are permanent 'liminoid' settings and spaces, too—bars, pubs, some cafés, social clubs, and so on. But when clubs become exclusivist, they tend to generate rites of passage, with the liminal a condition of entrance into the liminoid realm."[4] If, as Turner asserts, liminoid phenomena "are often parts of social critiques . . . exposing the injustices, inefficiencies, and immoralities of the mainstream economic and political structures and organizations,"[5] then the regenerative and transgressive properties of these city spaces within — and against—the larger organization of the city become evident. In *Middle Ground*, Kate Armstrong repeats Clara Maugham's journey to the metropolis in search of self-fulfillment, but she does not make as extreme a geographical leap from the north to the south. This is possibly one of the reasons for her disillusionment once she has arrived in the heart of the city. After progressing in telic fashion from a similarly confining suburb called Romley Fourways on the northern outskirts of London into the center of the metropolis, and after establishing herself there, Kate undergoes a crisis of direction. Kate Armstrong, feminist, mother, and successful commentator of women's issues, finds out that the center does not hold. Neither marriage, motherhood, nor her journalistic career—nor even her long term relationship with her married lover Ted Stennett—turn out to fullfil their initial promise as stable places of refuge from fragmentation, death, alienation. The London of *Jerusalem* was characterized by a succession of liminoid spaces that protect identity, from the public theater; to an actor's hangout; to the Denham's spacious, yet cheerfully cluttered house and parklike garden; to the Oriental corner of Liberty's—to name only a few. The city of *Middle Ground*, however, initially menaces Kate's renewed search for personal meaning. The London of the late seventies is seen as a confusing conglomerate of destabilizing multicultural political and commercial influences, and this is especially so for the women in *Middle Ground*, for they either originally belonged or still belong to a space on the periphery of culture.

This novel vividly portrays the female hero's dilemma of having arrived, and by all appearances belonging in the inner sanctum of the city, yet becoming too predictably defined by her chosen label of "angry feminist conscience," which has made her successful. The novel opens with Kate Armstrong's tragicomic cataloguing of her morning's mail. It is "a tribute to her Social Class B economic status,"[6] as her friend Hugo Mainwaring jokingly observes. There is, for instance, the following item:

> 1. A letter from the American Express, addressed to her ex-husband Stuart, asking him why he didn't give his wife the freedom of an Express card. The letter was illustrated by a photograph of an expensive-looking woman in a black evening dress and strings of pearls, standing in an expensive hotel foyer with a lot of shining matching luggage. (Kate had been a card holder for some years: Stuart's credit, as she had no need to explain to Hugo, was not good.)[7]

The hotel foyer is clearly liminal, an exclusive space of social ritual, and the "expensive-looking woman" bodies forth her husband's spending power as it derives from the glamourous cultural and social life of the metropolis. Far from providing the promised "freedom," the possession of the gold card actually seems to encumber the woman in the advertisement. She is laden with pearls and surrounded by a mountain of intimidating conventional "matching luggage." There is nothing "express," that is, dynamic about the woman, she is merely an emblem of luxury, static and statuesque at the same time. Even so, the added auctorial comment fullfils a truly liminoid narrative function: it subverts the liminal image by creating a liminoid space in the text.[8] This revealing incident is part of a larger liminoid setting: Kate and Hugo are having this conversation in a restaurant, and in the end it is she who again transgresses the prescribed male-female proprieties by her aggressive insistence on cutting up the man's meat and later paying for their meal. This may indicate in a small way that liminoid spaces engender transgressive behavior.

Drabble moves into perhaps the most liminoid of all city spaces: the London sewer system, and Kate, the journalist muckraker, is fascinated with it. Although the male characters in the novel link sewage to an underground lethal river of contamination and disease, Kate herself values "the companionable gutter"[9] and subconsciously recreates its ambiance in her "cramped and seething abode."[10] The symbolic significance of the sewer is much like that of the river—it observes no boundaries, it sweeps things along regardless of their origin, it subterraneously levels out all social distinctions and hierarchies constructed in the daylight world of the city. I refer here to the work of the anthropologists Peter Stallybrass and Allon White on the London sewer and its transgressive significance, which was seen as evil by nineteenth-century social reformers. Stallybrass and White claim: "At one level, the mapping of the city in terms of dirt and cleanliness tended to represent the discourse of colonial anthropology. . . . The nineteenth-century sanitary reformers mapped out the same division [between Christian and pagan, civilized and savage] across the city's topography, separating the suburb from the slum, the respectable from the 'nomad' along the same lines."[11] When her identity crisis eventually leads her back to her suburban origins, Kate also quite literally returns to the sewer that connects Romley Fourways to London. The sewer is both repellent and fascinating to her: "There had been something magical about the dark race of water and the powerful odour of London. She had lain there and thought of the mysterious network of drains and pipes and tubes and gulleys and sewers linking the underground city."[12] Contemplating the sewer triggers a return of the repressed: Kate remembers, for example, her love for, and sibling rivalry with, her brother Peter and realizes that their relationship as children determines their current extreme love-hate relationship. "I should never have looked. I should never have looked,"[13] repeats Kate, but, as Stallybrass and White point out, "The melodramatic coercion of extreme opposites into close intimacy here becomes the ultimate truth of the social. . . . The sewer—the city's conscience—insisted, as Freud said of the hysterical symptom, in 'joining the conversation.'"[14]

If the sewer represents the "true" city, its essential nature resists any attempts to coerce it into a pattern. Its meaning lies in its "shapeless diversity."[15] When Kate returns to Romley Fourways, she not only retraces her own origins, she also decides to investigate the lives of her former classmates and acquaintances for a television program "Women at the Crossroads." Although the male producer aims at reducing the contradictory statements of the various interviewees to a single cause, namely, "women's innate conservatism and resistance to change,"[16] Kate argues that there is "no recognizable pattern" and that it would be "much better to let them [the women] speak for themselves."[17] The pattern of the "crossroads" itself implies that society is structured according to a series of binary oppositions—success versus failure, telic progress versus passive acceptance of the status quo. Kate reveals the inadequacy of this male pattern of experience. It does not adequately contain female experience, as her research into the complex lives and motivations of her female contemporaries proves. A case in point is her own development, which suggests that progress does not have to be relentlessly telic and result oriented: "The easiest way out of the mistakes and embarrassments of a lower-middle-class life style was not upwards into the middle classes, but out as it were sideways, into a kind of comfortable uncompetitive Bohemia."[18]

In a parallel movement in the narrative, Drabble opens up the traditional marriage plot to a nonhierarchical multiple and permeable plot in which no one character is privileged at the expense of the others. In transcending the stalemate of her midlife crisis, Kate reaffirms her faith in the regenerative power of the liminoid, of personal, cultural, and social differences. This vision not only allows for a more flexible restructuring of female experience and female relationships, it provocatively imagines a utopian uncompetitive relationship between men and women. "After this, what could they feel but friendship of a most intimate nature? A friendship devoid of competition and desire. Are such things possible? Will they be so if we imagine them?"[19]

The "shapeless diversity" of the city on the other hand is profoundly ambivalent. Its menacing complexity produces real casualties, such as the bewildered old lady whom the social worker Evelyn Stennett encounters outside the casualty ward at the city hospital:

> It became clear . . . that the woman was in a state of shock: indeed, her mouth was covered in traces of dried blood, and she seemed to have lost some of her teeth. . . ."I'd better take you back to the hospital," said Evelyn, but the woman manifested intense alarm at this suggestion and refused to turn back. She wanted to get on a bus. "But you can't just go anywhere," said Evelyn. And they stood there, the tiny woman with her large shabby shopping bag, lost, adrift in meaningless London.[20]

Evelyn herself is ultimately victimized in a domestic dispute, a cultural misunderstanding between Irene (one of Evelyn's welfare clients) and her Rastafarian lover. It is ironic that Evelyn, whose job it is to sanitize the slums, has a bottle of cleaning fluid thrown in her face. Out of the bizzarre accident arises an unexpected social benefit: a spiritually wounded Kate and a physically wounded Evelyn are able to overcome their earlier sexual rivalry and form a bond of mutually supportive friendship. Their new-found sisterhood in turn lets them discover a redeeming spiritual vision of the city renewing itself:

> "It looked marvellous from up here," said Evelyn. "Yes, what a view you have," said Kate, wandering over to the window and gazing out over London. . . . From the twelfth-floor window, London stretched away, St. Paul's in the distance, and the towers of the City, and beneath them, nearby, the little network of streets, backyards, cul-de-sacs, canals, warehouses, curves and chimneys, railways, little factories tucked into odd corners; unplanned, higgledy-piggledy, hardly a corner wasted . . . the old and the new side by side, overlapping, jumbled, always decaying, yet always renewed; London, how could one ever be tired of it? . . . there it lay, its old intensity restored, shining with invitation, all its shabby grime lost in perspective, imperceptible from this dizzy height, its connections, clear, its pathways revealed. The city, the kingdom.[21]

The vision of the city as self-renewing also signals a return to the vision of the city as "*Jerusalem the Golden*." It equates the city with the liberating force of the liminoid: "As they drew nearer to Gabriel's house, they crossed a couple of squares with which Clara [Maugham] was vaguely familiar, squares once thoroughly decayed, and now full of the apparatus of demolition and construction; the area attracted her strongly, in its violent seedy contrasts, its juxtaposition of the rich and the poor, its rejection of suburban uniformity."[22] The rejection of the social order implied in these ambiguous, half-decayed/half-burgeoning city spaces emphasizes process and flux. Such a visible inversion of the social architectonics fuels Clara's iconoclastic desire to upset the "suburban uniformity" of her birthplace. For instance, Clara is strangely attracted to a Parisian bag lady who squats in the gutter to relieve herself. In marked contrast to the old woman lost in the London of *The Middle Ground*, this other peripheral character radiates energy and health precisely because she rebels against the laws of ordered city space. This dispossessed character confidently strides through *her* city space, she gives free rein to her natural urges, she transgresses the boundaries of the sidewalk. Her subversive action seems deliberate and willed. Clara herself is later emboldened to over come the hierarchical spatial divisions into high and low when she seduces Gabriel on the floor of his office: "They lay there together on the mock parquet tiles, lit by the band of fluorescent light, their heads in the space under his desk, staring upwards together, finally, at the unknown underside of the desk."[23] This view from the underside is also a *view of* the unknown, the neglected, the marginal. As Mikhail Bakhtin explains, the inversion of high and low plays a key role in the socially subversive and renewing ritual of carnival. Stally-brass and White interpret the notion of the carnivalesque as part of the phenomenon of social transgression: "we move . . . to a political anthro-pology of binary extremism in class society. . . . It reveals that the underly-ing structural features of carnival operate far beyond the strict confines of popular festivity and are intrinsic to the dialectics of social classification as such."[24] The carnivalesque city and carnivalesque sexuality are privileged in *Jerusalem*, but Drabble seems to qualify her earlier exuberant celebration of the carnivalesque and the liminoid in *Middle Ground*. Whereas Clara Maugham zealously champions the end of social and sexual hierarchies, Kate Armstrong has *become* that struggle in her own person and bodies it forth.

Middle Ground closes with a parody of Virginia Woolf's *Mrs. Dallo-way*: Kate, like Mrs. Dalloway, is giving a big party, but she turns it into a carnival. She accepts her Iraqi houseguest's gift of embroidered Arabian slippers, a symbol of colonized femininity. She integrates them into her costume, but she is free to improvise the rest of her garb:

> There she sits, Kate Armstrong, in her black Marks-and-Spencer petticoat, her feet dangling in their emerald Arabian slippers, won-dering what to wear, wondering what will happen at her party. . . . It is unplanned, unpredicted. Nothing binds her, nothing holds her. It is the unknown, and there is no way of stopping it. It waits, unseen, and she will meet it, it will meet her. There is no way of knowing what it will be. It does not know itself. But it will come into being.[25]

Kate's various male counterparts—her ex-lover Ted, her friend Hugo, her ex-husband Stuart, and her brother Peter—become casualties of the male ethic of success that they espoused, they are physically and mentally damaged by it. The phallic woman Kate, on the other hand, no longer feels guilty for possessing power, and she chooses to share it. The commu-nal feast, a collaborative model of society where each contributes accord-ing to his or her abilities, finally provides a model that moves from mere transgression to transcendence, in its acceptance of the Babylonian city as a nurturing matrix.

In her novelistic depiction of British society in the eighties, Drabble passionately indicts the personal greed, urban blight, and commercial overdevelopment promoted by Margaret Thatcher's economic policies. She focuses on the street, the public marketplace, the house, the prison as those urban sites that most clearly represent a society in crisis. If we want to measure the difference between the London of the sixties and seven-ties, which Drabble described so hopefully as a site of burgeoning change and renewal in *Jerusalem*, and the landscapes of devastation she sees as

129

representing the breakdown of the social contract, we need only look at her description of urban squares. Where *Jerusalem's* Clara Maugham romanticized poverty and the cramped living conditions of the working class, the middle-aged art historian Esther Breuer in *Radiant Way* experiences London as a squalid and horrifying purgatory, which after a serial killer has been discovered to be her upstairs neighbor, she ultimately flees:

> London has become difficult. Not impossible, but difficult. Even Esther, who likes urban life, is becoming slightly distressed by the visual impact of some stretches of Ladbroke Grove, by the apartment blocks of the Harrow Road, by the strange surreal landscape under the arches of the Motorway. . . . As the Harrow Road murders receded slightly in folk memory, Esther Breuer resumed her patrolling of the streets of West and North-West London . . . wondering why she stayed where she was. . . . She walked beneath the great strutting legs and curved segmented underbelly of the Westway, where a little herd of horses stood sadly in a dry ring of sand, like an abandoned circus: she wandered on waste grass near Wormwood Scrubs and found a woman's glove and a pair of shoes: she gazed at the bizarre, paint-dripping, surreal façade of the condemned house that called itself the Apocalypse Hotel: she bought prawns from the barrow, and peered through corrugated iron walls at building sites. Once she saw, swinging high from a crane, above a yard of scrap vehicles, a hanged man: a life-size dummy, in workman's green overalls, dangling against the sky. Alsatians roamed, cats scavenged, buddleias grew from abandoned rooftops. She walked past the Car Breaker Art Gallery, past a house that described itself as Interesting Books, past the Embassy Café. Once a small boy in a van drove past her, crazily red-bristle-haired, white-faced, hardly able to reach the wheel, but driving; he scraped along a row of parked vehicles, ripping from them expensive trim, dinting, and bashing and banging. . . . Giant graffiti marched and sprawled, machinery rusted, padlocked gates labelled *Reception* and *Welcome* led to nowhere, and in the midst of it a man sold lawnmowers from a tin hut, and a couple of girls were to be seen playing tennis in the rain.[26]

Whereas the first quotation characterizes the mix between gentrification and decay as companionable and promotes the area as a desirable place to live for a newcomer to the city such as Clara, the second quotation illustrates how unwelcoming, dangerous, and practically inaccessible the urban neighborhood has become, even to a loyal longtime resident like Esther. The development of ring roads around London—planned by the

GLC (Greater London Council) in the late seventies—was supposed to provide greater accessibility of the center to the outlying areas of the country and to transform the city into a bustling marketplace. Instead, the Motorway Drabble describes is a malevolent presence—it has cut off easy exploration by the pedestrian flâneur, one of the oldest pleasures associated with city dwelling, and furthered a segmentation of the city into separate zones: multilane thoroughfares, high-rise apartment blocks, junkyards, and squats filled with condemned buildings, juvenile delinquents, and abandoned pets. The worker who is hanged in effigy; the goblinlike little boy too short to control the wheel and steer the van clear of other cars; the mention of the prison site. Wormwood Scrubs (itself an apocalyptic reference to the *Book of Revelations*); the plants growing crazily from the rooftops instead of out of the ground—all conspire to create an eerie atmosphere of gloom and devastation. Against this backdrop, the examples of small businesses and individual entrepreneurship, which the Thatcher government had promoted as the panacea for all economic ills, stand out as incongruous and sham: the man selling lawnmowers from a shack fullfils no function as there are no decorative lawns, only building sites and fences; an "art gallery," a "bookstore" and a "café" are self-conscious postmodern simulations of the real thing—these are not the liminoid spaces whose transforming virtues Drabble celebrated in *Jerusalem* and *Middle Ground*. It is unclear for whose benefit these new commercial establishments are run because there are no shoppers, browsers, or walkers in this area; it is a limbo on the underside, unnoticed by the upwardly mobile commuters who speed over it on the Westway. It is particularly troubling that the squatters blame the demolition and construction workers for the process of gentrification that will end up displacing them and not the actual owners of the building sites. The real power dynamics are thus obscured by a vaguely glimpsed network of commerce, state subsidy, and private investment that is impenetrable to the individual observer who is merely at its mercy.

At the most basic subsistence level, it is still possible for Esther to purchase food in her neighborhood—prawns from a barrow, a sandwich and a cup of tea at a lunch counter, and it is still just barely possible for her to go on walks and peer curiously through barriers, iron gates marked *Reception* and *Welcome*, but leading nowhere. The whole scene is reminiscent of Marlow's arrival at the colonial station in the Belgian Congo in Conrad's *Heart of Darkness*—rusting machinery is sitting around, shadowy presences wander by, and like Marlow, Esther experiences a profound sense of alienation and doom. Esther's companions are only one or two old men, marginalized onlookers at the spectacle of futile shifting and carrying. No real transformation takes place in the wasteland, only a redistribution of space and the things in it—old women carry rubbish in

131

prams; young black men, another marginalized group excluded from finding meaningful employment, tote boom boxes; struggling pony-carts with Dickensian drivers haul scrap ajmlessly:

> She discovered a new café on the corner of Lykewake Gardens and Mortuary Road down by the gas station, wittily entitled the New Caprice, where she would sit with a cup of tea and a cheese sandwich, perched on a high uncomfortable stool at a narrow, smeared Formica ledge, watching the world go by, in the company of one or two old men, persistent regulars, and a shifting company of builders and roadworkers from nearby acres of demolition. One day they would rebuild, she supposed, but when? There was a lot to flatten first. Through the glass she stared at shabby grey old women with prams full of shopping or rubbish, and stylish young black men with huge transistors, wearing dashing woolen hats, and at the occasional pony and cart with a pale raw-nosed, hank-haired driver and a load of scrap. A landscape of nightmare, an extreme, end-of-the-world, dream-like parody of urban nemesis.[27]

What seems to disturb Drabble as much as the actual devastation she chronicles is the simulation, the "parody of urban nemesis." It seems stagey and exclusionary, it does not care whether it is being watched or not, thereby foreclosing any participation by concerned residents. Esther is powerless to affect or improve her neighborhood in even the slightest way, which is amply illustrated in a later scene when she is trapped inside her apartment while the police surround the house and attempt to arrest the serial killer upstairs. Drabble focuses here on the devastation at the margins of the city, which can be read as symbolic of the spiritual aridity at its center, where another one of the three female protagonists lives—the novel opens with a description of a dismal New Year's party at the psychiatrist Liz Headland's imposing house on Harley Street.

If we remind ourselves of the inner-city redevelopment that took place in London since the seventies, and look at some of the documentation, for instance on the redevelopment of Covent Garden, we come across clashing views on the function of public space, as exemplified by the following excerpt of testimony collected during an inquiry into that redevelopment:

> Not only is the street the place where the local pubs are, the local shopkeeper, but it is also the channel of local information. . . . It was . . . of some distress and concern to me to see this structure vitiated into . . ."pedways following lines of desire." What is pro-

posed is a series of urban foot roads carrying foot traffic along paths conditioned by the most minimal of activities—movement to and from work and to and from the lunchtime café. . . . Streets are for milling around in, hearing what's happening to family and friends, chatting about whatever interests people at any moment, in short for conveying a sense of belonging in local culture. It is not the speedway, motorway, freeway by which the pedestrian hurries through a "productive" life toward a premature coronary."[28]

Although the developers wanted to emphasize efficiency and transportation of people to and from their workplaces, it is also striking that they think of them as consumers of services and goods, and it is that aspect they want to facilitate by channeling and restricting foot traffic. The local resident whose testimony is quoted, however, wants the street to be a forum for exchanging information and personal news, he is in favor of crowds "milling around," "chatting," and "hearing what's happening to family and friends." Drabble clearly concurs with these goals, but in the London of the eighties she places her three central characters inside their houses in the city or at picnics out in the country as they communicate and uphold the integrity of the social fabric. Other characters abandon the city, even the country altogether, as they are lured away by promises of higher pay, more interesting work, higher social prestige. Drabble's examples are mostly upper-class or upper-middle-class males, like the journalist and television producer Charles Headleand, who departs London for a job in New York as he leaves his originally working-class wife Liz for Henrietta Latchett, a blue-blooded but anorexic socialite; or, the economist Otto Werner who despairs of solving Britain's economic ills and becomes part of the brain drain when he accepts a post in Washington to work on government policy there.

Women of the middle class like Alix Bowen and Esther Breuer remain in the city until they are confronted with murder. Were they to remain even longer, they would face a nervous breakdown or dismemberment and decapitation like the serial killer's victims. Ultimately, Esther relocates to a city in a foreign country—she moves to "Red Bologna. . . . A communist city. A well-run city. A civilized city."[29] Alix moves to Northam, an industrial city in the North of England, the only place where her husband can find a new teaching job after the government has cut subsidies to inner-city institutions and has phased out both their jobs. After failing to obtain government support, Alix is reduced to a more traditional and feminized form of work—she is hired as an amanuensis by "Northam's poet" to put his papers in order and edit his letters. Liz the psychiatrist is the only one to remain empowered and in the city, although she, too, moves out of its center—from Harley Street to St. John's Wood:

> The new house was irregular, and airy, and odd, and it had a garden. . . . It was a house of character. . . . It rambled, eccentrically, with strange-shaped rooms and alcoves. it had once been the home of an eminent zoologist. It had charm.
>
> . . . the house's undeniable attractions and the exclusivity of the neighborhood were doubly modified, partly by a Family Planning Clinic next door, occupying what had once been an equally attractive private house, and partly by an extremely ugly block of luxury flats opposite, built in the 1960s from a horrible pinkish stone, and known vulgarly in the district as Menopause Mansions on account of both its colour and of the average age of its inhabitants.[30]

Liz's private practice is sandwiched between a state-subsidized clinic that provides women with access to birth control and a block of condominiums that sequesters middle-aged women who have outlived their biological function to reproduce. Liz's identity is thus established "eccentrically," maintaining a middle ground between these two poles—as a feminist and a physician she positions herself closer to the progressive clinic, but as a middle-aged divorcée, she is socially positioned in contiguity to Menopause Mansions. It becomes apparent here as elsewhere in the novel that Drabble uses the house or a room within it to symbolize a woman's identity: Liz herself is an "irregular," an "odd" female because of her rise from humble origins to the top of the psychiatric profession; she has "character" because she successfully raised another woman's children while rising through the ranks of the medical profession, she has "charm" because guests willingly flock to her parties. In addition, Drabble equates the house with the female body, as she further equates the female body with urban society. In the opening scene, Liz claims: "The pattern is both one's own and not one's own, it is of the making of generations. One is no longer the hopeful or the despairing guest: one is host in the house of oneself. . . . There is a goal to this journey, there will be an arrival, Liz Headleand believes."[31] Liz learns to be both "host in the house of herself," that is, to share her life with others, and to arrive at the goal of her journey, which is to arrive at greater understanding of her origins and thus herself, to decipher the mystery of her own silenced memories of her father, who turns out to have been a child molester. In a sense, Liz comes to realize that there is no unspoilt Edenic past. The family romance of the picture-book family in her children's primer, *The Radiant Way*, turns out to be a compensatory fantasy masking the reality of the father's child abuse, the mother's depression and agoraphobia.

Given this crucial insight, which arrives towards the novel's end, I cannot concur with Valerie Grosvenor Myer's interpretation that "in [Drabble's] work, the real and the symbolic are blended, as she struggles to re-create an Eden in the slagheap which is still, in some respects, England's green and pleasant land."[32] It is true that Drabble, like Bunyan, is a moralist and does not give up her utopia of a more just and livable society when her alter ego Alix Bowen asks: "Where was a voice to speak to her, for her, for England? . . . Was the country done for, finished off, struggling and twitching in the last artificially prolonged struggles of old age?"[33] Like Bunyan's Christian in *Pilgrim's Progress* Alix has to leave London, the "City of Destruction," and embark on a journey of self-renewal. But that does not mean that Drabble abandons her utopia of the city as the center of civilized and caring social life altogether. In her next novel, *A Natural Curiosity* (1989) Liz visits an exhibit at the British Museum called "New Views of the Past," where she sees the mummified body of Lindow Man: "the strangely preserved, smooth, brown, plump, patterned immortal skin of Lindow Man. Bard or Druid, victim or sacrifice. Ageless, timeless, rescued from the bog."[34] And Alix ". . . had not quite detached herself from politics. She cannot wean herself away altogether. She cannot help looking for a way forward, for a new consensus that will unite her and Brian and Perry Blinkhorn and Stephen Cox."[35] Drabble once again invokes Bunyan's allegorical Englishman, Christian, who falls into the Slough of Despond but is rescued by Help, when she presents us with Lindow Man "rescued from the bog," and Alix like the true believer Christiana in the second part of the *Pilgrim's Progress*, who also "cannot help looking for a way forward" and who, together with her companion Mercy retraces Christian's journey to the "Coelestial City."

The premise of *Pilgrim's Progress* is a society in crisis, just as Drabble's contemporary London is described as teetering on the brink of destruction. The very title of her novel *The Radiant Way* suggests, like *Pilgrim's Progress*, the author's religious quest for a road to enlightenment, if not spiritual salvation. Bunyan uses allegorical figures, as Drabble uses allegorical names: Liz's maiden name is Ablewhite, suggesting both ability and innocence or blankness—as indeed she turns out to have built her identity around a memory blank; the Austrian-Jewish refugee Esther's last name is Breuer, the name of Freud's mentor, who together with his patient Bertha Pappenheim discovered the talking cure, but shrank away from its results just as Esther Breuer avoids talking about her true concerns, preferring to signify them by talking about what ails her potted palm.

Certainly Drabble's street and place names carry allegorical significance: Lykewake Gardens, Mortuary Grove, Apocalypse Hotel[36]—all connote an urban landscape of pervasive violence, paralysis, and death. Alix,

135

like Bunyan's Christian, is the one character who is from the start most self-aware and engaged in working for the social good, and she is therefore most disturbed by the evil she sees around her:

> Once, thought Alix, I had a sense of such lives, of such peaceable, ordinary, daily lives. I could envisage interiors, clothes drying on fireguards, pots of tea in the hearth, a pot plant on a window sill. Now I see them no more. I see horrors. I imagine horrors. I have courted horrors, and they have come to greet me. Whereas I had wished not to court them, but to exorcise them. To gaze into their eyes and destroy them by my gazing. They have won, they have destroyed me. There is no hope of a peaceable life, of a life for the people, of a society without fear. . . . That woman and her baby, they pause forever on their front step. The street will destroy them.
>
> I am defeated, thought Alix. We are defeated. But how can I admit defeat? Is it the wrong battle I have been fighting, all these years?"[37]

Violence is wreaked on the female body on urban ground, and the role of the social conscience/prophet of doom is also ascribed to women— perhaps the most noticeable difference from Bunyan, who foregrounds the struggle of the male citizen with various male tempter and helper figures—although in Part II he allows Christiana, Christian's wife, to make the journey following in his footsteps. Before Christian is persuaded by the angelic guide Evangelist to set out on his journey, he feels despair and asks himself and his family and neighbors what course he ought to take to avoid certain destruction. Christian admonishes Pliable and Obstinate, his neighbors, to come along on his quest for the heavenly city:

> "You dwell," said he, "in the City of Destruction. . . . I see it to be so; and dying there, sooner or later, you will sink lower than the Grave, into a place that burns with Fire and Brimstone: Be content good Neighbors, and go along with me."
>
> "You make me afraid, but whither shall I fly to be safe? If I go back to mine own Countrey. That is prepared for Fire and Brimstone; and I shall certainly perish there. If I can get to the Coelestial City, I am sure to be in safety there. I must venture: To go back is nothing but death, to go forward is fear of death, and life everlasting beyond it. I will yet go forward."[38]

Alix's loss of faith in the city echoes the malaise that Christian experiences during his own journey. In this light, Drabble's London corresponds to Bunyan's City of Destruction. It is a metropolis that exposes its residents to violent collisions with each other: from the relatively harmless collision of shopping carts at the supermarket[39] to the striking workers; to the police "in their riot gear" with their "charging horses," "blazing cars, upturned vans;"[40] as well as to acts of malice small and great, ranging from vandalism to cars to human carnage. Alix's exhaust pipe gets plugged up so that her car breaks down at night on the Motorway, her tires are slashed by a band of roving teenage delinquents, and ultimately, a gruesome murder is committed on one of Alix's former wards from the women's prison where she teaches English literature:

> And there, indeed, reposing upon the driver's seat, loosely wrapped but only partially concealed in a piece of mutton cloth, was the head of Jilly Fox. The eyes were open, and stared. Alix gazed at them, at Jilly's livid face, at the dishevelled hair. So this was it: death. Alix stared, and was not turned to stone. Her lips moved, drily. Good-bye, Jilly.[41]

> Who was she to flinch? And anyway, she had seen the worst already: Jilly's head, yellow-white, staring, handsome, livid, wrapped in grey muslin, mystic, wonderful.[42]

Alix comes face to face with a personalized death, the beheaded woman is not just any anonymous victim of urban violence, Jilly Fox was an unhappy middle-class girl who had looked to Alix for guidance and surrogate parenting, and the social network as well as Alix personally had failed her.

This example is the most graphic illustration of Drabble's use of the female body as a symbol of social malfunction. The breakdown of the social contract is enacted over and over and becomes visible on the bodies of marginalized women—be they "her mother, her gross mother swelling and aging in her traumatic den"[43] (namely, Liz's housebound mother, Rita Ablewhite, whose body swells up grotesquely after having been on a lifelong deprivation diet) or the young handicapped woman whom her family takes outside for a walk:

> [In the late spring, Liz and Esther go for a walk in Esther's neighborhood and observe] a strange, disturbing group of walkers: two men, and between them, struggling, and (they could dimly hear) moaning, a youngish woman. She stumbled and protested, one man gripped each arm. Liz and Esther slowed their already slow pace; the towpath was narrow, they were directly in line, they would have to pass within feet; intervention was, it would seem, forced upon them. The woman's legs were buckling and wandering splayed at angles, ungainly as she tried to free herself. "Christ," said Esther. . . . A father, a brother, taking for a walk, kindly, familiarly, a mentally, a physically handicapped young woman, who was strug-

gling against their benevolence, wanting to walk freely wanting to turn back, wanting she knew not what, wanting to kneel by the water and scoop up dead fishes. As they passed Liz and Esther, she lunged yet again for the water, mumbling about the fishes; and the two patient men held her and soothed her as they would have a frightened horse, calming her. . . . Her arms were everywhere, every now and then she gave at the knees and sank in a heap of sullen protest; firmly, not very gently, they would drag her up again and drag her on. The men looked exhausted: their faces were red and streaming with sweat: They did not look at Liz and Esther as they passed, and went their painful, struggling, desperate way.[44]

What we are shown here is an allegory of suffering, cast in the imagery of religious iconography as Christ's penitential walk through the stations of the cross. Like the disheveled hair of the Medusa-head placed in the driver's seat of a broken-down car, this woman's extremities are unruly, gangly— she has lost all motor control and is being propelled along a narrow towpath like a barge-dray, a beast of burden. Drabble condemns the dream of social progress through technology— the protagonist's car, often used as a symbol of advancement and personal progress, keeps breaking down. Unlike Christ's miracle of the loaves and fishes, which feed the community of believers, the water and the fishes in the London canal are poisoned, they cannot sustain anyone. Drabble deliberately makes this encounter of the two disparate groups of walkers inevitable ("they were directly in line . . . intervention was . . . forced upon them . . . ")[45] to criticize contemporary urban hardheartedness: typically, the well-off city dweller would ignore the presence of human misery and look the other way. As Valerie Myer observes: "as in *The Middle Ground*, the theme is health and sickness, and the pattern is the Quest Novel and the discovery of long-lost relatives: the family romance. . . . But despite the upbeat ending, the overriding impression is of a terrible world, through which the characters must pick their way as best they can. If harmony is achieved, it is at the cost of human sacrifice."[46]

I read Drabble's work as hortatory fiction—like Bunyan, she wishes to frighten her readers back into self-examination and an ethical sociality by holding up to them a terrifying spectacle of what their society is about to become. What is most troubling about her technique, however, is that this demonstration of urban corruption and decay is inscribed on the aging, medicalized female body—Drabble seems concerned with use-value and (re)productivity, even though she derides these as bourgeois values when they are associated with commerce. The interior spaces and tissues of the female body—the womb, the vagina, the breast tissue— retain their mystery for Drabble. Like the public spaces of the city, these private spaces— not easily accessible to the ordering human gaze—are felt to be dangerous. Freed of its biological capacity to reproduce, the middle-aged female body in Drabble's texts falls prey to diseases of the reproductive organs.

An example of this is Liz's sister Shirley who journeys from Northam to London to get a D and C and be sterilized, after which she stays at her sister's house to recover and be "on holiday."[47] Liz herself seems not to be living in her body and displaces all her remaining sexual feelings onto her newly adopted tabbycat. Liz's mother, freed by senility from all public constraints on her behavior, focuses obsessively on her bowel movements: "the even more unsavory and perplexing matter of the way in which she now appeared to wish to discuss her own bowel movements and body fluids with Shirley [her daughter] in the most embarrassing and uncalled-for detail, I really do draw the line, said Shirley, at having to gaze at her knickers: I mean, what next? And indeed, indeed, what next?"[48]

If we refuse to draw the line and ask ourselves what next, we are confronted with that dreaded and at the same time desired sight of the mother's genitals—not only the feared site of anatomical lack, according to Freud and Lacan, but also of biological origin. As Laura Mulvey puts it in a recent article on the trope of Pandora's box as symptom of cinematic distortion of female bodies and interior spaces, the mother's body becomes an enigma. Mulvey states:

> Enigmas and secrets generate the image of closed hidden spaces which generate in turn the divided topography of inside and outside. If a certain image of femininity is associated with mystery, its attendant connotations of a phantasmagoric division between an inside and an outside effects the iconography of the female body. . . . It is an image of female beauty as artifact or mask, as an exterior, alluring, and seductive surface that conceals an interior space containing deception and danger.[49]

The mother's body in Drabble's text is represented as unreadable, as an enigmatic entity that refuses finally to stay confined to the space it had allotted itself to take up, it expands and its fluids spread and enter discourse like a contagion. Drabble gives us the culturally accepted response of fear and revulsion to this scenario—the turning outward and bringing into speech and public space what was contained inside—in Shirley's reaction. Shirley is, after all, the submissive daughter who hands over her own womb to the doctors for sanitizing. But Drabble then goes on to supply a different response with her mocking authorial comment: "And indeed, indeed, what next?" Liz, the nonconformist daughter, is made curious and ends up investigating her mother's private spaces. As Mulvey interprets this desire to look for herself what the mother's enigma is about, it is self-reflexive and gets at the cultural concatenation of feminity and private, that is, domestic space: "Pandora combines the iconography of mystery with a narrative of curiosity. If the box is a reification and displaced representation of female sexuality as mystery and threat, Pandora's curiosity about its contents may be interpreted as a curiosity about the mystery she herself personifies. And her desire can be rerepresented as a self-reflexive desire to investigate feminity itself."[50]

Women are not only victims, they are also the viewers, the heroic questers in these traditionally male scenarios—as Alix gazes upon the Gorgon's head and is not turned to stone, Liz gazes at her mother's "privates" as well as her carefully secreted newspaper clippings about child abuse, and she survives the flood of shameful and potentially destructive memories. On the one hand, women like Rita uphold the family romance. On the other hand, like Liz, they dismantle it, making room for a new approach to reality that does not deny its ugly underside or (as Mulvey would call them) its "concealed spaces." Mulvey gives us a concise summary of Freud's view of the female body:

> In psychoanalytic terms, the female body is also a source of anxiety, constantly threatening to return the subject to an original, traumatic, repressed memory of castration. . . . This sight may well be of the mother's body, already the first locus of erotic feelings but also of disgust, the point where the subject first finds the need to draw lines of bodily separation and autonomy. . . . As the traumatic moment was itself born out of a perception of lack, of absence, the fetish object that is "concealing nothing" is a screen, protecting a void, simultaneously reassuring and terrifying. Nothing is there, so there is nothing to be afraid of, but it is nothingness, the void, that is the source of anxiety. . . . In this sense, the image of femininity as a mask facilitates the fetishistic fantasy, neutralizing and reproducing its anxiety. . . . I am arguing that the totality, the whole topography, would be seen to be a riddle, the solution of which points to the phantasmagorias generated by male castration anxiety. . . . While curiosity is a compulsive desire to see and to know, to investigate what is secret and reveal the contents of a concealed space, fetishism, on the other hand, is born out of a refusal to see, a refusal to known, and a refusal to accept the difference that the female body symbolizes.[51]

The daughter made curious about whose daughter she is faces the mother's void, her refusal to venture out into the street and thus subject herself to the public censure she fears, which leads to her nullity, her complete silencing as a public figure; but the daughter discovers who was responsible for it. It is not some intrinsic defect of Rita Ablewhite that has led to her erasure from public space, moreover, she has recognized the importance of public female speech and thus paid for her daughters' elocution lessons, which deliver them of their Yorkshire accents—they become urbanized, they learn to speak standard London English. Despite the city's many deficiencies, the daughter who moves to London does much better in life than the daughter who remains close to home in the small northern town. As the family home in the suburb or the small town, as Drabble sees it, is a contaminated space, the successful female protagonist removes herself from it initially and makes her home in a larger urban space. As the protagonist—and the author—enter middle age, a nostalgia for "home," for making it over as a safe interior space comes to pervade the narrative. Drabble wants her characters to be able to be "at home" in contemporary Britain, but this home has been turned inside out by the very forces that were intended to improve it: urbanization, technological networks, individualized transportation. The resulting urbanized landscape is experienced as fragmentary and dislocated, a "non-place urban realm" as Webber has aptly termed it.[52]

Drabble's attitude to women in this text is ambivalent (I would argue), but she codes them as more socially responsible because they stick closer to "home." Whereas the men join the brain drain and emigrate or absent themselves trying to solve global issues—like Charles Headland's best friend Dirk Davis, the journalist, who is kidnapped in Lebanon. Liz the therapist remains in London ministering to society's ills, and Alix the teacher delves into the local literary heritage: "But the poems live. . . . They are high art, and good. Alix has found her corner in immortality, in Beaver's attic. She is in a position of power: Beaver has conferred power upon her. She can destroy, edit, publish"[53] and, in the younger generation, Cynthia, Shirley's teenage daughter, enthuses over ancient British history and the example of the indigenous "Cartimandua, Queen of Queens" who repelled Roman invaders, and Cynthia's dedication to this interest wins her a place in university. Ultimately, Drabble sees feminized occupations like teaching or healing people's emotions and bodies through diagnosis and empathy as the sources of England's renewal—a turning away to personal agency because government and state-run institutions are characterized as tainted. She pits morality and personal engagement against corporate greed and privatization. Drabble therefore also turns away from the public marketplace and the street to reclaim private spaces of contemplation and learning: the study, the attic, the walled garden. But at least she delivers her female characters from the kitchen and the bedroom.

Sociologist Sharon Zukin states that contemporary postindustrial societies in the Western Hemisphere and their urban spaces are sharply

divided between landscapes of consumption and landscapes of devastation, a view borne out exactly by Drabble's recent fiction:

> The cultural understandings and social structures that constitute
> economic institutions are in disarray. These days, workers are im-
> portant because they consume, not because they produce anything
> the culture values. . . . The wealth of cities seeps out to border
> regions, and within the city, the center acquires a new aggressive-
> seductive lure. Place, moreover, is sharply divided between land-
> scapes of consumption and devastation. . . . Those places that
> thrive are connected to real estate development, financial ex-
> changes, entertainment—the business of moving money and
> people—where consumer pleasures hide the reins of concentrated
> economic control.[54]

In Drabble's 1975 novel *The Realms of Gold* the female hero, an
archeologist, returns to her grandparents' hometown to find it utterly
changed:

> She had remembered the route well, but it was utterly, utterly
> changed. Nothing was left as it had been. Landmarks had disap-
> peared, new ones in the form of garages and discount stores had
> risen. And, to her mounting dismay, she realized there was no
> country left. The whole road was built up, lined with houses. In the
> old days, it had taken five minutes to get out of the town, right out,
> into a dull but rural country. Now, it seemed, there was no country.
> After a quarter of an hour they were still driving through semi-
> detached houses, bungalows, and estates: where country roads had
> once led off the main road there were signposts saying Eastern
> Industry, Industrial estate, Priestman's Plant.
>   By the time they had reached Hesley, they had not passed a
> single field. . . .
>   She was about to turn back, judging that she had let enough
> time pass, when she saw ahead of her a sight that drew her forward.
> It was a field full of people, and the vision of it flashed across her
> unprepared eye, shaking her in a way that she could not compre-
> hend. A field full of people, only women and children, in a bare
> ploughed field. Stooping and bending under the large sky. They
> had baskets, they were filling the baskets. What were they doing, in
> that bare field? There were no crops, there was nothing. Small
> children stooped, women in head scarves stooped, like an ancestral
> memory. She shivered as she drew nearer, and her first impression
> dispelled itself—for of course, they were ordinary women and chil-

dren gathering stones, . . . they said they were clearing the new school playing field, and she could see that that was what they were doing, and that they were enjoying it—it was a voluntary effort, a communal effort, and the children were nicely dressed and the women were exchanging jokes as they worked. Why then had she seen something quite different? For what she had seen had been an image of forced labour, of barrenness, of futility, of toil, of woman and children stooping for survival, harvesting nothing but stones. The big field stretched aimlessly, the people at the far reaches looked small and aimless. Shivering, she went back and caught the bus to Tockley.[55]

As in the example I quoted earlier, of Alix Bowen observing the young black woman and her baby hesitating on the front steps of their tenement building, Drabble envisions the apocalypse being visited primarily on women and children, society's weakest members: as Sharon Zukin implies, they cheerfully participate in their own exploitation.

What is visually presented from the point of view of the distanced observer, like a mournful tableau of worker exploitation by Jean François Millet, is felt by its actors to be a meaningful activity of cultivation—they are in the process of producing a play space for their school children. The type of playing that will take place here, however, is not liminoid "free" play, but various forms of highly competitive, organized school sports. Drabble clearly describes her disillusionment with the landscapes of urban sprawl, which she sees as undefinable barren spaces—neither country fields nor city turf.

The inner-city space can be equally disconcerting and unreadable, even thought there is graffiti inscribed on it: "He told me [Esther said] that he knew of an Italian bank that would be only too delighted to sponsor my unwritten masterpiece on [Carlos] Crivelli. He said that in Italy all art books are sponsored by banks." "Absurd," said Esther. "Tax incentives, he spoke of . . ." The still hot air mocked. . . . *Kill the Mozart* [italics added], declared a large scrawled notice on the canal bridge. "Is that advertising? Or sponsorship? Or GLC popularist antielitism? Or what?" asked Liz as they paused to stare at it."[56]

The graffiti refers to a new housing complex that has arisen on the site of former squats and is thus intended as a politicized statement of protest, but its message is so cryptically condensed that even neighborhood residents like Esther cannot decipher it. At a deeper symbolic level, the graffiti reveals Drabble's fears for traditional mainstream culture: if we did go ahead to *Kill the Mozart*, we would deaden our sense of the cultural heritage.

The critics Valerie Myer and Michael Harper see a concern with culture as a typically middle-class obsession with holding onto privilege in the face of working-class dissatisfaction:

> Drabble's novels stretch "with difficulty from lower-middle to upper-middle class but [are] unable to comprehend radically different contexts." . . . The real empathy in *The Ice Age* is for the middle-class characters. . . . The book's message is the superiority of culture (which embodies spiritual values) to commerce. Culture is only safe in the hands of the children of the professional middle class. . . . [This] recapitulates the fear for traditional culture voiced in *The Ice Age*, in which the actuality of the world is pollution and rubbish.[57]

Increasingly, the space associated with pollution and the lower class is the outside: "[Esther's] niece Ursula, who has a taste for the louche, likes [the strange surreal landscape under the arches of the Motorway] immensely, strikes up terrible friendships in public houses and on street corners, sits drinking cans of beer with impossible people in condemned and boarded cottages in the middle of rubble wastes. The Apocalypse Hotel is her favoured rendez-vous. Esther, who once liked the louche herself, feels a little old for that kind of thing."[58] Her general questions about Britain in the eighties are "Does everything belong to something else? Is nothing what it is?"[59] and they betoken an anxiety about place and ownership as well as a wish for congruence between a given appearance (surface, exterior space) and the corporeal reality behind it (interior space, distinct bodily entities). Culture is linked to specificity, whereas commerce is linked to homogeneity, a leveling of differences, as the following example of a mundane trip to the supermarket illustrates:

> Alix hesitated, before a dizzying range of packets of orange juice. . . . [Otto] reached for the nearest, he did not know, they were all the same, surely, he said. . . . " 'Produce of several lands,' it says," said Otto, staring, thus prompted at the small print. "What can that mean?"
>
> "Engraved on my milkbottles this morning," said Alix, as they made their way towards the girl at the till, "there was an advertisement for the *Sunday Post*. In red lettering, on the glass of my milkbottle. What can that mean? Does the dairy belong to a newspaper consortium? Does the newspaper consortium belong to the dairy?". . . . "This is purgatory," said Otto, as someone in a hurry rammed, annoyed by their conversation, angrily into their trolley. "Is it always like this?[60]

This condemnation of Thatcherite economics and globalized production as far removed from everyday practices and individual needs (Otto, the economist, usually leaves the food shopping to his wife and so has no idea what an alienating space a supermarket is) goes hand in hand with an insistence on specificity, on Englishness, on legibility.

The biggest difference between Drabble's descriptions of social uniformity in the eighties versus the late sixties is that now it is cynical and fake, produced and streamlined by companies for their own profit, whereas back then, it was a counterculture uncompetitive Bohemia, produced by the working class and students together. Alix found a supportive community in the slums of North London that still bore the marks of a genuine neighborhood: communal spaces for relaxation (the pub, the park) and household chores (the launderette), such as laundry, usually kept out of the public eye in the middle-class family. Furthermore, she gets to know and like her working-class neighbors and they her, overcoming class barriers erected by the middle class of what is below it in the class structure. In the new world of the eighties, the hierarchy has gone underground, it has become an inscrutable network of big business and politics, which produces a sense of disaffection, not belonging:

> Alix, was at this stage, perhaps perversely, perhaps naturally, attracted by poverty. It seemed to her less alarming than it had seemed to her parents. She got on speaking terms with it. She discovered the art of sinking. She sank. Not very deep, but she sank. She and Nicholas in Clissold Park, eating crisps on a bench, feeding the ducks with crusts. Indistinguishable from her neighbours. Unrecognizable to her Cambridge friends. She walked for miles with Nicholas round North London tiring herself and him so that they would both sleep in the long nights.
>
> Gradually her fears of the rough and unmannerly faded, her expectations of the world adjusted. As a child, she had always had a secret yearning to enter the other city, the unknown city, beyond and within the suburbs, where nobody, middle-class folklore declared, read books or washed or cooked proper meals. She had sometimes, even as a child, wondered if it could be as fearful as its reputation. She disliked fear. Particularly she disliked being made to feel fear of her fellow men and women. Now she lived with these people, and was no longer afraid, for they were like herself in more ways than they were unlike herself. She faded into the background. Inconspicuous, accepted, she discovered new talents. She found she could teach.
>
> . . . At the end of Alix's road was a little patch of grass, on the corner in front of the launderette and the pub. A small patch, smelling of dog shit, in a heavily built area. On it was a bench, and on the bench sat, in fair weather and sometimes in foul, a row of strange-complexioned men, not all of them old though most of

them looked it, with bottles of wine, cider, and beer, sometimes with a half bottle of spirits. They accosted Alix as she passed, not for money—she no longer looked as if she had any money—but for company. . . . They rarely seemed drunk to Alix. They were past drunkenness, washed up on some far beach of harmless universal being, ground down to the bedrock of being, unstruggling, undemanding, unresentful. Dirty, ragged, high-smelling, communing with the Lord. They told her not to worry, the worst would never happen.[61]

Alix, precisely because she comes from, and is ultimately sustained by, the middle-class belief in personal betterment through education, is equipped to enjoy "sinking" into urban poverty. She sees it as a transitional stage for herself, a reprieve from the unremitting linear pursuit of middle-class success with its pitfalls: a good degree, a well-paying respectable job, a husband, house, and children. Her fraternizing with "the enemy" proves to be educational, because she can be one of the crowd, a group of forgotten men, who expect nothing out of life and demand only her occasional company. This romance with the underclass is strictly speaking a narrative screen, an avoidance of the living conditions and desires of the working class, who are at best a shadowy presence in Drabble's vignette of blissful urban squalor. It is precisely they who are unlikely to be "unstruggling, undemanding, unresentful," and indeed these are some of the attributes that resurface in Drabble's description of the new unemployed youth.

Submerging one's identity in the crowd, breaking middle-class taboos (especially) on women loitering "in the street," eating and drinking in public, dressing shabbily and not taking care of one's appearance are all experienced as liberating practices promoted by the liminoid spaces of "the other city, the unknown city, beyond and within the suburbs." That other city is subterranean, both outside and inside the known daily life of middle-class reality. By its very presence it shows up middle-class reality as a construct. Rather than debunk class ideologies altogether, however, Drabble puts another myth, another construct in their place, an ethical individualism that ultimately affirms rather than contests traditional middle-class values: thrift, education, instruction for the moral betterment of the less fortunate.

Drabble's utopian female community joins together individuals of roughly similar class background: both Esther's and Alix's families are solidly middle class, whereas Liz has raised herself into the middle class through her hard work in medical school, and she has cemented her position by marrying a wealthy widower who needs her to raise his three children. For Liz, identity constitutes itself in urban space, through naming and placing at the center of the city space, hence in the center of social power:

> Each time a shop assistant or a clerk or a tradesman wrote down Dr. E. Headland, Harley Street, the same thrill of self-affirmation, of self-definition would be reenacted. Liz Ablewhite of Abercorn Avenue had become Liz Headland of Harley Street, London W.1. Nobody could argue with that, nobody could question it, it was so. . . . The Headlands of Harley Street; resonant, exemplary. Myriad uncertainties and hesitations were buried beneath that solid pile, banished by the invocation of a street name. Vanished suburbia, vanished the provinces, vanished forever solitude and insignificance and social fear. No wonder that she and Charles felt they led a charmed life, that the times were on their side.[62]

Whereas Alix, whose origins are squarely middle class, seeks to merge and blend in with the working-class crowd at the margins of London, Liz, who hails from the working class, wants to belong to the elite in power and establishes her place as "exemplary," singular, in the center of the city. Locating the self out of the public gaze and merging with the background only comes as a release to those characters who were assured of their centrality in the social structure early on.

Whether they pursue a transitional marginality or permanent centrality, Drabble's female protagonists follow their desires in the city and experience their presence there as liberating and invigorating. From the vantage point of middle age, Esther remembers, for instance, her first trip to Italy as a young woman, mainly as a stay in Florence:

> She had stopped, then, in Florence, where her parents had arranged for her to spend the night, before catching the morning train to Perugia. She had been timid but reckless, exhilarated by freedom, unable to believe that she could go where she wished; that she was, at last, unobserved. She was booked into a small, safe, respectable hotel on the banks of the Arno, with a view of the Ponte Vecchio. She had left her luggage at the hotel, and had taken to the streets. She had wandered, past façades and windows, past shops selling marbled paper and tooled leather purses. She drank a small green drink in one bar and a small red drink in another bar. She had a conversation with a nun and was followed by a soldier. She sat on a bridge and watched the river. She walked through narrow streets, and saw a woman from an upper window lean over an array of geraniums and drying stockings. . . . She ended the evening in the Piazza della Signoria with an American student from Iowa. . . . She

had never eaten or even seen a pizza. They gazed at people, at the fountain, at Giambologna's statue of Cosimo I, at Michelangelo's David, at the Loggia, at the pigeons, at a man selling little painted mechanical flying birds. The American, who was gaunt and livid of aspect, with a long thin melancholy quixotic face, bought her a little bird (She has it still.) The American persuaded her to accompany him back to his pensione, where he attempted to seduce her, but she told him, primly summoning her meandering resources, that she was only seventeen and therefore beneath the age of consent. He received this information solemnly, with some relief and desisted. Nevertheless in the morning, after collecting her suitcase from her small hotel overlooking the Arno, she agreed to alter her plans and to hitchhike with him to Siena and Arezzo.

And so she made her acquaintance with Tuscany, with Umbria. And now was on her way to Bologna.[63]

The lure of the city, and especially the foreign (southern) city is that it seems to the English tourist a place for easy sociality and pleasure. The young Englishwoman, protected by her middle-class upbringing and her money, is free to stroll in the streets at her leisure, and she is depicted as a curious consumer, making her own choices about where to stop for a drink, whom to accost, with whom to eat and sleep (or not). She consumes the sights of Florence, but appears to derive the greatest pleasure from glimpses of small domestic or intimate scenes—the woman bending out of her window who calls out that the meal is ready, the American student who buys her a mechanical bird as a gift. Both those actions emphasize the liminoid and the visual—the window connects inside and outside, the bird takes flight and thus shares the ground and the space above it. The city architecture also allows for larger views, ranging from the birds-eye view to the view from below—of the river from the bridge, of the towering sculptures and buildings decorating the piazza. Diversity, color, a mingling of art and commerce that produces hand-crafted, playful, and highly ornamented surfaces (the marbled paper, the tooled leather, the painted metal) distinguish the idealized foreign city.

The built spaces of central London in the eighties, by contrast, emphasize mass ("the solid pile"), vastness, and blankness—the white and gold of Liz's house, for instance. Here, culture does not inscribe itself playfully by ornamenting surfaces or accenting a communal public space with sculptures and fountains. Instead of loosely gathering in the Florentine piazza, people come together to exhibit their façades, their public personae to each other, to mingle and talk at the Headland house, either for a specific purpose (the New Year's party) or for routinized monthly meetings of friends. A sense of the liminal prevails in both the architecture and the social rituals it sanctions. The only space left over for the potentially subversive liminoid is in women's talk and on women's faces—the visually accessible, communicative surface of the body:

> The faces of Alix and Esther were mobile, expressive, changeable; they were open to the weather, responsive, at least superficially, even open, she fancied. They had no public faces, the three of them, no public talk. So she fancied. . . . Chatter, chatter, female chatter, unstructured, shimmering, malicious, appreciative, acute, indulgent, shifting, rapid, unpunctuated, glancing, a light bright surface ripple on a deeper current, and Charles sat on, biting his inner lip.[64]

Women's talk is fluid, it has depth even when it skims the surface, it is like a body of moving water, as it shifts topics and location (the women take turns meeting at each other's apartments or houses in the city) and like the river in the Italian city, it is central to the city. The idea of communication on equal terms, without ownership or differentiation, among a triangle of three who over time become as one marks Drabble's ideal of sociality, depicted by religious iconography—the Divine Godhead, Father, Son and Holy Ghost have been replaced by three allegorical female divinities of learned knowledge—art, science, and literature. Furthermore, the three women speak in a tongue that silences the male observer—instead of pontificating, as is his wont, Charles Headland, the television producer who is an allegorical figure of the computer age, the age of the interface and the mediating screen, can only sit still and listen, "biting his inner lip." The shared thought-space, the shared information between the three women presents an alternative to the way information is processed and packaged by the modern media:

> They would eat, drink and talk. They exchanged ideas. Sometimes they exchanged them so successfully that a year later Alix would be putting forward a proposition that she had energetically refuted when Liz had proposed it a year earlier; only to find that Liz, influenced by Alix, had subsequently shifted her ground and herself reflected it. . . . Some of their notions swam, unallocated, in the space between them.
>
> . . . But one cannot really, wholly differentiate between these three women. In their mid-forties, after more than half a lifetime of association, they share characteristics, impressions, memories, even speech patterns; they have a common stock of knowledge, they have entered, through one another, worlds, that they would not otherwise have known. They have pooled their discoveries, have come back from other regions with samples of leaf, twig, fruit,

stone, have turned them over together. They share much. The barriers between them are, they think, quite low.[65]

Again, Drabble privileges liminoid space, even as thought-space which it renders more flexible, expanding the consciousness of those who share in it.

As Sharon Zukin has pointed out, the market economy and free enterprise have produced an exclusionary power structure and have limited the circulation of knowledge. Drabble reintroduces the element of time and historical consciousness into her concept of the mind, it frees the individual from the succession of present moments of stimulation and consumption that characterize the consumer in a market economy: "Tracing a critical social geography in landscapes of power challenges an ingrained belief in markets. Markets represent free movement and impersonal judgment, hallmarks of the American way of life from de Tocqueville to Reagan. By emphasizing earning over either giving or taking, markets satisfy Americans' moral yearning for a peculiar sort of social equality."[66] The epitome of this belief in the power of the market, which characterized the Thatcher era as it did the Reagan/Bush decade, is Charles Headleand, Liz's former husband. Drabble renders his stance profoundly ironic; all his mastery of modern technology—faxes, telexes, television, and cameras—cannot improve the fate of his friend and colleague Dirk Davis, kidnapped and presumably killed by Arab fundamentalists. Nonetheless, Charles launches himself on a quest to find Dirk and bring him back to England. The following excerpt shows Drabble's contempt for vicarious moral involvement, palliated by the belief in mediated knowledge—ultimately, Charles will turn away from his television screen to the Gideon Bible in his hotel room drawer to look for a clue to "the narrative of his own life, of his place in the history and geography of the world"[67]:

> Charles Headleand has got as far as the Gatwick Hilton. He is sitting on a king-size bed, by himself, in his maroon cotton pyjamas and his grey towelling dressinggown, playing with the remote control of his television. He summons up arcane messages, for he is a wizard with such machines, and they will tell him matters which they divulge only to the elect. . . . It occurs to Charles that he needn't go at all. He could just sit here for a week. Lying low. And return home, quietly, saying "mission accomplished." . . . Charles switches off the sound, and superimposes upon the picture some instant Global News. Over the flowing river [a nature program] appear newly calculated statistics of crime and violence in the inner cities, and predictable telespeak protestations of imminent action from the Home Secretary. Charles watches this combination with satisfaction. It is artistic. He has

150

made it. It occurs to Charles that we do not really need a Home Secretary any more: we could just programme a machine to issue statements, and another machine to issue equally predictable Opposition statements.

The river is subtle, supple, infinitely varied. No two days in time, no two minutes in time of its long, long history have ever been, will ever be repeated. Its patterns flicker, alter, flow, and each moment is unique.

. . . Charles can no longer pay attention to one source of information at a time. He is Modern Man, programmed to take in several story lines, several plots at once. He cannot quite unravel them, but he cannot do without the conflicting impulses, the disparate stimuli. Perhaps he hopes the alcohol will simplify them, will stick them together and fuse them all into one consecutive narrative. . . . Muslim extremists, the Koran, hostages, armaments. He knows fuck all about it.

All the programmes he's seen, all the reports he's read, have explained nothing. They are all biased, inevitably misinformed. How can one know what's going on in the mind of another culture?[68]

Drabble juxtaposes the sense of mechanized artistry, of simulated multiple presents mediated by the interface, with a belief in nature's cyclicality—the river's translucent flow—like the limpid female talk in the city of *Radiant Way* it is relegated to the background by superimposed "Global News," but the real meanings reside there.

Such a linkage of women and nature and men and technoculture is, of course, not new. For Drabble, the solution to modernity's ills lies in a turning away from technoculture to cultivation—a more organic metaphor for social innovation, cultivation as "study, care and practice to improve or advance something." Cultivation can also mean very literally a reshaping of the geographical space that surrounds us—as when Clive Enderby (another male whose belief in progress through a market economy is shaken) suddenly envisions grassing over the slagheaps and "abandoned acres" of northern England: "Of course one could not rebuild all these abandoned acres, modern industry did not need such spaces, but the sight of them crumbling and decaying was a deterrent. So—grass them over. Why not? Grass over what you don't need, and rebuild the rest. Landscape it, and rebuild. A sea of green. It would cost money, but not all that much money."[69] Drabble advocates a re-creation of liminoid space—to make urban industrialized wasteland over into a green space for public use. She wants to reintroduce depth perception through the creation of new landscaped vistas, get beyond the graffiti-covered surfaces, the stagnant canals and sewers of the modern city. Elizabeth Grosz draws our attention to the mutual constitution of cities and bodies through the architectonics of city space:

> The city helps to orient sensory and perceptual information, insofar as it helps to produce specific conceptions of spatiality, the vectorization and setting for our earliest and most ongoing perceptions. . . . Cities establish lateral, contingent, short- or long-term connections between individuals and social groups, and more or less stable divisions, such as those constituting domestic and generational distinctions. These spaces, divisions, and interconnections are the roles and means by which bodies are individuated to become subjects. The structure and layout of the city also provide and organize the circulation of information, and structure social and regional access to goods and services. Finally, the city's form and structure provide the context in which social rules and expectations are internalized or habituated in order to ensure social conformity, or position social marginality at a safe or insulated and bounded distance (ghettoization). This means that the city must be seen as the most immediately concrete locus for the production and circulation of power.
>
> . . . It follows that, corresponding to the dramatic transformation of the city as a result of the information revolution will be a transformation in the inscription of bodies. . . . [This development is subtended] the tendency towards hyperreality in cities today: the replacement of geographical space with the screen interface, the transformation of distance and depth into pure surface, the reduction of space to time, of the face-to-face encounter to the terminal screen. . . . The implosion of space into time, the transmutation of distance into speed, the instantaneousness of communication, the collapsing of the workspace into the home computer system, will clearly have major effects on specifically sexual and racial bodies of the city's inhabitants as well as on the form and structure of the city. The increased coordination and integration of microfunctions in the urban space creates the city not as a body politic but as a political machine—no longer a machine modeled on the engine but now represented by the computer, facsimile machine, and modem, a machine that reduces distance and speed to immediate, instantaneous gratification. The abolition of the distance between home and work, the diminution of interaction between face-to-face subjects, the continuing mediation of interpersonal relations by terminals, screens, and keyboards, will increasingly affect/infect the minutiae of everyday life and corporeal existence.[70]

152

Hyperreality as constituted by the electronic interface, Drabble believes, entails not only the disembodiment, but rather the evisceration of communication practices. As the case of Charles amply illustrates, the body that is produced by exclusive reliance on the interface is isolated, intoxicated, and in need of overstimulation. Charles avoids saying good-bye in person to the woman whose husband he is setting out to rescue, he only talks to his five children over the phone, he drinks, he is programmed for immediate gratification—for instance, he orders fast-food through room service, even though a real meal would be available in the hotel dining room. Far from being a British colonialist's dream of a desert oasis, the cityscape of Baldai in the Arabian desert echoes the wasteland of northern London, as it had been described in the previous novel:

> He does not like it in Baldai. There is nothing to see in the town but modern buildings of curious Texan structure, and a few palm trees that for all he knows may be made of plastic. Wide roads lead nowhere. The light is harsh. He cannot get the World Service, and Baldai TV, as he had feared, consists of long political and religious discourses in a foreign tongue, interspersed with Western commercials for soft drinks and soap and photocopiers.[71]

Bereft of a key for decoding a truly alien reality, Charles retreats into passivity and aborts his rescue mission, the journey failing even to effect a genuine transformation in himself.

Although Charles's heroic quest fails, and he does not recover any new information about his friend, let alone his body, Alix's quest to redeem "*her* murderer," the man who had cut off women's heads in the previous volume, is successful. She traces his sociopathic development through his family, and finds out a root-cause for his need to "castrate" women—inadequate mothering and abuse by his mother. Where Drabble fails, in my opinion, is that the mother is demonized and remains a paradox, Freud's riddle of femininity, as her very name already suggests: Angela Malkin contains conflicting "angelic" and evil attributes, she is "of bad kin." Her body is described mainly through its outward appearance, her clothes and cosmetics. She maintains a public façade, and Drabble condemns this enactment of femininity as studied masquerade with the intention to deceive, just as she disapproves of the manor house whose front rooms are "kept up" while bull mastiffs are kept caged and mistreated in the back of the house:

> Angela's voice was harsh, high pitched, monotonous, yet at the same time overlaid and affected. Like the house and its grounds, she presented an uneasy combination of the kempt and the unkempt. Her hair was varnished into its high crown, and she was

heavily made-up, with green eye-shadow, false lashes, dark red lips, a false complexion imposed upon a natural uneven pallor. But her feet were clad in old scuffed jewelled high-heeled sandals and her slacks were stained. She wore large stud earrings of yellow metal, and a thick yellow metal choker necklace. Her varnished nails were very long—were they false, too? A scar ran white and gleaming from her wrist up her inner arm, and vanished into the rolled-back cuff of her shirt.[72]

Femininity is visualized here as a nightmarish collage of false body parts—the false nails and skin, body ornaments that remind one of sadistic practices (body piercing and choking) and violent color clashes (mauve, green, red, yellow, black). Once again, it is the urbanized female body that brings forth the diseases of the body politic. This body looks bruised and constrained, but is at the same time a manufactured appearance of urban chic—the combined effect is that of a grotesque spectacle. Like Edmund Spenser's Babylonian whore, this woman is an archetype of corrupting female sexuality. She refuses the responsibilities of motherhood and wifeliness, her professional pursuits are criminalized—both the hairdressing and the dog-breeding are seen as distorting practices.

Although Charles never makes contact with his friend's captors, Alix braves her daunting specter in a face-to-face encounter and elicits a personalized conversation with it. This is reminiscent of the act of facing the Medusa in *Radiant Way*. Before it can be overcome, the urban nemesis needs to be faced and looked at. Drabble still believes, therefore, in the power of the analytical (female) gaze. Often, she locates that gaze as coming from below, which in turn echoes her early privileging of the underside and the subterranean in *Jerusalem*. In *Radiant Way*, Alix witnesses "strange sights" of private rituals and secret exchanges being performed in a parking garage, largely because she crouches on the ground and thus has a view from/of the underside of daily urban life:

Alix had found herself imprisoned at times in her own house, lying flat beneath the drawing-room window when she glimpsed Jilly in the street below; . . . once she dodged into the British Council car park in Spring Gardens when she saw Jilly stationed in a dark corner of Cockspur Court as she walked to the bus stop from work. Crouching there, hidden behind a red Triumph down at the seventh level, her heart beating fast with fear and humiliation and sorrow, she had witnessed strange sights, strange car park sights of the underground city: a dapper executive eating a hamburger from a square box with ravenous, with starving speed and a demented, hunted expression; a woman who removed her jersey, sniffed her armpits, sat there in her brassiere, applied deodorant, then reclothed herself in a blouse and jacket and calmly made up her face smiling at herself obsequiously, seductively, in her driving mirror; a strange, furtive interchange over an open car trunk between a policeman and a young man with an orange sports bag and a squash racket; a weeping older woman with an angry younger man. Half an hour she had crouched, hidden away, waiting for Jilly to move, waiting for Jilly to give up and grow bored and go away.[73]

Private rituals of illicit consumption and discarding; fast-food; clothing and cosmetics; money or drugs; and sexual favors are observed in this allegorical space "down at the seventh level" of the hellish city. The men are letting down their public façade by doing "forbidden" things—the yuppie executive eats tacky fast-food, the policeman accepts bribes of one kind or another, the young man is angry at an older woman. The single woman, on the other hand, reconstructs her public façade by changing clothes in her car and applying deodorant and cosmetics. She then fetishistically gazes at her new persona in her driving mirror. There appears to exist a gender split—men chafe under the demands of their public roles whereas women are complicit with them and use "dead time" to refashion themselves into even greater conformity with social standards. Alix, however, differs from these overly feminized narcissistic women in that she busies herself observing and chronicling what she sees, just as the author describes phenomena of urban life as she encounters them. She tries to construct meaning out of random details, to give a voice to those she sees and to tell their story insofar as it is emblematic of the current state of British society.

In Drabble's latest novel, *The Gates of Ivory* (1992), she pursues the archaeological metaphor—but widens it to a global scale. First, a British leftist writer, Stephen Cox, undertakes an odyssey to Cambodia, where he attempts a fictional reconstruction of the atrocities committed by the communist Khmer Rouge in the Killing Fields. There he hopes to penetrate the motives for human evil and mass slaughter in order to write a hortatory play about them. As an intellectual dissatisfied with consumerism and economic breakdown in the West, he also wishes to salvage the ideals of communism. He is fascinated by the Khmer Rouge's idea of starting over by wiping out an entire people reared in a capitalist system. As a European intellectual, Stephen feels guilty because their dictator, Pol Pot, was trained at the Sorbonne and my have become infected with his genocidal megalomania through the teachings of Western thought. Ironically, Stephen falls ill as soon as he reaches Khmer territory and ultimately dies there.

The second part of the archaeology focuses on Liz Headland's quest to retrace her friend's steps. She is finally unable to recover his body, but her quest is started off when she "inherits" his literary remains: a Pandora's box of a package, containing his notes and fictional fragments as well as the exotic detritus of tourist travel, postcards, ticket stubs, an amulet of finger bones. The pursuit of connection and information yields the story of Stephen's odyssey, and redeems it—Liz returns the vanished friend's memory back to his own society and to the city where she organizes a collective memorial service for him. What Valerie Myer claimed of *Radiant Way*, holds true for the third installment of this allegorical chronicle of our age: "Kinship and archaeology inform this novel. . . . The references to mythology and history are not excrescences, but an important part of the whole."[74] Drabble investigates what she sees as the root of society's ills in the age of technology—deliberate violence of humans against their fellow humans aided by modern technology—be they the Black & Decker chainsaw with which the serial killer severs the heads of his female victims in *Radiant Way* or the machine guns the Khmer Rouge turn on their own people. The second volume, *Natural Curiosity*, sought to explain the causes for human evil on a relatively small scale by delving into the personal history of P. Whitmore, the serial killer. Liz's quest to find Stephen Cox who was obsessed by a mass murderer and crowd violence is, in a sense, the large-scale complement of Alix's quest to reconstruct the origins of P. Whitmore's social deviance. Once again, Drabble opposes humanistic and religious values to the depersonalizing forces working to destroy society—she fosters a sense of communal purpose by uniting her characters in a quest for truth, she has her main protagonists undertake inward journeys of spiritual and moral self-evaluation, she believes in the mortification of the flesh through various illnesses—Brian Bown, Alix's socialist husband, gets cancer and is cured by an operation at a National Health hospital; Stephen Cox contracts malaria and, after being nursed back to a precarious state of health by a devoted Khmer woman, is then transferred to, and killed by, neglect in a Khmer Communist hospital; Liz gets toxic shock syndrome from an unraveling British-made tampon and gradually recovers in a Bangkok hospital. These trials of the flesh make people dependent on the help of others and force them to reevaluate the meaning of their lives. Their illnesses create a liminoid space, which removes them from ordinary social ritual and allows them to be reintegrated into the community in new roles; the survivors of those liminoid states are more willing to affirm their bonds with their fellow humans.

Nowhere does this become more evident than in the memorial service and party for Stephen Cox. Although the city, the emblem of the body politic, is still sick—its arteries clogged by stalling traffic and car pileups, Stephen's mourners do make it to his service on time and do manage to get to Liz's house for the celebratory party. Somewhere within the diseased body politic, healing rituals are taking place—close to the heart, the center, where Liz's new urban home is located.

So in the end, despite her misgivings, Drabble returns to the house in the city as a refuge and a place of renewal, and she restores her female protagonists' vision of the city as the Heavenly City. Alix is granted a sweeping view of London from a suspended point of view—a bridge, perhaps not from the underside, but from ground-level, as Clara Maugham observed Britain in the youthfully subversive sixties, but not quite from the controlling and distanced height of the bird's-eye view that Kate and Evelyn shared from the hospital window in *Middle Ground*, the novel that ushered in Drabble's chronicle of Britain in crisis during the eighties:

Alix Bowen stands on the bridge and stares at the Thames. The slate-grey ruffled water flows beneath her, the slate-grey sky dully swoons above her. An ancient flaking barge called Perseverance travels slowly upstream. . . . Alix gazes downstream, towards Chelsea, towards the distant Post Office Tower and the high rise of the city, towards the Buddhists of Battersea, towards the upturned stiff-legged dead sow of Battersea Power Station, and then she turns and leans on the low metal-studded parapet and gazes up towards Putney, Richmond, Kew and the mild light of the west. The river skyline is changing. Everywhere there are new developments; dinky, red-brick, paint-bright, triangle-and-porthole apartments, soaring superior icy glass-and-metal mansions, supermarkets, river walks, plazas, alpine towers, floating bubbles and insubstantial domes of paradise. Soon there will be river buses, the glossy brochures promise. Wandsworth by water! No more waiting at Waterloo! No more commuter chaos! No more queues at Clapham Junction! . . .

She thinks of Brian, and Paul Whitmore, and the old poet Beaver, and the Celts and the Romans, and the Battersea Shield. . . . Alix never crosses this bridge without thinking of that shield. It is part of her memory, part of her London. It is the Shield of Albion. From its dull drowned bronze, from its curves and roundels and prophetic swastikas, it reflects past, present, future. . . . The Child of Albion peers into the darkening glittering dance of light, into the bleeping, blinking, winking echo-located future.

The afternoon thickens, buses burst into cheerful and colourful illumination like cruising fun-steamers, cars confidently unlid their hooded metallic eyes, the city braids itself with moving jewels. The blooms and harsh yellow neon alarums, and red warnings and green invitations. The sky fills with the complex coded messages of aeroplanes. Descending westwards to the Gates of Empire at Heathrow. . . . As she begins to walk back across the bridge towards Wandsworth Town Station, she sees a cormorant. A neat, smart, sleek, snake-necked historic bird, its head held high above the shimmering effluent and bobbing polystyrene, it rides the flood, then dives, and then resurfaces. It knows the river. It risks the river. It knew Caractacus, it knew Captain Cook, it knew Conrad, it knew Stephen Cox, it knows Alix Bowen. It is a river-wise London bird. It cheers her. Her step quickens.[75]

For her sense of identity, Drabble's alter ego Alix relies on a sense of national pride in Britain's history—symbolized by the flow of the river Thames—on her flexible vision that can encompass the new and specious blandishments of postmodern architecture; delight in the neon lights and colors of the city at dusk; alight on natural details like the river's flow and the diving bird, and take comfort in them; look inward to remember individuals, both among the living and the dead, who are important to her. Like the "London bird," the cormorant so supremely adapted to its changing habitat, and surviving in the face of pollution, Drabble's aware and worldly-wise London women adapt to changes in their environment and chart their own course of exploration. The novel closes with the image of another survivor: the "lost" son of the dignified Cambodian refugee, Mme. Savet Akrun, making his way armed through a tropical forest. Like the cormorant, he is an equivocal figure in the Darwinian struggle for survival. Yet, in the full knowledge of human violence and of society at war with itself, Drabble strongly champions community and forward movement towards a better society. Bunyan's pilgrims finally enter the Heavenly City, just as Drabble's pilgrims Alix, Liz, and Esther resume their liminoid communal outings and are redeemed by "unclouded sunshine, an unimagined and unchanging radiance. They will be rewarded, as they walk along the green ceiling of the limestone and by the singing river, with the glory of Paradise. It will beat down upon them and reprieve them from mortality."[76] In the end, Drabble tempers a Rousseauian belief in human perfectibility and social change with the ironic realism of nineteenth-century realist novelists like Stendal and Thackeray. Drabble's London is Vanity Fair and Heavenly City all mixed up together, but it has not lost its centripetal pull.

The most striking difference between Rhys, Duras, and Drabble is her Protestant belief in moral betterment and overall improvement of social institutions emanating from the middle-class woman. Duras critiques the exploitiveness of the middle class and, furthermore, provides a thorough critique of the class and race barriers on which the colonialist enterprise relies. As a Creole colonial, Rhys is caught in the double bind of lashing out angrily against the middle-class British colonizers and at the same time she is reined in by having internalized their lesson of white middle-class superiority too well. She can only articulate her rebellion against this dogma somewhat successfully through the physical resistance of the Creole female body, but in growing up, that very body has already been coerced into the acceptance of white middle-class body regimes. Unlike Rhys and Duras, Drabble never seems to question her own class bias, which eerily reproduces a colonialist mentality, constructing the poor and the working class, or the economically underdeveloped north of England as "other" to the triumphantly analytical urban middle class. In *Gates of Ivory*, this binarism becomes especially grating. Apart from one brief journey into the general area of the "Heart of Darkness," where Stephen Cox had been lost, Liz remains safely ensconced in her London home, collecting and analyzing information that comes to her. In the end, Drabble affirms her vision of London as unifying center for a host of characters who converge there from the ends of empire, and this concluding move is tinged by colonialism. Drabble's focus on corrective institutions (women's prison, school, hospital) in her later novels further bespeaks her middle-class naiveté and faith in the redemptive power of such institutions. For all her initial fascination with the sewer and the liminoid potential of public urban spaces, Drabble finally retreats to the safe and narrow confines of the upper-middle-class urban home.

By contrast, the East German writer Monika Maron dissects the disciplining power of social institutions like the party and the collective under socialism. Resistance to surveillance is won through female mobility between administrative power centers and marginalized spaces. These are to be found not only on the periphery, but also within—in little enclaves under the very noses of the oppressors. Introspection, fantasy sequences, and the search for female alter egos who complement subversive desires are all evasion strategies that allow the protagonist to shore up rebellious strength, which finally leads to a death-dealing contestational dialogue with a Stalinist hardliner.

Maron demonstrates the subversive powers of verbalization and memory. Moreover, the protagonist seeks out connection to others whose rights have been violated by the regime, thus mobilizing a defense network. Together, they create disturbances of the public order and practice civic disobedience. The "killing" of a representative of the old guard signifies the end of a tyrannical regime. Through her critique of enforced consensus in the socialist collective, Maron rearticulates the need for democratic dialogue and true mediation of inevitably conflicting agendas within communities.

Monika Maron's Dissection of the Scarred Body Politic

In his recent biography of Michel Foucault, Didier Eribon quotes one of Foucault's favorite sayings culled from the poetry of the Provençal writer René Char: "Foucault aimait à utiliser cette formule de René Char: 'Développez votre étrangeté légitime' "[1] (Foucault liked to make use of the following motto by René Char: "Develop your legitimate strangeness"). I read this as an injunction to the individual to work at creating a distance to her society so that she may view it with greater critical accuracy—to develop a sense of deliberate alienation from a set of legitimating practices, out of which follows the freedom to argue for one's own difference—you are entitled to that foreignness, Char seems to say, make it yours and live it on the margins if need be, but own and defend your right to retain your difference. This kind of critical self-location is perhaps exemplified by Char's own geographical provence—he comes from and celebrates the South in his poetry, a border zone where North-African influences make themselves felt, as far removed from the centralized forces of French government as one can be and still remain on French soil.

For purposes of political resistance, the East German writer Monika Maron places her female protagonists in a different kind of geographical border zone—the space from which difference originates and may subsequently be spread is East Berlin, the capital, "Berlin-Hauptstadt der DDR," as the Ulbricht government had renamed it self-consciously. In her first novel *Flugasche*, for instance, Maron does not locate her journalist, Josefa Nadler, in the southern provinces of the GDR, instead she shuttles back and forth between Berlin and B., modelled on the industrial city Bitterfeld near Halle in the south, to report on living conditions there, "the filthiest town in Europe."[2] As a result of experiencing the dramatic contrasts between the two cities, the journalist begins to draw structural inferences between the two B's, the one in the north whose economic well-being is made possible by the ills people suffer in the southern B, and the presence of hermetically guarded buildings that dominate the two cities—the state headquarters in Berlin, the nuclear power plant in B. On account of her family history, Josefa is further predisposed to harboring a critical distance to the state and its mechanisms of power: her grandfather Pawel was a Polish Jew who was set on fire in a Fascist pogrom; her family is not fully synonymous with Prussian Germanness and the Berlin that was its capital.

In Maron's two subsequent novels, the protagonist is a historian, Rosalind Polkowski, who works in the state archives, squarely located at the center of the capital, tracing the historic roots of socialism in civic uprisings in the industrialized south. As her last name indicates, she like Josefa has Polish ancestry, she is not entirely identified with Germanness. Josefa's first name reminds the reader of Kafka's Josef K., whereas the name Rosalind alludes to the socialist politician Rosa Luxemburg, who was murdered in 1919 by right-wing extremists and whose body was thrown into the Landwehrkanal in Berlin. There is also an echo of Shakespeare's Rosalind from *As You Like It*, who is unjustly banished from the court and enters an alternate reality when she flees to Arden Forest, where fairer rules govern outlaw society. This allusion is further enhanced in *Die Überläuferin* when Maron's Rosalind withdraws for a time from the outside workaday world to an interior space peopled by phantasmagoric figures. Like her Shakespearean precursor, Rosalind at first manages to live under a repressive regime by silencing her disagreement, but ultimately she stand up for her beliefs during her period of exile when she oversees at least her imaginative return to a freer society. For Maron, freedom of expression is always linked to the city—the street, the marketplace—to pubic and accessible spaces. The kind of communication that goes on there represents largely a fantasized carnivalesque dissolution of the old order, the hierarchies between the haves and the have-nots, or making secret and isolated shameful processes public—such as sending off a petition to the government and receiving a reply in the form of a reprimand; or flagrantly drinking, peeing, being disorderly, and copulating in the gutter. All these acts represent a rebellion against a Prussian insistence on tight bodily discipline, public restraint, and *Untertanengeist* (unquestioning obedience, toadyism).

We now return to the historical view of Berlin as palimpsest, at least to those of its inhabitants who still remember their Prussian history. Despite the socialist regime's attempts to rewrite history by insisting on its own singularity and positing itself as having always been in command, past uses of the public spaces can still be glimpsed here and there—for instance, an old woman tells Josefa the nostalgic story of the Prussian king's visits to Niederschönhausen castle, where he had exiled his wife: twice yearly he would arrive by boat via the waterways. This story implies two things: first, it emphasizes the connection of the western and eastern halves of the city; second, it underlines the arbitrariness of the center's location by bringing to mind the vagaries of the powerful—Frederick the Great had at first made Charlottenburg into the seat of power; then he moved it westward to Potsdam, where he built Sanssouci castle; then he removed his wife from the court by establishing her at what was then the eastern margin of the city, and what now, at the time of the novel's action, is the new center of power of the Socialists. If boundaries can shift so much within one monarch's reign, what presents itself as immutable at present may not in fact be so securely entrenched. The Berlin where Josefa Nadler and Rosalind Polkowski live is characterized by its division—the East is cut off from the West by the Berlin Wall, yet the knowledge of another sphere, a formerly joined part still lingers on. This excluded forbidden city remains as a memento of the very artificiality of the totalitarian closed society: a citizen of the German Democratic Republic cannot move about freely in her city, but, as Maron describes in her third novel *Stille Zeile 6,* it is still possible to recover a historical sense of their connectedness. Bruno, the protagonist's former lover, has saved old maps and shows Rosalind how the streets in Pankow were laid out originally. Pankow is the part of the city where the Ulbricht government had created its seat of power in the fifties, and, in a gesture prefiguring the building of the Wall in 1961, had barricaded streets and walled off a large area around its compound:

Seit das Schloß 1949 zum Regierungssitz erklärt worden war, endete die Straße von beiden Seiten jäh an einem Zaun, der auf der Niederschönhausener Seite gänzlich verrammelt war und sogar die Sicht auf das Schloß versperrte und der auf der Pankower Seite von schwerbewaffneten Wachen gegen Unbefugte geschützt wurde. Um von dem einen Straßenstumpf zum anderen zu gelangen, mußte man nun fünf Haltestellen mit der Straßenbahn fahren oder eine halbe Stunde zu Fuß gehen. Ich wohnte in dieser Gegend seit dreißig Jahren und hatte die beiden Straßenenden nie in Gedanken zusammengefügt. Erst Bruno, für den Stadtpläne und Landkarten so interessant waren wie die wirklichen Landschaften und Wohnviertel, die in ihnen verzeichnet sind, rückte die Pankower Straßen in

163

meinem Kopf sinnvoll aneinander. Jedesmal, wenn wir unsere Spaziergänge dem Willkürakt der Schloßbesetzer unterwerfen mußten, fluchte er auf die verrückt gewordenen Machthaber und Straßenschänder, die nicht nur öffentliche Wege versperrten, wie es ihnen paßte, sondern obendrein einen unschuldigen Platz nach dem ehrenhaften Carl von Ossietzky benannten, um alle Welt glauben zu machen, Ossietzky sei ein guter Freund von Walter Ulbricht gewesen.

[Since the time the castle had been declared the seat of government in 1949, the street ended abruptly in a fence, which on the Niederschönausen side was totally boarded up and even blocked the view of the castle and which on the Pankow side was being protected against trespassers by heavily armed guards. To get from the one street-trunk to the other, you now had to take a tram for five stops or walk for half an hour. I had lived in this area for thirty years and had never joined the two street-ends in my mind. Finally it was Bruno, for whom city maps and maps of countries held the same fascination as the real landscapes and neighborhoods which are marked there, who moved the Pankow streets together in my head so that they made sense. Everytime we had to submit our walks to the caprice of the castle occupants, he cursed the crazy power-holders and street-violators, who not only blocked public paths according to their whims, but also named an innocent square after the honorable Carl von Ossietzky in order to make the world at large believe that Ossietzky had been a good friend of Watler Ulbricht's.][3]

Memory is the enemy of the omniscient state, which perceives the past as a competing authority. This is especially true in the case of the GDR with its slavish emulation of Stalinist historiographical models. The individual consciousness virtually displaces the archive as a source of accessible historical fact.

Foucault makes a very useful generalization concerning the administration of power in closed societies: "In this space of domination, disciplinary power manifests its potency, essentially, by arranging objects. The examination [as a ritual] is, as it were, the ceremony of this objectification."[4] As Maron describes the manipulation of public space in GDR society, the symbolic value of this precept becomes abundantly clear: the government demonstrates to the people that they have to do its bidding. They may only go along the prescribed paths where those in power want them to go. For instance, they may not look at a government building from the back, only from the heavily protected front. If we think for a moment of the seat of government as a body, we see that it wishes to preserve itself from contract with other bodies—especially from an exposing gaze directed at its less stringently controlled backside or underside. those who may approach it all, have to approach from the front where they are warded off by a whole defensive armature. A body politic overly concerned with keeping out, maintaining its excretionary processes invisible and regulating what enters it, is in psychoanalytic terms, a body caught up in orality and anal retentiveness. Recent sociological material published after the fall of the Wall bears this view out. The analyst Hans-Joachim Maaz wrote a study of the effects of various forms of deprivation in the GDR, and his insights are so compelling that I quote him at length:

> Eine wichtige Besonderheit des Lebens in der DDR war die ausgesprochene Infantilität: Ein ganzes Volk wurde in ewiger "Kindheit" gehalten, so wie man Kinder mit der "schwarzen Pädagogik" quält, verdummt und kleinhält. Der Staat war der große, allwissende immer recht behaltende, autoritäre, alles bestimmende "Vater." Gegen den Staat und seine Entscheidungen gab es praktisch keine Rechtsmittel. Verwaltungs- und Verfassungsgerichte waren abgeschafft. Es war klar, daß der Staatsapparat immer nur die Anweisungen der Partei umzusetzen hatte. . . . Dieses Verhältnis zwischen Staat und Partei nahm Formen an, wie sie häufig Ehebeziehungen in der DDR kennzeichneten: Die Mutter (Partei) dominiert und beherrscht den Vater (Staat), der seine Depotenzierung dann mit besonderer Strenge an den Kindern (Volk) ausläßt. In der Tat war uns ja das Eingaberecht "gewährt," und wenn wirklich mal zugunsten eines Bürgers entschieden wurde, war es in der Regel die Partei, die staatliche Entscheidungen korrigierte. . . . Die Unselbständigkeit und Abhängigkeit der Bevölkerung wurde als "soziale Sicherheit" glorifiziert. Für den DDR-Bürger wurde praktisch alles festgelegt, ohne daß er mitentscheiden konnte. Die Gesundheitsfürsorge, die Ausbildung, die Wohnungsfrage wurden administrativ geregelt. Der Entscheidungsfreiraum war minimal, die Freizeitgestaltung, die Beweglichkeit, die Gesinnung waren eingeengt und kontrolliert. . . . In der Sprache der analytischen Psychologie war die Entwicklung in der DDR auf einer oralen und analen Stufe stehengeblieben. . . . Am Anfang steht z.B. die Nahrungsaufnahme ganz im Vordergrund und der Mund wird das zentrale Organ, das Kontakt, Aufnahme, Befriedigung und Sättigung ermöglicht und vermittelt. Später richtet sich das besondere Interesse aud die Ausscheidungsfunktionen und die stolze Erfahrung, daß man zurückhalten und hergeben selbst bestimmen kann. . . . So werden in der oralen Phase die Erfahrung für Bekommen, Gesättigtwerden, aber

auch für Sich-Nehmen, für Zupacken und Kleinkriegen gewonnen. In der analen Phase werden die Urerfahrungen von Hergeben und Schenken, von Verweigern und Behalten, von Ja- und Nein-Sagen, von Sich-Gehenlassen und Sich-Beherrschen, von Ordnung und Disziplin, von Zwanghaftigkeit und Spontaneität gemacht und der Stolz des Machenkönnens und Aus-sich-heraus-Produzierens begründet. Und in der genitalen Phase schließlich wird die Geschlechtsidentität mit Eigenständigkeit, Selbstbewußtsein, kreativer und produktiver Potenz und sexueller Lustfähigkeit erworben.

[An important particularity of life in the GDR was its marked infantilism: a whole people were held back in eternal "childhood," just as children had been tortured, made dumb and held back by so-called "black pedagogy." The state was the great, omniscient "father" who would always be right, who was authoritarian and determined everything. There were practically no legal means that could be employed against the state and its decisions. Administrative and constitutional courts had been abolished. It was obvious that the state apparatus was merely there to carry out the instructions of the Party. . . . This relationship between state and Party took on characteristics of marriages as one could frequently observe them in the GDR: the mother (the Party) dominates and rules over the father (the State), who takes revenge for his loss of power by turning on the children (the People) with special strictness. In fact we did have the right to formulate petitions (Eingaben, literally, gifts to be ingested), and if ever something was decided in the citizen's favor, it was usually the Party which corrected decisions made by the state. . . . The lack of self-determination and the dependence of the population were glorified as "social security." Preventive health care, education, job training, the need for shelter were all regulated administratively. The freedom to make decisions was minimal, how to spend one's free time, mobility, one's state of mind were all curtailed and controlled. . . . In the language of analytical psychotherapy, development in the GDR had been arrested on an oral and anal level. . . . In the beginning for instance, taking in food is foregrounded and the mouth becomes the central organ which allows for and manages contact, ingestion, satisfaction and satiation. Later special interest is directed towards excretory functions and the proud experiencing of being able to determine independently when to hold in and when to give up something. . . . In the oral phase the following experiences are gathered: getting, being nourished to satiety, but also taking—for oneself, for seizing hold of, for breaking up into smaller pieces. The anal phase lays the foundations for the seminal experiences of giving up and gifting, of refusing and keeping, of saying yes and no, of letting oneself go and of self-restraint, of order and discipline, compulsiveness and spontaneity, pride in being able to manufacture something and of producing-out-of-the-self. And in the genital phase, at last, gender identity together with independence, self-confidence, creative and productive power and the capacity for sexual enjoyment are experienced.][5]

In the image of the heavily guarded state building, the state is pictured as a body who only wants to devour with its teeth, but does not want to give up its waste matter. And in fact, Maron takes up this negative symbol again in the image of the nuclear power station in B., which is too old and chronically malfunctions, emitting its waste by spewing forth toxic clouds of flying ash instead of cleansing itself internally and less harmfully for the bodies who surround it. The people of B. are caught up in a compensatory practice—they wash themselves and their clothes compulsively:

> Und wie die Leute ihre Fenster putzen. Jede Woche, jeden Tag am besten. Überall saubere Fenster bei diesem gottserbärmlichen Dreck. Sie tragen weiße Hemden, weiße Strümpfe die Kinder. . . . Weiße Pullover werder hier am liebsten gekauft, hat die Verkäuferin gesagt.[6]

> [And the way people clean their windows. Every week, better still every day. Everywhere clean windows in this god-awful filth. They wear white shirts, the children, white stockings. . . . The salesgirl said white sweaters sell best here.][7]

Other compensatory practices include scenes of journalists drunkenly bickering with each other after work because they cannot address their complaints to the government or to the readership of their paper:

> Vielleicht waren sie schon süchtig, nicht im Sinne der Medizin, aber süchtig nach der Leichtigkeit, dem Schwebezustand, dem Zustand der Kinder, in den sie sich nur noch künstlich versetzen konnten. . . . Sie spülten ihre Seelen vierzigprozentig, bis sie arglos waren vor Vergeßlichkeit.[8]

> [Maybe they were not yet addicts in the medical sense, but they craved lightness, the floating sensation, the childlike state they could only achieve artificially. They rinsed their souls with a forty percent solution until they were without fear out of forgetfulness.][9]

Orality takes its toll also through compulsive eating of sweets—Josefa's editor Luise always eats small chewy liquorice candies in the shape of cats in between phonecalls having to do with censoring practices at the paper; Rudi Goldammer, the next one up in the chain-of-command, is a hypochondriac who shirks conflicts at work by calling in sick and who can only eat ambrosial white cream soups from a gourmet restaurant because of a nervous stomach.[10]

Josefa is developed in contrast to these pathetic figures, she is a self-styled nonconformist who refuses to settle for stability and sameness:

> Was habe ich zu befürchten? Die Leben, die ich nicht leben werde. Das Bett, in dem ich sterben werde. Die Monotonie bis zum Verfall und danach.[11]

> [What do I have to fear? The bed I'll die in. The lives I won't be living. The monotony unto death and thereafter.][12]

She measures her own ambitions by a personal standard, elevating her family history into the place of lofty socialist ideology, which she experiences mainly in the guise of surveillance practices:

> Die Verrücktheit des Großvaters war verlockend. Verrückte Menschen erschienen mir freier als normale. Sie entzogen sich der lästigen Bewertung durch die Mitmenschen, die es bald aufgaben, die Verrückten verstehen zu wollen.[13]

> [My grandfather's madness was enticing. Crazy people seemed freer to me than normal ones. They escaped the irritating value judgments of other people, who quickly gave up trying to understand madmen. They're crazy, they said, and left them in peace.][14]

When Josefa is advised by her colleagues not to write an article about the pollution in B., as she had witnessed it with her own eyes, she decides to tell it as it is and fight it out rather than fabricate a more palatable version and see it get published without a hitch. In a way, Josefa embodies some of the "Prussian" qualities she so resents—she demonstrates "courage before the enemy" and does not choose the easy way out. Through critical introspection, Josefa realizes that she has been guilty of compensatory living—she had fantasized egotistically about living in exotic forbidden Western cities like Venice and New York, precisely because the travel restrictions place them out of her reach, but she had not been curious about how people live in other cities in her own country:

> Ich schäme mich, weil ich gewußt habe, daß es diese Stadt gibt, und gegeizt habe mit meiner Phantasie, auf die ich so stolz bin. Auf der bin ich inzwischen durch Venedig gegondelt oder hab mich in New York zu Tode gefürchtet oder habe in Marokko die Orangen von den Bäumen gepflückt. Aber in dieses jederzeit betretbare B. habe ich sie nicht gelassen.[15]

> [I'm ashamed because I knew that this town existed and I was stingy with my imagination, which I'm so proud of. No doubt I've taken gondolas through Venice in my imagination, or been scared to death

in New York, or picked oranges from the trees in Morocco. But I didn't let it into this B., where I could have gone all the while.][16]

Telling the truth about the city becomes a touchstone for Maron, whose subsequent novels attempt variations on this theme in a mix of social documentary and fantasy and fairy-tale elements. The truth relies on the communication of personal vision that is opposed to the controlling glance and inward-directed censorship of the conformist.

Vision is also predicated on gaining an overview, being allowed to occupy the all-seeing position of the birds-eye viewer. Josefa mentions a recurring dream that shows her desire for the mastery such a view would bring with it:

> Bevor ich einschlafe, werde ich in roten und goldenen Farben meine Zukunft träumen. . . . Ich gehe wieder durch die sand-farbene Ruinenstadt. Sie muß weit im Süden liegen, in Spanien oder Italien, vielleicht sogar in Afrika, denn es ist irrsinnig heiß dort. Und der Himmel ist blau, so blau wie über dem Meer. Er scheint gleichmäßig durch die leeren Fensteröffnungen der Ruinen, als hätte man einen blauen Prospekt hinter die Wände gestellt. Die Straßen sind schmale steile Treppen aus gelbem Sandstein, denn die Stadt liegt an einem Hügel. Ich bin immer allein dort, aber es stört mich nicht. Ich steige langsam die Treppen zur höchsten Stelle des Hügels, weil ich von da auf die Stadt sehen will. Jedesmal. Aber jedesmal, wenn ich oben angelangt bin und mich umdrehe, zer-springt das Bild oder schrumpft zusammen, und ich finde mich wieder auf einer Treppe, die auf halber Höhe des Hügels liegt, und ich beginne meinen Aufstieg von neuem.[17]

> [I'll dream about my future in red and gold before I fall asleep. . . . I walk through sand-colored runs again. The city must lie far to the south, in Spain or Italy, perhaps even in Africa, as it's incredibly hot there. And the sky is blue, as blue as it is over the sea. It shines uniformly through the empty windows of the ruins as if someone had placed a blue backdrop behind the walls. The streets are nar-row, steep steps of yellow sandstone, as the city lies on a hill. I'm always there alone, but that doesn't bother me. I slowly climb the steps to the highest point on the hill because I want to view the city from there. Every time. But every time I've gotten to the top and turned around, the image flies apart or shrinks to nothing, and I find myself again on a step that is halfway up the hill and I start climbing again.][18]

The dream conveys a sense of numbed isolation, a Sisyphean struggle to the top, and a sense of unreality—the sky and the empty windows create a cheerfully monotonous backdrop, but there is no visual access to what lies behind or beyond them. One might read this dream as symbolic of Josefa's work at the newspaper, which after all, is called *Illustrierte Woche*, (*The Week in Pictures*). Josefa is expected to provide a pretty picture, a sense of escape to her readers, to let them be tourists in their own country. The southern city only reminds one of grimy, toxic B. by its heat and deadness—an eerily beautiful apocalyptic city, but a hallucinatory vision of a devastated ghost town nonetheless, which unfailingly explodes or shrivels up at the climactic moment of the dream, just before the promise of the climb is fulfilled. Enlightenment does not come after a laborious climb to the top, the dream predicts; perhaps one must get to the top in a different manner or, possibly, this quest is going in the wrong direction and should be reoriented in another direction. Ultimately, Maron's protagonists obtain enlightenment when they take themselves out of the upward climb altogether, when they choose immobility for a time. They stay in bed like Josefa at the end of *Flugasche* or are paralyzed from the knees down like Rosalind in *Die Überläuferin*, or they idle away time in cafés and pubs observing and talking to the people around, as Rosalind does in *Stille Zeile 6*. A chance encounter at the café leads to her confrontation with, and ultimate victory over, the Stalinist past, represented by Beerenbaum, a retired high-ranking party official. This chosen immobility is a survival strategy of the weakened individual in the Darwinian struggle for supremacy, waged by the Socialist party against the subject. What looks like paralysis and deathlike stasis may camouflage a gathering of subversive forces within.

Maron privileges liminoid spaces that allow a retreat into a private domain, reminiscent of Günter Gaus's characterization of the GDR as a *Nischengesellschaft* (society of little niches) be they apartments, corners of public parks, neighborhood pubs. Despite their affinity to provincialism, it is important to emphasize that for Maron, these spaces of retreat are only to be found in the urban realm. They are pockets of difference and pleasure right in the center, under the nose of the powerful.

> Hier merkt man es nicht so—diesen Satz hatte der Graf vor einiger Zeit während eines Spaziergangs durch den Park wie einen Seufzer ausgestoßen. Seitdem zitierten wir ihn, wann immer wir eine halbwegs unverdorbene Oase entdeckten. Da merkt man es nicht so. Was das war, das man nicht so merkte, bedurfte keiner Erklärung, auch das "so" erschöpfte sich in der Andeutung: Nicht so schlimm wie anderswo. Seit jeher wunderte ich mich, daß sie dem Park nichts angetan hatten, seine Wege nicht betoniert, seine zweihundert oder sogar dreihundert Jahre alten Bäume mit den ausgemauerten Stämmen nicht gefällt. Sie hatten ihn nicht einmal eingezäunt wie das

Schloß oder das "Städtchen." Wo wir hinkommen, welken die Blätter, soll Anna Seghers einmal gesagt haben. Auf wundersame Weise hatte das Segherssche Wir den Pankower Schloßpark verschont. An den Sträuchern suchte ich nach den ersten Knospen, wie winzige harte Bäuche wölbten sie sich an den Zweigen.

[Here, you don't notice it quite as much—this sentence had been uttered like a sigh by the Count some time ago. Since then we quoted him whenever we discovered a halfway unspoilt oasis. There you don't notice it as much. No explanation was needed for that "it" one didn't notice as much, even the "so much" was only hinted at: not as bad as elsewhere. I had always wondered anyway why they had not laid their hands on the park, had not cemented over its paths, had not felled its trees with their trunks propped up by little walls which were two hundred, perhaps even three hundred years old. They had not even fenced it off like the castle or the "little city." Wherever we arrive, the leaves wither, Anna Seghers is supposed to have said. In some miraculous manner the "We" of Seghers had spared the Park of Pankow Castle. I looked for the first buds on the bushes; like tiny hard bellies, they sat rounded on the twigs.][19]

Maron connects heat and sun imagery with the socialist regime of total social control, as we have seen in the dream about the ruined city. "They" are so powerful that the very leaves wither, they bring the death of the old order, even tampering with the seasons and unsettling nature. The irreversible destructive act of the "we" is the ultimate and punishable blasphemy, not the victimized individual's wishful dreaming about flying (Josefa), looting a supermarket (Rosalind, Martha, Klärchen) or acts of terrorism (Thekla Fleischer).

It must be noted that in Maron's texts, only the women dream such dreams, the men are content to sublimate their frustrated desire for social change in drinking and ritual sparring with each other. The neighborhood pub is a male domain, but women like Rosalind are tolerated there:

Die Kneipe war, profan und geheimnisvoll zugleich, eine Gegenwelt, ein Orkus, wo andere Gesetze galten und ein urbanes Naturrecht herrschte. Wes das Kneipenreich betrat, entzog sich der Schwerkraft der Oberwelt und fügte sich einer anderen Ordnung. . . . Kutte Kluge, Rentner, ehemaliger Kellner. . . . war nicht nur, wie Bruno, eine Kneipenperönlichkeit, er war eine Schachperönlichkeit. . . . Kutte Kluge schlug Lateiner und Nichtlateiner, Studierte und Promovierte, alle, denen er ein Leben lang flambierte Enten vorgelegt und anschließend für das Trinkgeld gedankt hatte.

Die Kneipe, schien es, verhalf dem Leben zu einer höheren Gerechtigkeit, die mich zwar nicht einschloß, mir aber dennoch ein Trost war. In der Kneipe endete Beerenbaums Macht, hier hatte er genau so wenig zu sagen wie in der Wohnung von Thekla Fleischer, als deren Mutter noch lebte.

[The pub was, profane and mysterious at once, a counterworld, an Orcus, where different laws counted and an urbane law of nature ruled. The one who entered the realm of the pub withdrew from the laws of gravity of the world above and submitted to a different order.... Kutte Kluge, retired and a former waiter ... was not only, like Bruno, a pub personage, he was a chess personage.... Kutte Kluge beat those who knew Latin and those who did not, those who had studied and gotten advanced degrees, all those whom he had served up flambéed duck and whom he had thanked for his tip.

The pub, it seemed, brought out a higher justice in life, which, although it did not include me, was a consolation to me. Beerenbaum's power ended here, in the pub, here it wasn't his place to order around, just as little as he would have had that right in Thekla Fleischer's apartment when her mom was still alive.][20]

It is striking evidence of the internalized watchful eye of the censor that repression can be circumvented only by instituting another reality, a zone of make-believe and play, by deliberately making life theatrical: in pursuing a game of mental skill, like chess, or in communicating subversive emotion through bursts of operatic song in a foreign tongue, like Italian; or in quoting Latin mottoes to each other; or in speaking to each other in very exotic languages—Chinese, or even Eskimo. All these activities have in common that they require an idle urban(e) audience educated enough to appreciate these miniature performances. They are more than mere escapism because they contain subversive messages. When Bruno breaks into operatic song, for instance, he smuggles the following message past his inner censor: "E non voglio più servir / und ich möchte nicht mehr dienen / e non voglio più servir / und ich möchte nicht mehr dienen."[21] When the Count tells a fairly trivial story about Brunos' cat allergies he suddenly proclaims in Latin: "Corpus nos veritatem cognoscere docet, oh, Verzeihung, Madame Rosalie, ich vergaß, der Körper sagt uns die Wahrheit, übersetzte er." ["...,oh, I beg your pardon, Madam Rosalie, I forgot, the body tells us the truth, he translated,"].[22] That is exactly the motto Maron wants the reader to take to heart when she presents us with the puzzle of malfunctioning bodies—Rosalind's temporarily numbed legs, Beerenbaum's paralyzed right hand, Rudi Goldammer's upset stomach, the thin red scar that runs across Jauer's forehead on his return to work after a nervous breakdown that had necessitated a stay in a state-run psychiatric clinic.

Socialist officialese is not the only language, but it is the one associated with dissection and the deadening microscopic gaze. It acts on bodies just as it rearranges space, with the intent to wither and eradicate what is already growing there. The overriding metaphor is that of the invaded, violated body: Jauer's head was opened up and his brain operated on, we are left to surmise. While he is dying in the hospital, the unrepentant Stalinist Beerenbaum snatches at Rosalind's breast as if groping for her heart. And the Chinese scholar Karl-Heinz Baron, the "Count," as his friends, have renamed him, is incarcerated for three years and his academic career ruined because he went to a post office and forwarded a manuscript to its owner who had left the GDR. If passing on messages for others or sending them under one's own name is followed by such swift and severe punishment, it follows that the individual is cautioned by the authorities and their internalized version in his superego to refrain from sending messages altogether, or that the individual must convince the outer and inner censors that he is really doing something else, something harmless and inconsequential—in the words of Stevie Smith's poem, "not drowning, but waving"—quoting Latin to boast his erudition, or, as Rosalind does, learning the libretto to *Don Giovanni* by heart "because it is classical music, learning to play the piano 'to fill up idle time.' "

Aside from her daydreams, the journalist Josefa increasingly has no recourse, no language that is safe from the censors. She lives to report on the day-to-day and cannot escape into a bygone era, a different civilization, as Bruno, Rosalind, and the Count do in Maron's later texts. It is surely no accident that Maron makes all her subsequent protagonists into historians, linguists, artists—Dadaist-inspired painters like Herr Solow in *Silent Close 6*, or poets like Martha in *The Defector*. All these characters have in common an archaeological occupation, they piece together collages of what matters to them. The journalist, however, is expected to observe linearity in the retelling of her day, use socialist catch phrases and produce a glossy picture like a travel brochure. As the dream of the ruined city shows, her new reality is an opaque cardboard backdrop that is purely self-referential and entraps the subject in the circular pursuit of a specious visionary goal.

Josefa has a prophetic vision about her fate and that of her article about B. when she imagines a bunch of dead fish lying spread out on the conference table at the editorial board meeting:

Alle lagen sie vor ihr wie sezierte Fische. Luise, Strutzer, Rudi Goldammer, Ulrike, Hans Schütz, sie selbst—alle lagen kunstvoll

173

zerteilt in Köpfe, Gräten, Filets und Häute auf dem hufeisen-
förmigen Versammlungtisch aus hellem Holz.[23]

[They all lay in front of her like dissected fish. Luise, Strutzer,
Rudti Goldammer, Ulrike, Hans Schütz, she herself—they all lay
artfully carved up into heads, spines, filets and skins on the
horseshoe-shaped conference tables made out of blond wood.][24]

Taken together, Maron's three novels almost function as a casebook of
Foucauldian disciplinary technologies-—from the surveillance rendered
possible by Panopticon architecture to bodies regimented and compartmentalized in space. The anthropologists Dreyfus and Rabinow sum up
Foucault's analysis of body control very succinctly:

> According to Foucault, discipline operates primarily on the body at
> least in the early stages of its deployment. Of course, the imposition
> of a form of social control over the body is found in all societies.
> What is distinctive in disciplinary societies is the form that this
> control takes. The body is approached as an object to be analyzed
> and separated into its constituent parts. The aim of disciplinary
> technology is to force a "docile [body] that may be subjected, used,
> transformed and improved." . . . First, the body is divided into
> units, for example, the legs and arms. These are then taken up
> separately and subjected to a precise and calculated training. The
> aim is control and efficiency of operation both for the part and the
> whole.[25]

Bearing in mind Foucault's analysis of the mind-set behind surveillance
practices, one sees that Josefa attempts to overcome her own demise by
initially identifying herself with the disciplinarian: she has become the
pathologist, forestalling her own victimization by eviscerating her professional superiors.

Maron finds in humor, Dadaist montage techniques, surrealist fantasy, and the use of grotesque imagination useful tools for subverting
from within the drabness of a realist, often documentary narrative of
daily humiliations and invasions of the self under socialism. Opposing
the image of the sectioned fish spread open for examination is a powerful
metaphor for the writer/journalist as a phantasmagoric marine creature—
a squid with wings like the leaves of a maple tree. This animal can both
swim and fly, thus survive in two difference spheres, and when it is
attacked it is more flexible in seeking an escape because it can squirt its
ink and obscure the attacker's vision:

> Ein Tintenfisch hält mich in den Armen und treibt mit mir auf dem
> Ozean. . . . Er hält mich fest, damit ich nicht ertrinke. Er hält

meinen Mund zu, damit ich kein Wasser schlucke. . . . Er drückt mir die Luft ab mit seinen Armen. Schwimme, sagt er und läßt mich los. Nur an einem seiner Arme hänge ich noch und gehe nicht unter. Aus dem Kopf des Tintenfisches wachsen Flügel. Jetzt fliegen wir, flüstert er und hebt sich in die Luft. Er soll mich nicht fallen lassen. Höher, schneller, schneller. Wir fallen, ruft der Tintenfisch. Im Sturzflug rasen wir auf die Erde. Jetzt wachsen mir Flügel, große Flügel aus Ahornblättern. Wir fliegen dicht über dem Wasser, und die Wellen klatschen gegen unsere Bäuche. Meine Arme sind weiße weiche Schläuche mit Saugnäpfen an den Innenseiten. Ich habe viele Arme. Ich bin ein Tintenfisch.[26]

[A squid is holding me in its arms and drifting with me on the ocean. . . . He's holding tight so I won't drown. He's keeping my mouth closed so I won't swallow water. . . . He presses the air out of me with his arms. Float, he says, and lets me go. I'm holding onto only one of his arms and don't go under. The squid's head has sprouted wings. We're flying now, he whispers and lifts himself into the air. He mustn't let me fall. Higher, faster, faster. We're falling, the squid cries. We race to earth in a nose dive. Now I sprout wings, large winds of maple leaves. We're flying just above the water, and the waves are splashing against our stomachs. My arms are soft white tentacles with suckers on the inside. I have many arms. I am a squid.][27]

Desire for emotion-driven action is symbolically expressed in animal symbols like the flying squid or the rearing white horse, their movement is sudden, transformational, and scary at the same time. The human form is associated with being fixed under the hypnotic medical gaze, therefore, to avoid mutilation, it becomes essential to transform the self into multiples—many arms instead of two, wings sprouting out of the head to keep the self from being submerged—"Imädshineischen, Rosi, . . . halb jewagt, is janz verloren."[28] ["Imagination, Rosi, . . . something ventured, nothing gained."][29] as Rosalind's body self, Claire, helpfully interjects in *The Defector*.

In that text, Maron experiments with splitting the self three ways: a massive body she calls Claire Winckelmann; a poetic shadowy artistic self she calls Martha Mantel, clearly an analogue to her own name (Monika Maron); and the everyday self, Rosalind Polkowski, who goes to work reliably but suppresses her real needs and impulses to the point where she becomes incapacitated. Restrictions and wounds the self suffers in the straitjacket of social control and supervision are always inscribed and rendered visible on the *female* body. Rosalind becomes paralyzed, Claire commits suicide by hanging herself in a chestnut tree in the park, Josefa becomes addicted to tranquilizers and sleeping pills and stays in bed all day.

In *Flugasche*, Josefa tells a Western journalist the story of Heidi Arndt, a young woman who had fallen in with a bad boyfriend, had his baby, had dropped out of her work training, and was arrested by the police for her disorderly lifestyle; sent to prison for two years, she was not seemingly rehabilitated, had remarried, held down a job. While she was in prison, she got tattoos all over her body, which she is now having removed in an equally painful procedure that leaves thick burn like scars:

> Das Kind kam zu den Eltern, Heidi kam in eine Zelle mit zwanzig anderen Frauen, Prostituierten, gescheiterten Republikflüchtigen, Alkoholikern. Ein Jahr lang versuchte sie, gut zu arbeiten. Am Tag schaffte sie die Norm, in der Nachtschicht nicht. Ab drei Uhr morgens kämpfte sie mit dem Schlaf, manchmal schlief sie auch ein. Sie war gerade achtzehn. Von den anderen Häftlingen wurde sie gemieden wegen ihres Wohlverhaltens. Die meisten Frauen in der Zelle waren lesbisch. Heidi wollte nicht. Obwohl es streng verboten war, ließen die Frauen sich tätowieren. Heidi nicht. Nach einem Jahr teilte ihr die Anstaltsleitung mit, sie könne noch nicht entlassen werden, weil sie die Norm nicht erfüllt hätte. Es werde überlegt, ob ihr Kind zur Adoption freigegeben werde. Die Eltern schrieben ihr nicht. Heidi wußte nicht, wo ihr Kind war. Kurz darauf erklärte man ihr, das Kind sei nun adoptiert. An dem Tag ließ Heidi sich tätowieren. Sie begann ein Verhältnis mit einer Frau, die, wie Heidi sagte, sehr klug war und sehr lieb. . . . Als die Freundin aus dem Knast kam, hatte sie eine andere. Heidi heiratete den Kohlenträger. Sie verstanden sich gut. Aber mit ihm schlafen konnte sie nicht. . . . Sie hatte sich vorgenommen, zu einem Psychiater zu gehen und ihre sexuellen Neigungen korrigieren zu lassen. . . . Sie war am ganzen Körper tätowiert. Einmal in der Woche ging sie zu einem Arzt, der ihr die Tätowierungen aus der Haut schliff. Das machte der Arzt ohne Betäubung, es hinterließ Narben, die Brandnarben ähnelten. Sie hatte ein Jahr warten müsen, um als Patientin angenommen zu werden, manche müßten noch länger warten, sagte sie.[30]

[The baby went to her parents. Heidi was put in a cell with twenty other women: prostitutes, unsuccessful emigrants, alcoholics. She tried for a year to do good work. She filled her quota during the day, but not on the night shift. She had to fight off sleep at 3:00 A.M., sometimes she did fall asleep. She had just turned eighteen. She was shunned by the other prisoners because of her good behavior. Most of the women in the cells were lesbians. Heidi didn't want to. Although it was strictly forbidden, most of the women had themselves tattooed. Not Heidi. She was told after a year by the institution that she could not be released yet because she had not filled her quota. They were considering whether to put her child up for adoption. Her parents didn't write to her. Heidi didn't know where her child was. Shortly after that she was told that her child had just been adopted. The same day she had herself tattooed. She began an affair with a woman who was, according to Heidi, very smart and loving. . . . When her girlfriend got out of jail she had another woman. Heidi married the coal heaver. They understood each other . . . but she couldn't sleep with him. . . . She took it upon herself to see a psychiatrist to correct her sexual preference. . . . She went to the doctor once a week to have the tattoos rubbed out of her skin. The doctor did it without anaesthetic and it left behind scars that looked like burn marks. She had to wait a year until she was accepted as a patient; many had to wait longer, she said.][31]

This bleak anecdote is reminiscent of Kafka's "In the Penal Colony" where a convict's punishment consists of having the text of his sentence tattooed into his body by a harrow and dying as the machine finishes inscribing the text. Heidi Arndt chooses the tattoos as a last expression of protest when the state authorities tell her that they have given away her child. This shows that the state treats the individual as a disposable body, it can tamper with even the most personal relationships like the mother—child bond. The cruelty of this judgment is rendered worse by the fact that they lie to her in order to break her down. In the end, the epidermis is the only barrier left between the self and the carceral system. Once outside, Heidi attempts once more to fit in, to erase the visible marks of her otherness. But the price she pays is yet another disfigurement—the tattoos are gone, but the treatment leaves large burn marks. Heidi, her body brutally marked by decay and violence, represents an aggravated case of the daily oppression visited on an individual's desires by a totalitarian regime.

To this end, the GDR rulers established a Panoptic architecture, with their central watchtowers for easy and round-the-clock surveillance. In the cityscape of East Berlin, this architecture was best represented by the Wall itself: its double set of walls, the floodlit death strip in between, the watchtowers spaced at regular intervals along it; and by the dominating TV tower at Alexanderplatz, which resembles a large eyeball pierced by a needle, and was revealed to have infrared TV cameras hidden in its base, that transmitted pictures to Stasi headquarters in Normannenstraße, allowing the State Security forces to monitor the plaza around it for public activity day and night. In *Discipline and Punish*, Foucault describes Bentham's plan for the Panopticon, which originated around the time of the French Revolution when crowds were becoming more restless and urban populations started to grow dramatically:

> It consists of a large courtyard with a tower in the center and a set of buildings divided into levels and cells on the periphery. In each cell, there are two windows: one brings in light and the other faces the tower where large observatory windows allow for the surveillance of the cells. The cells are like small theatres in which each actor is alone, perfectly individualized and constantly visible. . . . He is the object of information, never a subject in communication. . . . The inmate cannot see if the guardian is in the tower or not, so he must behave as if surveillance is constant, unending and total. The architectural perfection is such that, even if there is no guardian present the apparatus of power is still operative. . . . [The Panopticon] is a mechanism for the location of bodies in space, for the distribution of individuals in relation to one another, for hierarchical organization, for the efficient disposition of centers and channels of power.[32]

In Maron's fiction, the surveillance tower is present wherever there are walls and barriers, and high-rise buildings like the newspaper tower in *Flugasche* resemble a gigantic prison: a glass front makes it visually accessible from the outside, each floor is a series of cell-like offices connected by a corridor, and Josefa works in a *Großraumbüro*, where every worker's desk is placed in such a way that she only sees her coworker's back and cannot make eye contact. Such an office space is, once again, an easily surveyed controlled environment:

> Auf dem Gang waren alle Tage gleich. Die weiße endlose Eintönigkeit, Kaffegeruch, klappende Türen. Nichts, das einen Tag von dem anderen unterschieden hätte. Der Großraum gab Gedächtnishilfen durch leere oder besetzte Schreibtische: An dem Tag war Günter nicht da, also Donnerstag. Auch das Wetter half: der Tag, an dem das Gewitter war. . . . Es war kaum möglich, sich in diesem Haus vor den Blicken der anderen zurückzuziehen.[33]
> . . . Auf dem Treppenabsatz blieb sie stehen, lehnte die Stirn an die kalte Glaswand, dann den ganzen Körper. Wenn sie bricht, falle ich, dachte sie, ohne Angst zu fühlen. Durch das Glas roch sie die staubige Luft, die in der Sonne von den Straßen aufstieg, hörte sie, wie die winzigen Menschen unter ihr lachten und sprachen. Ich bin lange nicht mehr geflogen, dachte sie. . . . Als sie sich von der Glaswand löste, hatte sie das Gefühl, sie stünde in einem Käfig:

rechts und links massive Mauern, einsehbar von vorn, der Rückzug nur möglich nach hinten über die Treppe.[34]

[Every day was the same in the hallway. The white endless monotony, smell of coffee, doors opening and closing. Nothing that would have made one day different from any other. The open-plan office provided memory aids with its empty or occupied desks: Günter wasn't here on that day, then it's Thursday. The weather helped too: the day of the storm. . . . It was difficult to avoid the view of others in this building.[35] . . . She stopped on the landing, leaned her forehead against the cold glass wall, then her whole body. If it breaks I'll fall, she thought without feeling any fear. Through the glass she smelled the dusty air, drawn by the sun from the streets, she heard the tiny people below laughing and talking. It's been a long while since I've flown, she thought. . . . When she pulled herself back from the glass wall, she had the feeling that she was in a cage: massive walls left and right, you could look in from the front, retreat was possible only backwards and down the stairs.][36]

The metaphor of a hermetically closed interior space recurs with great frequency in Maron's fiction: in *The Defector*, Rosalind has a dream in which she approaches a female figure from the back:

Ist die Figur nicht, wie erhofft, Martha, sondern sie selbst, Rosalind sitzt vor einer weißen Wand, die eine Gefängniswand ist. Der Raum, in dem ich mich befinde, ist grellweiß getüncht, die wenigen Möbel . . . sind ebenso weiß. Alles ist sehr sauber. Trotzdem ist das ein Gefängnis, weiß ich, die Fenster vergittert, die Tür verriegelt, von außen. Ich weiß nicht genau, wie lange ich schon hier bin, nicht sehr lange, aber länger als nur einige Stunden. Ich muß hier schon die Nacht verbracht haben, denn das Bett ist zerwühlt, und ein Nachthemd, mit einem schwarzen Stempel am Saum, hängt über dem Stuhl. Ich versuche, die Stempelschrift zu entziffern, aber sie ist unleserlich vom häufigen Waschen.[37]

[Except the figure is not, as she had hoped, Martha, but herself, Rosalind, sitting in front of a white wall, the wall of a prison. The room in which I find myself is painted a harsh white, the few pieces of furniture . . . are also white. Everything is very clean. But it is still a prison, I know. The windows are barred, the door locked from the outside. I don't know exactly how long I've been here, but longer than a few hours. I must have spent the night here because the bed is rumpled and a nightgown, with a black mark on the hem, is hanging over the chair. I try to decipher the writing on the mark, but frequent washing has made it illegible.][38]

In the subject's imagination, the awareness of being held prisoner in a room is constructed around the blank wall. The blinding white of the wall is reminiscent of the white paint on the Berlin Wall—defacing it with graffiti was punished with hard labor. The exaggerated cleanliness and monochromatic whiteness harken back to the citizen's efforts to cover over pollution in B. by compulsive washing and wearing white, the color of innocence and purity. In this white space, nothing can be deciphered by looking/inspecting or reading, the privileged analytic techniques of the twentieth century. The prison cell is furnished remarkably like a hospital room in an asylum.

Maron drives home the symbolism of the state as a prison in another dream sequence in *Flugasche*, where the "prison room" is staged in a theater space, an amalgam of Brecht's Berliner Ensemble, located near the wall at Schiffbauerdamm and border watchtowers spaced evenly every three hundred meters:

Der Fluß war die Spree. Die Spree war so breit wie die Donau. Über eine riesige Treppe konnte man auf drei Brücken gelangen, von denen eine gerade, die beiden anderen in schrägen Bögen nach links und rechts über den Fluß führten. Auf der anderen Seite mündete jede Treppe in ein Haus wie in einen Tunnel. Die Häuser lagen jeweils dreihundert Meter voneinander entfernt und waren Theater. . . . Das Spiel hatte begonnen. Auf der Bühne standen zwei Frauen. Sie waren lila. Auch das Licht, das von oben auf sie fiel, Tapeten, Vorhänge, die seidene Decke auf dem Bett waren lila. Die Frauen waren uralt, die eine war älter. Die alte war groß und hager, die jüngere trug Zöpfe, die auf ihre schlaffen Brüste fielen. Haut, Haare, Zähne waren lila. . . . Die jüngere setzte sich der alten auf den Schoß, streichelte ihr die faltigen Wangen und sagte mit einer quengligen Kinderstimme: "Ich kann immer noch nicht schreiben, Mama." Die Alte ordnete die Schleife am Zopf der jüngeren.

"Du hast noch Zeit," sagte sie, "du bist noch nicht einmal achtzig."

"Ich will so gerne lesen können," sagte die jüngere, "es ist so langweilig."

"Du hast deine Bilderbücher."

"Ich will nicht immer in dem Zimmer sein, Mama, es ist so lila." . . . Aus den Kratern im Gesicht der alten sprühte es. Sie griff nach einer lila Glasschale und zerschlug sie auf dem Kopf der jüngeren. "Warum lügst du?" schrie sie. . . . Durch eine Tür, die bislang nicht sichtbar war, trat eine Frau in Schwesterntracht. Die Tracht war weiß. "Er kommt," sagte sie. . . . Er kam. Er trug einen Zylinder und einen Frack. Beides war schwarz. Er ging vorbei an den Frauen bis in die Mitte des Raumes. Die beiden Alten an der Tür erstarrten wie am Anfang. Auch der schwarze Mann erstarrte. Sie zischten etwas, das Josefa nicht verstehen konnte.

Hinter ihr weinte jemand. Sie drehte sich um, aber es war niemand zu sehen. Niemand war im Theater außer ihr. Das Theater war lila.[39]

[The river was the Spree. The Spree was as wide as the Danube. You could get to three bridges via a huge staircase. From there the bridges led across the river: one straight, the others leading left and right in sloping arches. On the other side each bridge ended in a building as if it were a tunnel. Each of the buildings was three hundred meters from the next. They were theaters. . . . The play had already begun. There were two women on stage. They were purple. The light that fell on them from above, the wallpaper, the curtains, the silk bedspread were all purple, too. Both women were very old; one was older. The older one was tall and gaunt, the younger one wore braids that fell across her flabby breasts. Skin, hair, teeth were purple. . . . The younger one sat on the old one's lap, stroked her wrinkled cheeks and said in a whiny child's voice: "I still don't know how to write, mommy." The old one fixed the ribbon on the younger one's braid. "You still have time," she said. "You aren't even eighty yet." "I'd so much like to be able to read," the younger one said, "it's so boring." "You have your picture books." "I don't want to be in this room all the time, Mommy. It's so purple." . . . You could see the sparks flying out of the craters in the old one's face. She grabbed for a purple glass bowl and smashed it over the head of the younger one. "Why are you lying?" she screamed. . . . A woman in a nurse's uniform stepped through a door, which hadn't been visible until then. The uniform was white. "He's coming," she said. . . . He came. He wore a top hat and tails. Both were black. He walked past the women to the middle of the room. The two old women at the door stood as stiffly as they had in the beginning. The black man also stood stiffly. They whispered something that Josefa couldn't understand.

Someone behind her was crying. She turned around but she couldn't see anyone. There was no one in the theater except her. The theater was purple.][40]

There is a widening of space (the river, the giant steps) combined with a rising movement, then a constriction of space and downward movement (the straight bridge, the tunnel-like houses). On this stage, the protagonist has a choice of three similar boxes to enter, they are labeled "theaters," but in the end, stage action and audience space merge—they are truly traps for those who enter.

Maron uses surrealist techniques to create a nightmarish scenario of claustrophobic sameness despite the passage of time: the artificial lighting that distorts actors and objects alike as if they were in an aquarium, oxymoronic figures like the withered ancient little girl, the unnurturing mother, the climactic arrival of a father figure, promising resolution of the struggle between mother and daughter, but leading right back to the frozen positions of the opening scene. The dilating then contracting perspective, which is once more dilated—only to be contained in the darkened purple room at the very end of the dream—evokes a sense of being lured into a labyrinthine body system, being inside the pupil of the eye or trapped in the expanding and contracting lungs. The outside becomes the inside, the city space turns into the caverns of an engulfing body, only we cannot classify this body, we don't know whose it is, animal or human.

Maron plays upon the double symbolism of the *golem* and Frankenstein, both of whom she craftily introduces as part of asides in *Flugasche*, both are monsters invented by men who run amok. The *golem* seems especially relevant in this context because it is an "embryo or anything incompletely developed . . . an automatonlike servant made of clay and given life by means of a charm"[41]—it is very much like a design for a human being gone wrong. We might read the female protagonists's episodic outbursts of wanton destruction and havoc in that light—the automaton's rebellion against its masters. These upheavals occur significantly not in *Flugasche*, with its frustrated but ultimately powerless daughter figure Josefa, but in the following texts, which are more outspoken efforts at emancipating the female self from outwardly directed patterns of thought and action. For instance, Rosalind wishes at first for an earthquake[42], then goes about producing one of her own when her aunt Ida, the last link to her childhood and her earliest timid nurturer, dies:

> Atemlos tobte ich durch das kleine Zimmer, bis ich Idas Handgriffe alle zurückgenommen hatte und Idas Ordnung durch ein namenloses Chaos getilget war. . . . Nie zuvor hatte ich eine innigere Übereinstimmung mit einem Raum empfunden, nie hatte eine vorgefundene Ordnung meinem inneren Zustand deutlicher entsprochen als dieses von mir selbst errichtete Chaos.[43]

> [I raged through the small room out of breath until I had undone all of Ida's work and had obliterated her order. . . . Never before had I felt a deeper harmony with a room. Never before had any

order expressed my inner state as faithfully as this self-created chaos."].[44]

The libidinally charged chaos Rosalind unleashes when she is united with Martha and Claire, her poetic and body selves, is another example of the *golem* automatization: the threesome refuses to wait in line at the supermarket and encourages the other customers to loot the store, provoking a comical fight between the state police and the people, in which much gets smashed and the people carry the day.[45] This carnivalesque interlude attains greater subversiveness when we read it in conjunction with the exposure scene in the purple theater, in which the infantilized daughter rips open the mother's dress to reveal a lack. The "mother" has no breasts, she is not equipped to be a mother—her body tells the truth about who she really is—she is a cruel disciplinarian masquerading as a maternal caregiver, an allegory of the Party, who does not even allow the individual access to the equally ossified authoritarian father figure, the State, to whom she herself is enslaved. Analogously, the shop which Rosalind, Martha, and Claire loot is called in official socialist jargon *die Zentrale Versorgungseinrichtung Becherstraße, Stadtbezirk Pankow* (the Central Provisions Facility Becherstrasse, Pankow district).[46] The term *Versorgungseinrichtung* implies a similar relationship of basic caregiving by dispensing food, but instead, the hungry have to line up and wait endlessly in front of closed registers. Maron denounces this scenario as a Kafkaesque "Before the Law" and devises ways of circumventing the impasse, the wall erected by the law to preserve its hegemony.

This is made possible by a retreat to the individual's interior space, which signals to the State's external controls that all is in order because the subject is locatable. Actually, the subject begins to contemplate, to expand her thought-space, to make abstractions about her living conditions, which leads up to her decision to perform an act of resistance in "thinking her way through the wall." This will lead, among other things, to the rediscovery of what belongs uniquely to the self and will enable the subject to perform a more comprehensive critique of the mechanics of power:

> Rosalind lernt zu verstehen, was eine Wand ist. . . . Eine Wand, die in keiner Beziehung zu einer anderen Wand steht, ist eine Mauer. Ein System aus vier Wänden und einem Fußboden, einzig nach oben mit einer Öffnung versehen, ist ein Loch. Ein Raum aus vier Wänden mit Decke, Fußboden und einer Tür, die durch den Insassen nicht zu öffnen ist, ist ein Gefängnis. Ein Raum mit Fenstern und einer Tür, die nach Belieben von beiden Seiten geöffnet und geschlossen werden kann, ist ein Zimmer. Die Wand kann den Betrachter von etwas abschirmen oder etwas vom Betrachter. Wände trennen das

eine vom anderen, man kann an eine Wand klopfen. Die Wände um Rosalind trennen sie von dem Nachbarn, vom Hausflur, vom Korridor und von der Straße. Sie hält sie alle für unverzichtbar. Je länger sie ihre Wände betrachtet, um so sicherer wird sie in der Annahme, daß Wände zu den wichtigsten Regulatoren des menschlichen Zusammenlebens gehören.

Und jetzt, sagt Rosalind, werde ich mit dem Kopf durch die Wand gehen.[47]

[Rosalind is learning to understand what a wall is. . . . A single wall that exists in no relation to another single wall is a partition. ("Mauer" suggests the Wall and is more appropriate here.) A system consisting of four walls and a floor, which has no ceiling, is a hole. A room with four walls, a ceiling, floor and a door which cannot be opened by the inhabitants of the room, is a prison cell. A room with windows and a door, which can be opened and closed at will from both sides, is a room. The wall can protect the observer or the observed. Walls separate one from the other; you can knock on a wall. The walls around Rosalind separate her from her neighbor, from the hallway, from the corridor and from the street. She thinks that she cannot do without any of them. The longer she observes her walls, the surer she becomes that walls are the most important regulators of human life.

And now, Rosalind says, I'm going to put my head through the wall.][48]

Putting one's head through the wall finds its equivalent in another metaphor, walking the city streets, but new, less obviously prescribed paths need to be discovered:

Wie sollte sie auch so schnell ein anderes Denken lernen, dachte sie, Denkwege sind wie Straßen, gepflastert oder betoniert, unversehens ging man sie wie gewohnt, . . . Ihr verzweigtes System aus Haupt-und Nebenstraßen, Gassen und Trampelpfaden, für ihr bisheriges Leben durchaus tauglich, erwies sich nun als Falle, in der sich jeder Gedanke fing. . . . Geheimpfade, Schleichwege, unterirdische Gänge und Gebirgsgrate brauchte sie. Früher hatte sie solche Wege gekannt.[49]

[How could she learn a new way of thinking this quickly? she wondered. Paths of thoughts are like streets, paved with cobblestones or concrete, one went along them as usual, unawares, . . . Her articulated system of main and secondary streets, alleys, and trails, quite adequate for her life up until now, turned out to be a trap for every one of her thoughts. . . . She needed secret tracks, hidden paths, subterranean passageways and mountain ridges. She had once known such paths.][50]

The first prerequisite for unlearning the familiar routines is leisure, being forced to stop hurrying about in a crowd. Josefa discovers this in one of the rare moments when she imagines herself soaring over the city and scans the streets from the controlling birds-eye view:

> Wir haben keine Zeit zum Fliegen. Wir müssen uns beeilen, immerzu beeilen. Zum Wurstladen, zur Sparkasse, ins Büro, in den Kindergarten, zur S-Bahn. Überall könnten wir zu spät kommen. Das Geld ist ausverkauft, die Sparkasse abgefahren, der Chef hat geschlossen, das Kind weint."[51]

> [We don't have any time to play. We have to hurry, keep on hurrying. to the butcher's, to the bank, to the office, to the kindergarten, to the elevated train. We might be late everywhere. The money is sold out, the bank has driven off, the boss is closed, the child is crying."][52]

Such an analysis demonstrates Maron's effective use of Dadaist montage techniques—by displacing he participles out of their customary context, the daily grind is rendered grotesque and shown up in its absurdity. The next step, according to the advice her poetic alter ego gives Rosalind is: "du mußt deine nutzloseste Eigenschaft herausfinden" ["you have to find out your most useless quality].[53]Rosalind no longer asks wistfully like Josefa: "Warum können sie mich nicht gebrauchen, wie ich bin?" ["Why can't they use me the way I am?"][54] She is far angrier at being regimented and infantilized, she refuses to be "used" at all by society.

A likely cause for this radicalization is the change in governmental policy towards women in the eighties: as the economy worsened, they were being shunted back into the home and to childbearing,[55] they were being offered a second *Babyjahr* (maternity-leave year), for instance. Maron condemns this overplanning because its linearity leaves no room for personal decisions:

> Denn schoen ehe du geboren wurdest, hat man dich statistisch aufbereitet und deinen möglichen Nutzen errechnet: die durch dich verursachten Kosten im Kindesalter, die Verwendbarkeit während der Arbeitsphase, die zu erwartenden Nachkommen, die wieder entstehenden Kosten im Alter bis zum statistisch ausgewiesenen Sterbealter, kurz: diene Rentabilität ist veranschlagt und wird erwartet. Du kannst aber die Statistiker überlisten, indem du etwas in dir findest, was sie nicht verwenden können. Deinen Kopf bauen sie einer Maschine ein, deine Arme machen sie zu Kränen, deinen Brustkorb zum Karteikasten, deinen Bauch zur Müllhalde. . . . das

Besondere, das Unberechenbare, Seele, Poesie, Musik, ich weiß keinen passenden Namen dafür.[56]

[For even before you were born you were included in a statistical survey in which your potential utility was calculated: the cost you incur as a child, your usability during your work phase, expected progeny, the expenses incurred in old age up until your statistically forecast age of death, in short: your profitability is estimated and is taken for granted. But you can outwit the statisticians by finding something within yourself that they can't use. They'll install a machine in your head, they'll transform your arms into cranes, your chest into a card catalogue, your stomach into a dumping ground. . . . The special, the unpredictable: soul, poetry, music, I don't know a suitable name for it.][57]

Maron suggests that a new language that is both playful and poetic can be a tool for the rebuilding of a sense of privacy, a sense of inalienable selfhood. It comes into being spontaneously, when the individual overcomes isolation and seeks out the city's liminoid spaces—cafés, pubs, parks. Owning the self thus involves both the setting up of barriers against state intervention and supervision and the breaking down of barriers between the self and others—for the first time in ten years, Rosalind decides to ring her neighbor's doorbell and enters into conversation with her, which reveals Thekla Fleischer as far more interesting and dignified than she had seemed earlier when Rosalind would just observe her leaving the building:

"Ich bekomme niemals Besuch," sagte sie, "außer meinen Schülern besucht mich niemand. . . . Ich möchte Terrorist sein, sagte sie plötzlich, Terroristen sind nie allein. Wenn sie ihre Bomben schmeißen, sowieso nicht, und später, im Gefängnis, regt sich die ganze Welt darüber auf, wenn sie allein sitzen müssen. Ich sitze hier jeden Tag allein und niemand regt sich darüber auf."[58]

["I never have visitors," she said, "except for my pupils, no one visits me. . . . I would like to be a terrorist, she said suddenly, terrorists are never lonely. When they throw their bombs they're not, and later, in prison, the whole world gets annoyed about their having to be in solitary confinement. I sit here by myself every day, and nobody gets worked up over that."][59]

Rosalind and Thekla establish real neighborliness by sharing their worries with each other and establishing a friendship based on reciprocity— Thekla teaches Rosalind the piano, Rosalind helps Thekla get married illegally.

186

This relationship is contrasted to the foregrounded relationship in the narrative, the exploitive connection between Beerenbaum and Rosalind. In listening to him talk callously about the history of the State and the necessity for building the Wall, Rosalind realizes that she won't be free until the generation of Stalinist hardliners is dead, and she eventually "slays the Father" by confronting him with his crimes:

> Ich hatte nichts zu verteidigen als mich, während Beerenbaum einen ganzen Radschwung der Geschichte als sein Werk ansah, das er zu beschützen hatte, wenn nötig, mit der Waffe in der Hand, wie mein Vater oft gesagt hat und vermutlich auch Beerenbaum sagen würde. In dieser Minute begriff ich, daß alles von Beerenbaums Tod abhing, von seinem und dem seiner Generation. Erst wenn ihr Werk niemandem mehr heilig war, wenn nur noch seine Brauchbarkeit entschieden würde über seinen Bestand oder Untergang, würde ich herausfinden, was ich im Leben gern getan hätte. Und dann würde es zu spät sein. Manchmal fielen mir Sätze ein, die ich nicht gedacht hatte. Sie stiegen auf aus der Heimlichkeit, die irgendwo nistete in meiner Leber, Milz oder in anderen Eingeweiden, wo sie nachts, wenn ich träumte, rumorte. Und sehr selten, unverhofft, schickte sie in mein Wachsein Sätze wie eine Flaschenpost.[60]

> [I had nothing to defend but myself, whereas Beerenbaum conceived of a whole turn of the wheel of history as his oeuvre, which he had to protect, if need be, with his gun at the ready, as my father often put it and doubtless Beerenbaum would say that, too. At this moment I understood that everything depended on Beerenbaum's death, on his death and that of his generation. Only once their work would no longer be sacred to anyone, once only its usefulness would govern whether it lasted or went down, only then would I find out what I might have liked to do with my life. And then it would be too late. Sometimes I discovered sentences I had not thought. They arose out of the secrecy which had eaten itself into my liver, my spleen or some other part of my entrails, where it clamored for attention at night, while I was dreaming. And very rarely, unhoped for, it sent me sentences into my wakefulness like a message in a bottle.][61]

In terms of psychological growth, the individual has reached another important growth step, the Oedipal phase. She is fully conscious of her wish to kill the father, and, unlike the standard Freudian scenario, no castration fear supervenes to inhibit this impulse. Nonetheless, after Beerenbaum's death, the narrative loops around to its premise in an equivocal closing movement: just as she deigned once again to think for pay, Rosalind still takes home his legacy—the manuscript of his autobiography, which she had typed for him:

Als ich die Straße erreiche, sehe ich auf dem Parkpatz das karmesinrote Auto von Michael Beerenbaum, der in diesem Augenblick die Wagentür öffnet und aussteigt. Er kommt auf mich zu. In der Uniform hat er plötzlich das Gesicht eines Militärs, nicht mehr das eines Pfarrers oder Pathologen. Auch der Gang wirkt verändert, soldatisch. In der Hand hält er ein in Zeitungspapier eingeschlagenes Paket. Hier, sagt er, als er vor mir steht, er hat gewollt, daß Sie es bekommen. Seine Stimme verrät nicht, ob er den Willen seines Vaters billigt. *Ich weiß, was in dem Paket ist. Ich will es nicht haben. Ich will damit nichts mehr zu tun haben. Trotzdem greife ich dananch.*

Ich stehe noch vor dem Friedhof, als das karmesinrote Auto hinter der Kurve verschwindet, in der Hand das dünne Paket, eingewickelt wie ein Pfund Heringe in die Zeitung vom Vortag. *Ich werde es nicht öffnen. Ich werde es in die nächste Mülltonne werfen. Ich werde es zwischen den Papierbergen im unteren Fach meines Bücherregals begraben. Ich werde es auf keinen Fall öffnen.*[62]

[When I reach the street, I see in the parking lot the dark red car which belongs to Michael Beerenbaum, who opens the car door just now and gets out. He is coming towards me. In his uniform he suddenly wears the face of a military person, no more than of a minister or of a pathologist. Even his walk seems different, like that of a soldier. Here, he says, when he is standing in front of me, he wanted you to have it. His voice does not give away whether he approves of his father's last will. *I know what is in the package. I don't want it. I don't want anything more to do with it. Still, I reach for it.*

I am still standing in front of the cemetery when the dark red car disappears around the bend, in my hand the thin package, wrapped up like a pound of mackerel in yesterday's newspapers. *I shall not open it. I shall throw it out into the next trashcan. I shall bury it between the mounds of paper in the lowest shelf of my bookcase. On no account shall I open it.*][63]

It is fitting that the autobiography of the socialist oldtimer returns to his former amanuensis like an obligation. She won't be able to wash her hands of his legacy and will have to come to terms with it, just as GDR citizens in the now unified Germany still have to process the mountains of Stasi files left behind after the collapse of the Honecker regime.

In *Stille Zeile 6*, the destructive aspects of the regime are personified in the figure of Beerenbaum, which allows the author to assign responsibility for her own malaise and contemporary socialism's ills to a specific generation, to "name" the originators of the deathlike paralysis that holds her city in thrall. In Maron's earlier novels, the source of evil was mythologized as either a repulsive Nazi bugaboo or a mysterious official of "the Association of Male Poets" in *The Defector*; or the source had been located at too low a level, that of relatively lowly bureaucrats like Josefa's editor Strutzer in *Flugasche*. The Rosalind of *Stille Zeile 6*, however, assigns blame to a leading *Politbüro* member. Unlike the vaguely defined enemies whom she confronted by proxy (the Male Poet for instance is sent to kill Martha, not Rosalind herself) or who seem to be chimeric constructs—the clone who has escaped from an asylum or the old Nazi who haunts the streets—the protagonist firmly locates herself and her enemies in the daytime city, in a specific place (in the *Städtchen* [little city: the former residential quarter of the government in Niederschönhausen), and she pursues her confrontations with her enemy regularly, only gradually building in intensity; they always take place in a realist setting (Beerenbaum's house) and are narrated in realist language. The most probable external reason for this shift may be the author's 1985 move to West Germany, with a special three-year visa that allowed her to travel to the GDR for visits and did not foreclose the possibility of returning there to live. From a distance in space and time, it becomes possible to assign responsibility where it is due, and it becomes possible to face one's own complicity with the system through cowardice. Rosalind expresses this to herself in an imaginary dialogue with her blood, which symbolizes her instinctual drives: "Ich sage nicht, daß du ängstlich warst oder feige, du hast zu wenig gewollt." "I'm not saying that you were afraid or, much less, cowardly; you simply wanted too little."[64] From Rosalind's period of physical breakdown follows the imperative, still formulated somewhat tentatively, to return to a sense of ownership of the self by turning aggression back outwards towards its sources instead of directing it inward against oneself: "Die Dinge zerschlagen und weiterleben, dachte ich, irgendwie, anders, auf eine Art, die sich finden würde." "To destroy the things and go on living, I thought, somehow, in another way, differently, in a way still to be seen."]^[65] This commitment to enable the self to survive leads to another decision: "Ich darf hier nicht bleiben, . . . ich muß gehen, ich muß diese Wohnung verlassen, endgültig." 'I mustn't stay here, . . . I have to go, I have to leave this apartment for good."]^[66]

Once she carries out the decision to leave and makes her way to the station, Rosalind is confirmed in her decision by an allegorical scene of mass carnage she witnesses in the streets. A large group of civilians tried to storm the Wall leading to the West or were trying to run away to the East and were killed by the police. They are now being walled up in the dead of night, no trace of their insurrection will remain:

> Am Morgen würden vorübereilende Passanten erstaunt oder gleich-
> mütig wahrnehmen, daß dort, wo gestern eine Straße war, nun eine
> Mauer steht. . . . Früher war da mal eine Straße, werden die Leute
> sagen, bis auch das in Vergessenheit gerät."[67]

> [The next morning pedestrians rushing by would be amazed or
> note indifferently that where there had been a street the day before,
> there was now a wall. . . . There used to be a street here, the people
> will recall, until that too fades into oblivion.][68]

In her memory, Rosalind reenacts the moment of the building of the Wall in 1961, only now there is a personal sense of being hurt by this action. Maron describes watching the police build the wall in claustrophobic imagery, it is like being buried alive:

> Polizeiwagen standen nebeneinander über die ganze Sraßenbreite.
> Davor uniformierte Männer Schulter and Schulter. . . . Ein Schein-
> werfer überflutete die Straße mit bleichem Licht und schien auf die
> Körper zahlloser, eng nebeneinander liegender Menschen. Männer
> und Frauen in weißen Kitteln, auch Zivilisten, beugten sich über
> sie, aber Rosalind konnte den Zweck ihrer Bemühungen nicht
> erkennen. Am Eingang der Straße, gleich hinter den Einsatzwagen,
> bauten mehrere Männer an einer Mauer, die über Fahrbahn und
> Gehwege von einer Hauswand zur anderen reichte. Sie arbeiteten
> ohne Hast, einen Stein auf den anderen, die Mauer reichte ihnen
> schon bis an die Hüfte. . . . Die Eberswalder Straße wurde in
> westlicher Richtung durch die Stadtmauer vom angrenzenden
> Bezirk Wedding getrennt. Nördlich und südlich bildeten vier-
> stöckige Häuser lückenlose Wälle. Und jetzt vermauerten sie den
> östlichen Zugang. Oder Ausgang. Dazwischen die Menschen,
> tausend zweitausend, wer wußte, wie viele.[69]

> [Police cars barricaded the street. In front of them were men in
> uniform standing shoulder to shoulder. . . . A headlight flooded
> the street with pale light and shone on the many bodies lying
> closely, one next to the other. Men and women in white gowns,
> civilians as well, were bent over them, but Rosalind could not make
> out what they were doing. At the entrance to the street, next to the
> emergency vehicles, men were building a wall that cut across the
> road and walkways from one building to the other. They placed one
> brick on top of the next without haste; the wall was already up to

their hips. . . . Eberswalder Straße was divided in its western part from the bordering district of Wedding by the town wall. On both the northern and southern sides, five-story buildings formed unbroken barriers. And now they were walling up the eastern entry. Or exit. In between were people, a thousand, two thousand, who knew how many.][70]

For the first time, the protagonist overcomes her scruples and places herself outside with the mass of people who want to flee, whom the state would label criminals. By identifying the socialist police with piles of bodies they become the opposite of what they claim to be: that is, the evil Fascists against whom the *Antifaschistischer Schutzwall* (antifascist protection wall) was supposedly erected. The city periphery turns into an apocalyptic war zone, reflecting the increased despair of reforms within the GDR after 1984. GDR citizens were acutely conscious that Gorbachev had begun to liberalize in the Eastern block states, but that this did not result in a liberalization of GDR policies. Honecker's *Politbüro* member Kurt Hager tellingly confirmed Maron's allegorical description of the country as a room in his 1987 statement, "Würden Sie wenn Ihr Nachbar seine Wohnung neu tapeziert, sich verpflichtet fühlen, Ihre Wohnung ebenfalls neu zu tapezieren?" ["Just because a neighbor is changing his wallpaper doesn't mean we have to put up new wallpaper ourselves."][71] GDR policy became once again less flexible, more reminiscent of the founding years of the republic.

If we compare the endings of Rosalind's 1986 and 1991 identity quests, we notice a transformation from her imaginary escape into being a bag lady on the Bowery in New York City—where she is reunited with her poet self and undergoes a carnivalesque self-debasement and dissolution—to a more realistically narrated and more enduring rebirth of the self. This is achieved by making good use of those means for experiencing difference as pleasurable and capable of producing a new expressive language for the self as are accessible to it in everyday reality: less fair-flung real travels—to Prague instead of the Bowery, drinking tea, listening to Mozart's *Don Giovanni*, and practicing the piano—music as a new language opposed to the instrumentalized language of power. "Das strikte Einhalten der aus Interessen erwachsenen Spielregeln" ["Strict observance of the rules of the game born out of self-interest"] is replaced by "erleben . . . wonach ich mich sehne . . . den schönen Rausch des Fremdseins" ["experiencing . . . what I long for . . . the beautiful intoxication of strangeness (being strange)"].[72]

The translation of the beleaguered female self into an other takes the twofold form of a quest for mythic models and the search for an

191

ancient language of prophecy and spirituality. In *The Defector*, the Antigone becomes an important model of female heroism in the face of a crushing Law.[73] The salient features of the Greek myth are: Antigone's courageous upholding of civilized standards and ethical action when she insists on performing the funeral rites for her brother, despite the tyrant Creon's order to let the body decay like carrion outside the city gates; her horrible punishment—being walled up alive; and her tainted origin from the fated incestuous marriage of Oedipus and Jocasta. Maron denounces the founders of the Socialist State as power-hungry greedy tyrants, her Rosalind successfully fights servility within herself, thus overcoming her early indoctrination to be submissive to the Party line. Moreover, Rosalind stands up to the tyrant in defense of, as the avenger of, a brother—the sinologist Karl-Heinz Baron, affectionately known as "the Count," whose career and life were ruined by Beerenbaum's caprice. She rights the wrong Beerenbaum has done by forcing him to remember the victim, to reveal his guilt. "Ich wollte es zu einem Ende bringen. Ich wollte Beerenbaum besiegen. . . . Gegen Beerenbaum wollte ich einen verlorenen Kampf nachträglich gewinnen." ["I wanted to finish it. I wanted to vanquish Beerenbaum. . . . I wanted to win a lost fight against Beerenbaum after the fact."][74] Rosalind formulates her attack against the repressive government of the Stalinists in the words like blows, language that speaks the truth and has the power to kill:

> Ihr habt Hirnmasse konfisziert, weil ihr selbst zuwenig davon hattet. Im nächsten Jahrhundert hättet ihr sie amputiert und an Drähte gehängt, um die Gefängniskosten zu sparen. Hirneigenschaft statt Leibeigenschaft, ihr Menschheitsbefreier. . . . Nichts wissen wir . . . weil wir nicht leben durften. Euer eigenes Leben hat euch nicht gereicht, es war euch zu schäbig, ihr habt auch noch unsere Leben verbraucht, Menschenfresser seid ihr, Sklavenhalter mit einem Heer von Folterknechten.

> [You confiscated brain cells because you yourselves did not have enough of them. In the coming century, you would have amputated brains and hung them on wires to save the cost of a prison term. Servitude of the brain instead of servitude of the body (bondage), you liberators of humanity. . . . We know nothing . . . because we weren't allowed to live. Your own life wasn't enough for you, it was too mean for you, you are ogres, slave owners with an army of torturers at your command."][75]

Her passionate indictment leads to Beerenbaum's fatal heart attack. Rosalind then goes to see him be buried, and, for the first time, she assumes the gaze of surveillance when she observes the funeral guests, who represent the apparatus of power:

> Ich war froh darüber, daß ich hinter diesen Leuten stand, statt unter ihnen zu sitzen. Obwohl ich ihre Gesichter nicht sehen konnte, blieb mir keine Regung ihrer Körper und Köpfe verborgen."

> [I was glad to be standing behind these people instead of being seated among them. Even though I could not see their faces, no movement of their bodies and heads was hidden from me.][76]

She survives the visual running of the gauntlet over the open grave—the toadies and cronies are the ones who avert their eyes from hers, Beerenbaum's son, the Stasi official, even turns away altogether, which we can read as an admission of impotence—here is one whom his gaze cannot fix to kill:

> Es ist vorbei. Als ich mich umdrehe, stehe ich ihnen allen gegenüber, und sie alle richten ihre Augen auf mich. Auch Michael Beerenbaums Augen mit dem matten, gläsernen Schimmer blicken auf mich. Ehe ich die drei Schritte auf ihn zugehen kann und ihm meine Hand entgegenhalten kann, wendet er sich ab. Ich bin erleichtert."

> [It is over. When I turn around, I face all of them, and they all are training their eyes on me. Michael Beerenbaum's eyes, too, with their (tired) matte, glassy gleam are looking at me. Before I can make the three steps towards him and hold out (hold up) my hand, he turns away. I am relieved."][77]

Apart from assuming the power of the gaze, the protagonist is beginning to learn a new more expressive language. In *Flying Ashes* it was the mystical love poetry of the Song of Solomon that voiced Josefa's resistance to being instrumentalized; in *The Defector*, it was a nonsense language patterned on Inuit[78] and Martha's poetry, which emphasized feeling in a baroque mixture of styles;[79] and in *Stille Zeile 6* it is the language of Mozart's opera *Don Giovanni*. These languages of protest have in common that they resist categorization by being replete with images and sounds.

> "Eine neue Sprache ist wie ein neues Leben," sagte der Graf. . . . So redeten sie eine Weile, jeder in seiner Sprache, und das Gelächter, mit dem sie ihre Reden begleiteten, rührte sowohl von der Gemeinsamkeit her, jeder eine eigene Sprache zu haben, als auch von dem Vergnügen, so den anderen die schaurigsten Geheimnisee mitteilen zu können und sie zugleich für sich zu behalten. Daß keiner von

ihnen ein wirkliches Geheimnis aussprach, hinderte nicht den Spaß
an der Möglichkeit, es zu tun.[80]

["A new language is like a new life," the Count said. . . . They
talked this way for a while, each in his own language, and the
laughter with which they accompanied their talk came from both
the common fact of each having a language of his own, and from
the fun of thus being able to tell the others the most gruesome
secrets while simultaneously keeping them to themselves. The fact
that none of them actually voiced a real secret did not diminish the
enjoyment in the possibility of so doing.][81]

In "*Coming to Writing,*" Hélène Cixous performs that kind of
celebratory joyful writing that in its use of biblical imagery and cadences
is akin to the "private" yet shared language of Maron's survivors in/of an
unjust society. Cixous uses the language of prophecy to speak lyrically of
change and a new perception of the other, one that lets the other be
distinct without wanting to limit and contain:

This is what my body teaches me: first of all, be wary of names;
they are nothing but social tools, rigid concepts, little cages of
meaning assigned, as you know, to keep us from getting mixed up
with each other. . . . *But, my friend, take the time to unname yourself
for a moment.* Haven't you been the father of your sister? Haven't
you, as a wife, been the husband of your spouse, and perhaps the
brother of your brother, or hasn't your brother been your big
sister? . . . *Writing and traversing names are the same necessary gesture.* . . . As soon as you let yourself be led beyond codes, your
body filled with fear and with joy, the words diverge, you are no
longer enclosed in the maps of social constructions, you no longer
walk between walls, meanings flow. . . . And you are returned to
your innocences, your possibilities, the abundance of your intensi-
ties. . . . *Woman, for me, is she who kills no one in herself, she who gives
(herself) her own lives: woman is always in a certain way "mother" for
herself and for the other.* . . . There is something of the mother in you
if you love yourself. If you love. If you love, you love yourself as
well. This is the woman who belongs to love: the woman who loves
all the women inside her. . . . She doesn't watch herself, she doesn't
measure herself, she doesn't examine herself, not the image, not the
copy. . . . Plenitude, she who doesn't watch herself, doesn't reappro-
priate all her images reflected in people's faces, is not the devourer
of eyes. *She who looks with the look that recognizes, that studies, respects,
doesn't take, doesn't claw, but attentively, with gentle restlessness, contem-
plates and reads, caresses, bathes, makes the other gleam.* Brings back to

light the life that's been buried, fugitive, made too prudent. Illuminates it and sings its names.[82]

Maron's Rosalind learns to listen to her body self, "to look with the look that recognizes." This new attitude is fleshed out by the character of the ungainly Claire who represented Rosalind's suppressed sense of her physicality. Claire returns to Rosalind in two inspiring visions to praise the power of imagination, which lets her body transform itself: grow new limbs or acquire new skills.[83] These fantastical metamorphoses light the way for rebirth and change on the level of realist narrative and the "real" person—in *Stille Zeile 6*, Rosalind proclaims her new credo: "Ich glaube, sagte ich, die Freiheit ist enso ein Ort wie der Mensch ein Ort ist." ["I believe, said I, that freedom is just as much a place as the human being is a place.][84] Freedom is to be found in one's head and in the free movement of one's body, and in a society still limited by having been shut-in upon itself, Berlin, the metropolis is the space for these growth experiments. Ultimately, Maron privileges memory and introspection as fostering self-awareness, and she sees the female body as a site that may signal social repression, but which also has the power to regenerate itself through temporary regression and fantasmatic transformations. Introspection for Maron is a refuge, because in her society, authority is easily identifiable. It is, in some sense, an escape that is easier to effect than that in Western capitalist societies where authority is more often internalized than it is objectified.

CONCLUSION
Managing Alterity

We have seen a progression from tentative and un-heard expressions of resistance against commodification toward a vision of agency that redeems the subject's power to choose alliances and to implement these in a communal but highly specific local agenda. This vision of social interaction does not rely on the objectification of others and therefore presents a viable alternative to social models that encourage a false equation of agency and consumerism or create a divisive sense of agency as radical opposition between specific groups or classes in society. Ultimately, Maron's fiction contains perhaps the most nuanced examples of democratic dialogue across class, age, and gender boundaries. Such dialogue respects and does not try to erase or cover over differences.

Although in many instances this journey towards self-understanding and purposive acting culminates in the city, it does not necessarily end there. The city is the center of myriad transactions and therefore offers women opportunities for education, work, and social engagement they would not have outside it, but it also offers up the possibility of alienation. Rhys and Maron (at least initially) represent the city as a labyrinthine closed space, whereas Drabble and Duras, and eventually Maron as well, figure the city as palimpsest in which traces of its history can be read and reincorporated into new designs, and can even become the basis for a subversive new understanding of community. Drabble and Maron especially rediscover interiority and the subterranean space as ways of grounding and liberating female identity. This process of sympathetic exploration and observation began in the work of Marguerite Duras. She stresses female mobility that includes a shifting perspective of the city—she affords her female protagonist both the controlling birds-eye view and the view from the underside. This view from below becomes shared by other marginalized characters who seek out the city's liminoid spaces as sites of transformation and playful exploration.

197

Drabble mythologizes the urban working class and a less driven sideways progress in an uncompetitive Bohemia in her earlier novels. She sees this as the social environment most conducive to finding new hitherto unsuspected professional skills, just as it seems to her the most suited to liberate the individual from supervision by family and government agencies. In her later fiction, however, she increasingly comes to identify the street as a dangerous public space for her female protagonists, regardless of their class background. Beginning with her novel *The Radiant Way* (1987), women are at risk of being threatened, victimized by drugs or even dismembered in the city's border zones and wastelands, which is what happens to neglected and pathologically ill Jilly Fox. Younger members of the middle-class who drop out of the social net are contrasted with the redemptive archaeological work that is performed by older female members of the middle class. Many of Drabble's central female characters are in the healing professions and devote themselves to interpreting and reassembling the lives of individuals overlooked or penalized by the rest of society. They uncover genealogies of evil, as Alix Bowen does in tracing "her" murderer's history of childhood abuse, or as Liz Headleand does in clearing up the journalist Stephen Cox's disappearance during his investigation into Pol Pot's mass murders in Cambodia. These ethically committed female characters attempt to reintegrate such lost members of society where possible, or, if that fails, at least guarantee their place and value as individuals in communal rituals of remembrance.

Both Drabble and Maron value the verbalization of unspoken motivations for social behavior: they bring them into a shared language and thus transport them into other people's consciousness. Drabble's characters look into the sewer and the river running through the city; they also inspect family taboos and secrets and gradually become interested in psychological explanations of social ills on a larger scale: they move from an absent father who is revealed to be a child molester (in *Radiant Way*) to the broader canvas of third-world dictatorships and colonialism (in *Gates of Ivory*).

Maron privileges interiority and the liminoid as spaces of contemplation that enable the unveiling and shattering of surveillance regimes. Rosalind in *The Defector* and *Silent Close 6* exposes the Communist state's control mechanisms as socially and individually crippling. Her female protagonists suffer from various physical ailments that can be read as somatic illnesses produced by oppressive social constraints on the individual: paralysis of the legs (Rosalind), the grotesquely obese (Klärchen)—or its observe, the anorexic body (Martha). It is only the empathetic and projective labor of imagination coupled with the exploration of utopic social possibilities that can restore these bodies to wholeness. Ultimately, Rosalind succeeds in "thinking her way through the wall." She overcomes her sequestration. She begins to re-form society by creating neighborly bonds with other isolated individuals, she bridges with a personal network of niches and forgotten historical meeting places the artificial distance and ahistoricity maintained by the police state in the public sphere.

Drabble, Maron, and Duras elaborate on the importance of physical mobility for the female protagonist in the city. The self-authored mobility they advocate for their protagonists is quite different from the urban hauntings of Rhys's characters. Rhys maintains her female protagonists in endless circulation through labyrinthine spaces, but they never attain an empowering view of the city, nor do they manage to sustain nurturing female friendships. They are trapped in a specular economy, forever checking their appearance or their body surfaces (skin, fabric, hair) to present a smooth and youthful exterior to the men who are their financial supports. Nonetheless, their insistent ghostlike haunting of the city spaces disturbs the semblance of propriety and stability at these centers of empire. Rhys contributes the unsettling view of the colonial subject traveling from the periphery of empire to its center, and her inability to make a place for her there. Her subject's hysterical speech and somatic language convey an encoded rebellion against repressive social norms, but it cannot be brought to the level of complete verbal expression. Rhys's female characters—like Charcot's hysterical patients who were exhibited in the operating theater—are carefully presented demonstration objects who cannot speak their own symptoms, they can only mutely act them out. Rhys retain control of the narrative through her repetition of ever-similar scenarios of humiliation and exploitation. By making these happen to her female protagonists, she inverts her original position of social powerlessness and her own objectification as a young unskilled woman from the colonies, but in doing so, she fails to open up possibilities for innovation regarding these predetermined gender roles. Duras, however, allows her female character a more positive experience of the mother–daughter bond than Rhys, and consequently lets her test different social roles through trial and error combined with mimesis. Where Rhys's characters cling to the femininity they understand to be a masquerade as their only chance for survival in the urban setting, Duras allows her protagonist to play with femininity, to experiment with setting the standards for her own merchandising, and opens up the possibility of leaving the market altogether as a conscious choice.

In stark contrast to Duras's conviction that resistance needs to locate itself outside oppressive social practices, in some kind of a detached beyond. Drabble, and, even more outspokenly, Maron asserts that resistance has to be practised from within these parameters, that there is no "outside" vantage point. In postmodernity, everything becomes a potential commodity, absolutely every agenda may be reappropriated and become a fashion trend, a lifestyle, or some other form of consumer commodity. So it is even more urgent at the present moment to critique consumerism as the basis of our late capitalist society, because this widespread practice is hollowing out and has come to be confused with other, more profound and politically engaged notions of community and democracy. It is, however, impossible to locate such a systemic critique outside the realm of commodification. Maron understands this contingency most fully, for example, when her protagonist is faced once more with the scathing biography she had written, only now it presents itself to her as a product, an information package about the socialist past of her society which she has to disseminate. Nonetheless, her agency is not denied, the protagonist will decide what to do with the package, she knows she will face up to her responsibility to find the proper evaluative context for it. By extension, we as readers may feel that Maron herself has already successfully performed what her protagonist has yet to carry out at the end of her novel: She has presented her readers with a personalized and contextualized account of corruption under socialism. The words of the novel's title, *Stille Zeile* (Silent, Quiet Line), may symbolize that empty line between the lines of text that make up personal and national narratives, a dead space that needs to be filled with meaning, and may then subvert the narrative from within. That lacuna may further be a space for listening, of opening up to difference, and learning about societies that are different from our own experience.

Female mentoring becomes an important source of alternatives for female agency in the work of Drabble and Maron. By creating protagonists whose stories change and are followed over the course of several novels, these authors open up the narrative—in the case of Drabble even sustaining a plurivocal narrative in which no one character remains privileged. None of the women writers I analyze abandon the notion of female subjectivity. They are not interested, however, in refashioning a monolithic female subject to imitation of the male model of identity. In her latest work, Drabble seems compassionate towards masculinity as a masquerade as well, in short, to the subject's enacting what Judith Butler has termed gender as performance. As the philosopher Jana Sawicki rightly points out in her recent book on Foucault, we must not overlook "the complexities of institutional mediation which are surely also a part of the story of male domination. . . . A Foucauldian feminist would stress the sheer variety of ways in which effects of male domination are produced and gendered identities constituted."[1] She further cautions that identity is not a superannuated concept in postmodern feminist discourse: "[Foucault] believes that humanist discourses that place the subject at the center of reality or history have failed to grasp the extent to which the subject is fragmented and decentered in the social field. But to

200

describe the ways in which individuals have been dominated through a rigid attachment to particular modern identities is not equivalent to rejecting identity *tout court*."[2] Implicitly following this social constructivist argument, Iain Chambers locates identity in the body and our consciousness of it: "It is the body, as individual history, memory and trace, which sets in play the possibility of dialoguing with our being—in-difference. Here a surplus of specificity, an excess of details and sense, points towards the impossibility of erasing difference, where difference functions not simply as a rhetorical or stylistic trope, but, above all, as a historical experience."[3] In cities that increasingly turn into homogenized "nonplace urban realms" or theatrical simulations of historically specific places, "ageographical cities, Cyburbia" as the architect Michael Sorkin labels them,[4] the body is our visible, tangible guarantor of specificity. From Rhys to Duras, from Drabble to Maron, the authors I analyze all inscribe social ills on the female body in the metropolis. In unfolding the story of the female body as it ages, falls ill, is healed, is tortured, gives birth, or sometimes dies, the significance of the body as the outward shape of our identity in society, as constituted by social norms as well as personal experience, is illustrated. Late-stage capitalism and Soviet-style socialism converge in medicalizing and disfiguring the female body as an allegory for political processes gone awry. Both of these apparently competing political systems have, with the aid of surveillance regimes, dismantled the idea of community as interactive among its members. In both societies the individual is isolated and compartmentalized, a powerless recipient of the dissecting gaze of authority.

A new kind of "embodied thinking" would bring up the question of borders, of coming to terms with an irreducible alterity. For bodies are "less separate than it might seem, and . . . are, before anything else, excrescences of other bodies."[5] This germination of one body from another necessarily unfolds in time and therefore is historical as well as somatic. Historical consciousness is a necessary underpinning of systemic critique, without which there can be no social transformation. If we can accept the interdependency of bodies over time and at any given moment, we can also create more ethical relationships with each other as a social body. "The irreducibility of the world to a single, comprehensible totality, map, or source of 'authentic' being, forces us to recognize its incalculable alterity: the differences we need to respect."[6] It is precisely this more inclusive view of self as both part of society and at the same time distinct in living in its specific body, gender, and historical moment that Irigaray wants to promote.

All the authors ranging from Rhys to Maron invoke city spaces—cinemas and pubs, cafés and squares, streets and parks—as scenes of the civic. They provide a new picture of women's cultural relations to a space traditionally gendered as male, a decentralized view of the city as male construct, not demonstrating the impossibility of metaphorizing the city, but a feminist resistance to a totalizing rhetoric about city space and, by extension, culture. Iain Chambers argues in a more recent volume on migrancy in late modernity that:

> In signifying limits, we already expose ourselves to the possibility of an opening. For we are thrown into that ambiguous space where differences are permitted a hearing, in which both speakers and the syntax of conversation run the risk of modification. . . . It signals the boundaries of that particular sense of belonging in language and encourages us to venture abroad with a weakened and more restricted sense of one's own idiom. To entertain this other sense of community, one not necessarily inscribed in the confines of a national language, literature and identity, is to grasp that side of modernism in which the historical tropes of migrancy and movement become central[7]

What does agency mean in the age of the computer and the worldwide web? The need for human responsibility, critical awareness, and action is not obviated by these technological advances. We evolve as subjects in movement and the articulation of our experience, subtended by memory, and shaped by dialogue with an increasingly larger group of others, and thanks to new information systems we are today perhaps more aware of the contingency and interdependency of our cultures and communities. This awareness must include the persistent reality of others who are excluded and marginalized, and whose existence as potential or actual agents we must respect.[8]

NOTES

Introduction: Transaction, Exchange, and Female Agency

1. Richard Rorty, *Contigency, Irony and Solidarity* (Cambridge: Harvard Univ. Press, 1989).
2. Jean Baudrillard, *La Société de consommation* (Paris: Denoël, 1970), 17, 43.
3. See Michel Foucault, *Discipline and Punish: The Birth of the Prison* (New York: Vintage, 1977).
4. Jürgen Habermas, *Towards a Rational Society* (Boston: Beacon, 1970).
5. Terry Eagleton, *Ideology: An Introduction* (London: Verso, 1991), 37.
6. Ibid., 47, 49.
7. György Lukács, *History and Class Consciousness* (Cambridge: MIT Press, 1971), 59.
8. Ibid., 101.
9. Ibid., 171.
10. Ibid., 168.
11. See, for example, Adelheid Popp, *Jugend einer Arbeiterin* (Berlin: Dietz, 1983).
12. Judith Butler, *Bodies That Matter: On the Discursive Limits of Sex* (New York: Routledge, 1993), 9.
13. Ibid., 15.
14. Elizabeth Grosz, "Bodies–Cities," in *Sexuality and Space,* ed. Beatriz Colomina (New York: Princeton Architectural Press, 1992), 241–53, 242.
15. Ibid., 244.
16. Ibid., 249.
17. Fredric Jameson, *Postmodernism Or, The Cultural Logic of Late Capitalism* (Durham: Duke Univ. Press, 1991), 41.
18. Ibid., x.
19. Ibid.
20. See also W.J.T. Mitchell, "The Violence of Public Art," *Critical Inquiry* 16 (Summer 1990): 880–99; 894–95.
21. Susan Bordo, *Unbearable Weight: Feminism, Western Culture, and the Body* (Berkeley: Univ. of California Press, 1993), 30, 189.

22. Ibid., 30–31.
23. Ibid., 191.
24. Walter Benjamin, "On Some Motifs in Baudelaire," in *Illuminations* (New York: Schocken, 1978), 155–200; 172–73.
25. Cf. Daphne Spain, *Gendered Spaces* (Chapel Hill: Univ. of North Carolina Press, 1992), xiv, 3.
26. Ibid., xiv.
27. William Sharpe and Leonard Wallock, eds. *Visions of the Modern City: Essays in Art, History, and Literature* (Baltimore: Johns Hopkins Univ. Press, [1983] 1987), 1, 26.
28. Ibid., 25–30.
29. See Judith Kegan Gardiner, *Rhys, Stead, Lessing and the Politics of Empathy* (Bloomington: Indiana Univ. Press, 1989).
30. See Anthony Giddens, *Modernity and Self-Identity: Self and Society in the Late Modern Age* (Stanford: Stanford Univ. Press, 1991).
31. See Iris Marion Young, *Justice and the Politics of Difference* (Princeton: Princeton Univ. Press, 1990), 123.
32. Cf. my work on the Faust myth in nineteenth-century realist fiction; Helga Druxes, *The Feminization of Dr. Faustus: Female Identity Quests from Stendhal to Morgner* (University Park: Pennsylvania State Univ. Press, 1993).
33. Sophocles, *The Oedipus Cycle,* Dudley Fitts and Robert Fitzgerald, trans. (San Diego: Harcourt Brace Jovanovich, 1977), *Antigone,* ii, 203.
34. Ibid., 212, 214–15.
35. See also Iain Chambers, "Some Metropolitan Tales," in Chambers, *Border Dialogues: Journeys in Postmodernity* (London: Routledge, 1990), 57. Chambers discusses the sources of democratic change in the contemporary city as coming from inside the structure rather than relying on a metaspace outside it. He sees this as a return to the ancient Greek concept of civic discourse.
36. Luce Irigaray, "Droits et devoirs civiles pour les deux sexes," *Le Temps de la différence* (Paris: Le Livre de Poche, 1989), 82. My translation; all subsequent translations from *Le Temps* are also mine.
37. See my discussion of Irigaray's "essentialist" early writings as reaction against Jacques Lacan and Simone de Beauvoir in Druxes, *Feminization of Dr. Faustus* 12.
38. Luce Irigaray, "Love between Us," in *Who Comes after the Subject?* Eduardo Cadava, Peter Connor, and Jean-Luc Nancy, eds. (New York: Routledge, [1989] 1991), 167–77; 172–73.
39. Cf. Margaret Whitford, *Luce Irigaray: Philosophy in the Feminine* (London: Routledge, 1991), 44; for a fuller account of the psychoanalytic model of identity, see 48–49.
40. Ibid., 48–49.
41. Sophocles, *Oedipus Cycle: Antigone* ii, 204.
42. Ibid., 212.
43. Ibid., 213.
44. Irigaray, *Le Temps,* 25, 35, 36.
45. Ibid., 37.

46. For a more detailed discussion of the scientific parallels to Irigaray's concept of feminist subjectivity, see Druxes, *Feminization of Dr. Faustus,* 12–15.

47. See Luce Irigaray, *Speculum. De l'autre Femme* (Paris: Minuit, 1974); ibid., *Ce Sexe qui n'en est pas un* (Paris: Minuit, 1977).

48. Chambers, "Some Metropolitan Tales," 54–55.

49. Whitford, *Luce Irigaray,* 44.

50. Irigaray, "Love Between Us," in Cadeva et al., "Who Comes After the Subject." 176.

51. Ibid.

52. William Connolly, *Identity/Difference* (Ithaca: Cornell Univ. Press, 1991), 20–21.

53. Whitford, *Luce Irigaray,* 29.

54. Connolly, *Identity/Difference,* 64–65.

55. Whitford, *Luce Irigaray,* 91–92.

56. Connolly, *Identity/Difference,* 178–79.

57. I take the concept of the double character of the network from Chambers, "Some metropolitan Tales," 79.

58. Ibid.

59. Celeste Olalquiaga, *Megalopolis: Contemporary Cultural Sensibilities* (Minneapolis: Univ. of Minnesota Press, 1992).

1. Somatic Rebellion in Jean Rhys

1. Jean Rhys, *After Leaving Mr. Mackenzie* (London: Penguin, [1930] 1988). All subsequent quotes are from this edition and will be cited as *Mr. Mackenzie.*

2. Ibid., 49.

3. See Elaine Showalter, *The Female Malady: Women, Madness, and English Culture* (New York: Pantheon, 1985), 158–59; cf. also "Male Hysteria," 167–94. For further information about the urge to heroism as a denial of death see Ernest Becker, *The Denial of Death* (New York: Free Press, 1973). For the class politics of warfare and the British war experience, see Paul Fussell, *The Great War and Modern Memory* (London, Oxford: Oxford Univ. Press, 1975).

4. Mary Lou Emery, *Jean Rhys at "World's End": Novels of Colonial and Sexual Exile* (Austin: Univ. of Texas Press, 1990), 24.

5. Rhys, *Mr. Mackenzie,* 68, 69, 73, 88, 89.

6. Ibid., 57.

7. Jean Rhys, *Good Morning, Midnight* (New York: Norton, [1939] (1986), 75.

8. See John Berger, *Ways of Seeing* (London: BBC, 1972).

9. See Sander Gilman, "Black Bodies, White Bodies: Toward an Iconography of Female Sexuality in Late Nineteenth-Century Art, Medicine, and Literature" in *"Race," Writing and Difference,* ed. Henry Louis Gates (Chicago: Univ. of Chicago Press, 1986), 223–61. On 234–35 Gilman describes the nineteenth-century identification of the black woman and sexuality through focusing on her buttocks and genitals as overdeveloped compared to those of white women. He discusses the case of the Hottentot, Sarah Bartman, who

was exhibited as a curiosity in nineteenth-century Europe. Then he goes on (238, 248–51) to analyze the conflation of the black woman and the European prostitute:

> It is a commonplace that the primitive was associated with unbridled sexuality. . . . It is exactly this type of uncontrolled sexuality, however, which is postulated by historians . . . as the sign of the "swamp," the earliest stage of human history. . . . Manet employs the stigmata of fatness to characterize the prostitute. This convention becomes part of the visualization of the sexualized female even while the reality of the idealized sexualized female is that of a thin female. . . . It is thus the inherent fear of the difference in the anatomy of the Other which lies behind the synthesis of images. The Other's pathology is revealed in anatomy. . . . The "white man's burden" thus becomes his sexuality and its control, and it is this which is transferred into the need to control the sexuality of the Other, the Other as sexualized female. The colonial mentality which sees "natives" as needing control is easily transferred to "woman"—but woman as exemplified by the caste of the prostitute. This need for control was a projection of inner fears; thus, its articulation in visual images was in terms which described the polar opposite of the European male (256).

10. Rhys, *Mr. Mackenzie*, 49.
11. Ibid., 44.
12. See Jean Rhys, *Smile Please: An Unfinished Autobiography* (New York: Harper & Row, [1979] 1980), 80–81. Rhys describes taking her first bath on English soil, after she had arrived in London chaperoned by her aunt. The passage makes it clear that her bathing was considered excessive and self-indulgent by the boardinghouse society that she entered unaware of its rules. It also emphasizes the strict social surveillance of what would be private and self-determined rituals:

> On my way to my room I passed a bathroom and thought it would be a good idea to have a bath. I felt not hot, but sticky and a little tired. So I went in and turned the hot water tap on. When the bath was half full I undressed and got in, thinking it very pleasant. I began to feel rather happy and thought that when the water got cool I would turn the hot tap on again. I began to sing. Then above the noise of the water came a loud voice. "Who's that in there?" I answered with my name. "Turn that tap off," said the voice. "Turn that tap off at once." I turned it off. All my pleasure had gone and I got out of the bath and into my clothes as quickly as I could. When I reached my room my aunt was waiting for me. . . . "What possessed you to go into the bathroom and take all the hot water?" . . . "I've already noticed," said my aunt, "that you are quite incapable of thinking about anyone else but yourself." . . . All through breakfast the landlady glared at me. My aunt wouldn't speak to me. I could hardly swallow my eggs and bacon.

Rhys remembers this episode as characteristic of the sense of alienation she was made to feel at points of transition into an ostensibly more grown-up and properly British lifestyle. I shall discuss other examples later on in my analysis.

13. Gilman, in Gates, *"Race," Writing and Difference*, 242.
14. Rhys, *Mr. Mackenzie*, 54.
15. Ibid., 53, 54.
16. Jean Rhys, *Voyage in the Dark* (London: Penguin, [1924] 1986), 120.
17. Ibid., 112, 113, 114, 119.
18. Ibid., 122–23; italics mine.
19. See Judith Kegan Gardiner, *Rhys, Stead, Lessing and the Politics of Empathy* (Bloomington: Indiana Univ. Press, 1989), 12. Gardiner argues that the relationship between author and female character is that of mother to daughter: "This reading is congruent with current French-based theories that see the feminine as the silent suppressed childhood memory of maternal plenitude that cannot be fully expressed in the paternal realm of symbolic discourse. . . . Although the overtly maternal is absent . . . , one might say that its hero acts like her author's daughter, not merely because she is more than a generation younger but rather because the narrator steps into the vacant maternal position to instruct us daughterly readers in catching men and avoiding harm. She encourages us to treat her young hero as she does, with compassionate empathy and also with detachment."
20. Rhys, *Voyage*, 124.
21. Erving Goffman, *Encounters: Two Studies in the Sociology of Interaction* (New York: Macmillan, [1961] 1985), 133.
22. Rhys, *Mr. Mackenzie*, 39–44.
23. See Emery, 126–27.
24. See Rhys, *Smile Please*, 40; 13–14.
25. See Sandra Bartky, *Femininity and Domination: Studies in the Phenomenology of Oppression* (New York: Routledge, 1990), 99–119. Bartky discusses the female "ethic of care." On 102–3 she analyzes verbal and physical signs of "sustained sympathetic listening," which is the hallmark of traditional femininity.
26. Rhys, *Mr. Mackenzie*, 44.
27. See *Smile Please*, 40; *Voyage*, 41,90; *Mr. Mackenzie*, 90–91, 125.
28. Rhys, *Smile Please*, 118, gives another example of this attitude: "Listening to a piano being played very far off one day, Germaine said that her sister, Madame Bragadier, was one of the best amateur pianists in Paris."
29. Ibid., 103.
30. Ibid., 103–5; italics and underlining mine. Italicized statements are qualifications, whereas underlined parts are assertions. See also Laura Tracy, "Transference Theory in Literature," *Catching the Drift* (New Brunswick: Rutgers Univ. Press, 1988), 26–27: "Her career asks an implicit question about female writers in a patriarchal culture. To become speaking subjects, what are women required to give up?. . . . Despite her compulsion to write, then, she does not seem to have identified herself as a writer. Instead, she remained "feminine," that is, passive, submissive, out of control, creative apparently despite herself." Tracy takes a more critical attitude than I do to Rhys's

amateurism. Unlike Tracy, I see it as even more of a pretense than fact, and more caused by the white Creole Rhys's wish for social acceptance in Europe through her feigned adherence to white upperclass standards of ladylike comportment.

31. Giddens, *Modernity and Self-Identity*, 3.
32. Gardiner, *Rhys, Stead, Lessing*, 21.
33. Ibid., 2, 3.
34. Ibid., 6.
35. Ibid., 18.
36. Giddens, *Modernity and Self-Identity*, 5–6.
37. Emery, *"World's End,"* 23.
38. Deborah Kelly Kloepfer, *The Unspeakable Mother: Forbidden Discourse in Jean Rhys and H.D.* (Ithaca: Cornell Univ. Press, 1989), 51, 52.
39. Emery, *"World's End,"* 14.
40. Gayatri Spivak, "Three Women's Texts and a Critique of Imperialism," in Gates, *"Race," Writing and Difference*, 262–80.
41. Young, *Politics of Difference*, 111.
42. See Rhys, *Smile Please*, 17, Rhys mentions the gifts mailed to Dominica by "Irish Granny," her father's mother, ". . . boxes of chocolate, crystallized fruit, Carlsbad plums, and a jar of Stilton cheese for my father"; see also p.30, where two dolls arrive for the girls.
43. Gardiner, *Rhys, Stead, Lessing*, 22.
44. Judith Butler, *Gender Trouble: Feminism and the Subversion of Identity* (New York: Routledge, 1990), 99.
45. Ibid., 24–25.
46. Bartky, *Femininity and Domination*, 72–73.
47. Rhys, *Smile Please*, 16.
48. Ibid., 13.
49. Ibid., 16–17.
50. Ibid., 14.
51. Bartky, *Femininity and Domination*, 72–73.
52. Rhys, *Smile Please*, 44–45.
53. Bartky, *Femininity and Domination*, 80.
54. Ibid., 80–81.
55. Rhys, *Smile Please*, 14.
56. See my analysis in chapter 2 of Duras's *Un Barrage Contre le Pacifique* (Paris: Gallimard, 1950) 77: "Peut-être serait-il devenue d'une transparence de vitrine vide, parfaite."
57. Rhys, *Smile Please*, 33.
58. See Rhys, *Smile Please*, 18.
59. Wade Davis, *Passage of Darkness: The Ethnobiology of the Haitian Zombie* (Chapel Hill: Univ. of North Carolina Press, 1988): 207. I am indebted to Holly W. Fils.-Aimé for this and other references related to the zombie.
60. Rhys, *Voyage*, 19.
61. Ibid., 20.
62. Ibid., 59.

63. Ibid., 63.
64. Ibid., 62–63.
65. Ibid., 61.
66. Ibid., 134.
67. Ibid., 159. See Emery, *"World's End,"* 80–81. Emery analyzes the ending in terms of carnival logic, giving Anna's return to life a hopeful valence with which I disagree. The zombie returned to life never regains social acceptance, therefore, if we read Anna's wanderings in the context of zombification instead of Bakhtinian carnival, we cannot find subversive or innovative potential there. It is tempting, as Emergy does, to posit "multiplicitous identities" and "Caribbean heritage" as sources of redemption and strength for female character, but this view is not borne out once we really delve into Vodoun concepts of identity and social control. After reading Davis's account of Haitian society, I simply find a statement like ". . . [Anna] sustains her multiplicitous identities. She has not triumphed as an individual, up against society, but rather found the place and the people from which she can envision a new life." (Emery, 81) to be wishful thinking. There is no countersociety that does not also have its sanctions and regulations for the individual.
68. Rhys, *Mr. Mackenzie,* 61–62.
69. See Davis, *Passage of Darkness,* 62–85.
70. Ibid., 196.
71. Emery, *"World's End,"* 124.
72. Ibid., 65.
73. See Davis, *Passage of Darkness,* 15–55; Maya Deren, *"Divine Horsemen: The Living Gods of Haiti"* (video) (New York: Documentext/McPherson, [1970], video 1985).
74. Cf. Butler, *Gender Trouble,* 54–56: "Lacanian discourse centers on the notion of a divide, a primary or fundamental split that renders the subject internally divided and that establishes the duality of the sexes" (54). "Although one can argue that for Lacan repression creates the repressed through the prohibitive and paternal law, that argument does not account for the pervasive nostalgia for the lost fullness of *jouissance* in his work. Indeed, the loss could not be understood as loss unless the very irrecoverability of that pleasure did not designate a past that is barred from the present through the prohibitive law. That we cannot know that past from the position of the founded subject is not to say that that past does not reemerge within that subject's speech as *fêlure,* discontinuity, the prejuridicial past of *jouissance* is unknowable from within spoken language; that does not mean, however, that this past has no reality. The very inaccessibility of the past, indicated by metonymic slippage in contemporary speech, confirms that original fullness as the ultimate reality" (56).
75. Davis, *Passage of Darkness,* 186.
76. Ibid., 189, 190, 191.
77. See Deren film, "Divine Horsemen": "around the centerpost (*poteau mitan*) all ritual movements and davne revolve. . . . through its centerpost, the gods enter."

78. Rhys, *Mr. Mackenzie*, 106–8.
79. See Davis, *Passage of Darkness*, 180.
80. Rhys, *Mr. Mackenzie*, 118.
81. Davis, *Passage of Darkness*, 179.
82. Rhys, *Mr. Mackenzie*, 119–20.
83. Ibid., 71.
84. Emery, *"World's End,"* 24.
85. Rhys, *Mr. Mackenzie*, 96.
86. Mary Douglas, "External Boundaries," in *Purity and Danger* (New York: Praeger, 1966), 124.
87. Rhys, *Voyage*, 15, 30, 30.
88. See Young, *Politics of Difference*, 123: "Pulses of attraction and aversion modulate all interactions, with specific consequences for the experience of the body. When the dominant culture defines some groups as different, as the Other, the members of those groups are imprisoned in their bodies. Dominant discourse defines them in terms of bodily characteristics, and constructs those bodies as ugly, dirty, defiled, impure, contaminated, or sick. Those who experience such an epidermalizing of their world . . . discover their status by means of the embodied behaviour of others: in their gestures, a certain nervousness that they exhibit, their avoidance of eye contact, the distance they keep."
89. Rhys, *Voyage*, 8.
90. Ibid., 90.
91. Ibid., 62.
92. Douglas, "External Boundaries," 123.
93. Rhys, *Mr. Mackenzie*, 12.
94. Rhys, *Smile Please*, 23–24.
95. Cf. Deren, *Divine Horsemen*, where the Vodoun dancers have apronlike pieces of fabric sewn onto their clothes and twirl them upwards and out when the *loa* descend on them.
96. Rhys, *Voyage*, 100.
97. Rhys, *Mr. Mackenzie*, 50.
98. Rhys, *Voyage*, 93–94.
99. Butler, *Gender Trouble*, 139–41.
100. Rhys, *Voyage*, 69–70.
101. Rhys, *Mr. Mackenzie*, 133.
102. Ibid., 135.
103. Rhys, *Voyage*, 74.
104. Rhys, *Mr. Mackenzie*, 25.
105. Ibid., 45.
106. Showalter, *The Female Malady*, 147.
107. Quoted in Showalter, *The Female Malady*, 157.
108. Rhys, *Mr. Mackenzie*, 45.
109. Ibid., 38.
110. Giddens, *Modernity and Self-Identity*, 54.
111. Rhys, *Voyage*, 13.

112. See Showalter, *The Female Malady,* 162–63. She describes the imprisonment of suffragettes in Holloway Gaol in 1912, and points out the hys-
tericization of their bodies: "Ridicule, shaming, and physical abuse culmi-
nated in forcible feeding . . . , a technique which had been employed with
lunatics in the old madhouses."

2. Jamming the Exchange Machinery in Duras

1. M. Duras, *Un Barrage contre le Pacifique* (Paris: Gallimard, 1950); translated
as *The Seawall,* Herman Briffault, trans. (New York: Harper & Row, 1986).
Subsequent quotes from these editions are cited respectively as *Barrage* and
Seawall.
2. Duras, *Barrage,* 13.
3. Ibid., 13. It occurs to me that this statement could be read as a negative
creation myth: the family tries to create a link to the world, whereas God
created the world in seven days. This is another example of Duras's laconic
undercutting of readerly expectation for an unfolding quest pattern, which is
rewarded with success.
4. Duras, *Seawall,* 9.
5. Duras, *Barrage,* 9.
6. See Chris Gregory, *Gifts and Commodities* (London: Academic Press, 1982),
12. Gregory offers a concise discussion of Marx's approach to the origin of
commodities. Marx studied the anthropological literature of his time and
developed the theory that simple communities do not trade within the society but at its margins. ". . . the exchange of commodities evolves originally
not within primitive communities, but on their margins, on their borders,
the few points where they come into contact with other communities. This is
where barter begins and moves thence into the interior of the community,
exerting a disintegrating influence upon it" (Marx, 1859, 50).
7. Duras, *Barrage,* 51.
8. Duras, *Seawall,* 40.
9. Duras, *Barrage,* 40–41.
10. Duras, *Seawall,* 31.
11. Duras, *Barrage,* 73.
12. Translation mine; Briffault's translation is too focused on M. Jo's reaction
rather than Suzanne's realization of her own value.
13. Pierre Bourdieu, *Outline of a Theory of Practice* (Cambridge: Cambridge
Univ. Press, [1972] 1977), 5.
14. Duras, *Barrage,* 59.
15. Duras, *Seawall,* 47.
16. Duras, *Barrage,* 72.
17. Ibid.
18. Ibid., 73–74.
19. Micheline Tison-Braun, *Marguerite Duras* (Amsterdam: Rodopi, 1984), 15.
20. See Lewis Hyde, "Introduction," in *The Gift: Imagination and the Erotic Life*

of Property (New York: Vintage, 1969); xiv. Hyde states: "It is this element of relationship which leads me to speak of gift exchange as an 'erotic' commerce, opposing *eros* (the principle of attraction, union, involvement which binds together) to *logos* (reason and logic in general, the principle of differentiation in particular). A market economy is an emanation of *logos*."

21. Marcel Mauss, *The Gift: The Form and Reason for Exchange in Archaic Societies* (New York: Norton [1950] 1990); 14.

22. Sherry Ortner and Harriet Whitehead, "Introduction: Accounting for Sexual Meanings," in *Sexual Meanings: The Cultural Construction of Gender and Sexuality* (Cambridge: Cambridge Univ. Press, 1981); 5, 12.

23. Bourdieu, *Theory of Practice* 56.

24. Duras, *Barrage*, 76,.

25. Ibid., *Seawall*, 59–60.

26. Jane Collier and Michelle Rosaldo, "Politics and Gender in Simple Societies," in Ortner and Whitehead, *Sexual Meanings*, 281.

27. Duras, *Barrage*, 45.

28. Duras, *Seawall*, 35.

29. Duras, *Barrage*, 49.

30. Duras, *Seawall*, 38.

31. Sherry Ortner, "Gender and Sexuality in Hierarchical Societies," in Ortner and Whithead, *Sexual Meanings*, 368.

32. Ibid., 373.

33. Mauss, *The Gift: The Form*, 37.

34. Ibid., 40.

35. Douglas Cole. "The History of the Kwakiutl Potlatch," in *Chiefly Feasts: The Enduring Kwakiutl Potlatch*, ed. Aldona Jonaitis, (New York: Univ. of Washington Press, 1991); 135.

36. Ibid., 140.

37. Duras, *Barrage*, 68.

38. Duras, *Seawall*, 53.

39. See Salvatore Cucchiari. "The Origins of Gender Hierarchy," in Ortner and Whitehead, *Sexual Meanings*, 58.

40. See *Le Petit Robert* (Paris: Société du Nouveau Littré, 1969); 1811a: "*trafic*: 1. commerce plus ou moins clandestin, honteux et illicite; 2. mouvement général des trains; frequence des convois sur une même ligne." ["traffic." 1. more or less clandestine, illicit or shameful commerce; 2. general circulation of trains, spacing of convois on the same line."]

41. Ortner, "Gender and Sexuality," 372–73, 375.

42. Duras, *Barrage*, 89.

43. Duras, *Seawall*, 69.

44. Duras, *Barrage*, 99.

45. Duras, *Seawall*, 78.

46. Duras, *Barrage*, 90.

47. Duras, *Seawall*, 70.

48. Nicholas Thomas, *Entangled Objects: Exchange, Material Culture, and Colonialism in the Pacific* (Cambridge: Harvard Univ. Press, 1991), 15.

49. Cf. The film *Hiroshima mon amour*, where the cat's eyes look at the incarcerated woman in the basement and that look restores her sanity; or the scene in which the Japanese sits opposite the woman in a bar and looks at her, which enables her to tell the story of her victimization. She begins to recover from that destructive moment in her personal history, just as the city of Hiroshima is beginning to recover from the bombing.

50. Duras, *Barrage*, 77.

51. Duras, *Seawall*, 60.

52. Duras, *Barrage*, 79.

53. Duras, *Seawall*, 62.

54. Duras, *Barrage*, 84.

55. Ibid.

56. Duras, *Seawall*, 66.

57. Ibid., 68.

58. Duras, *Barrage*, 86.

59. Duras, *Seawall*, 67–68.

60. Cf. Sharon Willis, *Marguerite Duras: Writing on the Body* (Urbana: Univ. of Illinois Press, 1987), 76–77. Willis states that identity is always developed by becoming conscious of being able to manipulate the space surrounding one's body (a reiteration of Freud's *fort/da* game played by his young grandson with a spool): "The separation between inside and outside, necessary to speech, is precipitated from a primary spatial mapping that begins with points of discharge for the excitations of the anaclisis [propping]. . . . These points of fixity are engaged in an alternating process of stabilization-destabilization, and participate in the indifferentiation of the semiotic chora, which includes the maternal body and the space surrounding the infant as well. As the first mappings of differentiation, they mark both the cut and the threat of absorption into indifferentiation; for example, the look is indistinguishable from its capture, by absorption, in the bright spot that attracts it."

61. Duras, *Seawall*, 100.

62. Duras, *Barrage*, 126.

63. Duras, *Seawall*, 100.

64. Ibid., 105.

65. Thomas, *Entangled Objects*, 28.

66. Ibid., 206.

67. Duras, *Barrage*, 134 and *Seawall*, 106.

68. Duras, *Barrage*, 164.

69. Duras, *Seawall*, 131.

70. See Anthony King, *Urbanism, Colonialism and the World-Economy* (London: Routledge, 1991), 120, 129. King has an enlightening discussion of the colonial bungalow as it was reimported as the model for a second home in the colonialists' home country. I am indebted to John Calagione for this reference. King states:

Everything about [the bungalow's] form, utilization, land use, and sitting is evidence that they are essentially building forms geared to consumption—of space, views, scenery, time, consumer goods, and money—and this was consumption in agricultural areas, previously devoted to production. They were also, obviously, evidence of accumulation in that they were a second dwelling. Moreover, the 'spilling out,' or expression of that surplus was, again, not in Scotland, Wales, or the Midlands, but on the reachable margins of the centre of capital accumulation—London. . . . Especially from the nineteenth century onwards, and in particular in the present day, that mode of production has been a capitalist world-economy. . . . architectural forms extending through the colonial urban system provide evidence, not only of the change from one mode of production to another [industrial to service-oriented], but of the emergence of such a global system of production. . . . The transformation of the physical and spatial environment, especially in the form of cities, was a prerequisite, on one hand, for establishing 'Western' (that is capitalist) patterns of consumption and culture in the 'non-Western' world. On the other, it also provided possibilities for different kinds of consciousness for the representation of different kinds of cultural, ethnic or national identities. The outcome is a mixture of both.

71. See ibid., 136–137.
72. Duras, *Barrage*, 210.
73. Duras, *Seawall*, 168.
74. Duras, *Barrage*, 169.
75. Duras, *Seawall*, 136–137.
76. Ortner and Whitehead, *Sexual Meannings*, 25.
77. Duras, *Barrage*, 172–73.
78. Duras, *Seawall*, 139–40.
79. Duras, *Barrage*, 170.
80. Duras, *Seawall*, 137.
81. Duras, *Barrage*, 168.
82. Duras, *Seawall*, 136.
83. Duras, *Barrage*, 170.
84. Duras, *Seawall*, 138.
85. King, *Urbanism*, 1.
86. Ibid., 19.
87. Ibid., 14.
88. Cf. King, *Urbanism*, 14–15.
89. Ibid., 18.
90. Ibid., 18–19.
91. John Berger, *Ways of Seeing* (London: BBC, 1972), 45–64, especially 46–47.
92. Duras, *Barrage*, 184.
93. Duras, *Seawall*, 148.
94. Ibid.
95. Duras, *Barrage*, 185–86.
96. Duras, *Seawall*, 150–51. Ellipsis points mark where the translation is more verbose than Duras's original, and so those lines are omitted.

97. Duras, *Barrage*, 167–68.
98. Duras, *Seawall*, 135–36. Cf. *Le Petit Robert*, 1599b gives two meanings for *salissant:* "1. Qui se salit aisément, qui est difficile de tenir propre; 2. Qui salit; où on se salit." ["1. that which gets soiled easily, which is difficult to keep clean; 2. which makes dirty; where one gets soiled."]
99. Duras, *Barrage*, 188.
100. Duras, *Seawall*, 151.
101. Duras, *Barrage*, 189.
102. Duras, *Seawall*, 152–53.
103. Deborah Gaensbauer, "Trespassing and Voyeurism in the Novels of Virginia Woolf and Marguerite Duras," *Comparative Literature Studies*, vol. 24, no. 2 (1987), 192–201.
104. Marcelle Marini, *Territoires du Féminin* (Paris: Minuit, 1977), 50.
105. Gaensbauer, "Trespassing," 192, 193.
106. Luce Irigaray, *This Sex*, trans. Catherine Porter (Ithaca: Cornell Univ. Press, 1985), 144–45.
107. On the use of twinning and "creating an inner twin through dialogue," see Simone de Beauvoir, "The Narcissist," in *The Second Sex* (New York: Knopf [1949] 1971), 633.
108. Duras, *Barrage*, 168.
109. Duras, *Seawall*, 135.
110. Gregory, *Gifts and Commodities*, 19–21.
111. Duras, *Barrage*, 226–227.
112. Duras, *Seawall*, 180. Here I am substituting my own translation for a mistranslated passage.
113. Duras, *Barrage*, 228.
114. Duras, *Seawall*, 181.
115. Duras, *Barrage*, 324.
116. Duras, *Seawall*, 256. In French, Susanne's first statement is closer to something more vulgar, like "I am nicely stacked."
117. Duras, *Barrage*, 210.
118. Duras, *Seawall*, 168.
119. Duras, *Barrage*, 225.
120. Duras, *Seawall*, 179.
121. Duras, *Barrage*, 353.
122. Duras, *Seawall*, 278.
123. Duras, *Barrage*, 322.
124. Duras, *Seawall*, 254.
125. Duras, *Barrage*, 365.
126. Duras, *Seawall*, 288.
127. Duras, *Barrage*, 226.
128. Duras, *Seawall*, 180.
129. Collier and Rosaldo, in Ortner and Whitehead, *Sexual Meanings*, 307.
130. This becomes very clear in the film *Hiroshima, mon Amour* (1959), where the colonial city is not only a bombsite, but because of its still visible ravaging becomes the site of "re-membering," healing the wounded female

protagonist of the war wounds she obtained at an earlier time in a small provincial town in France.

3. Female Community in Drabble's Fiction

1. Margaret Drabble, *Jerusalem the Golden* (New York: Fawcett, Popular Library, 1967). All quotations are from this edition.
2. Margaret Drabble, *The Middle Ground* (New York: Bantam, [1980] 1982). All quotations are from this edition.
3. Victor Turner, "Liminal to Liminoid, in Play, Flow, and Ritual," *From Ritual to Theatre* (New York: Performing Arts Journal Publications, 1982), 25.
4. Ibid., 55.
5. Ibid., 54.
6. Drabble, *Middle Ground*, 4.
7. Ibid., 3.
8. The French feminist critic Luce Irigaray advocates the use of this technique as a necessary subversive practice of rereading the founding texts of patriarchy. Her book *Speculum* consists of such a rereading of Freud's and Plato's writings on femininity where she appropriates their discourse, then breaks it up and interjects her subversive comments.
9. Drabble, *Middle Ground*, 139.
10. Ibid., 105.
11. Peter Stallybrass and Allon White, "The City: The Sewer, the Gaze and the Contaminating Touch," in *The Politics and Poetics of Transgression* (Ithaca: Cornell Univ. Press, 1986), 125–48.
12. Drabble, *Middle Ground*, 107.
13. Ibid., 124.
14. Stallybrass and White, "The City," 141.
15. Drabble, *Middle Ground*, 213.
16. Ibid., 202.
17. Ibid.
18. Ibid., 29.
19. Ibid., 169.
20. Ibid., 55.
21. Ibid., 225–26.
22. Drabble, *Jerusalem*, 161.
23. Ibid., 189.
24. Stallybrass and White, "The City," 26.
25. Drabble, *Middle Ground*, 257.
26. Drabble, *Radiant Way*, 198, 249–50.
27. Ibid., 250.
28. See H. V. Savitch, *Post-Industrial Cities* (Princeton: Princeton Univ. Press, 1988), 219.
29. Drabble, *Radiant Way*, 362.
30. Ibid., 256.
31. Ibid., 17.

32. Valerie Grosvenor Myer, *Margaret Drabble: A Reader's Guide* (New York: St. Martin's Press, 1991), 168.
33. Drabble, *Radiant Way*, 353.
34. Margaret Drabble, *A Natural Curiosity* (New York: Viking, 1989), 22.
35. Ibid., 56.
36. Drabble, *Radiant Way*, 250.
37. Drabble, *Radiant Way*, 347.
38. John Bunyan, *The Pilgrim's Progress* (London: Oxford Univ. Press, 1960), 11, 43.
39. Drabble, *Radiant Way*, 325.
40. Ibid., 352.
41. Ibid., 343.
42. Ibid., 348.
43. Ibid., 233.
44. Ibid., 251–52.
45. Ibid., 251.
46. Myer, *Margaret Drabble*, 149–50.
47. Drabble, *Radiant Way*, 231–33.
48. Ibid., 232.
49. Laura Mulvey, "Pandora: Topographies of the Mask and Curiosity," in Colomina, *Sexuality and Space*, 58–59.
50. Ibid., 66.
51. Ibid., 68–70.
52. Melvin M. Webber, "The Urban Place and the Nonplace Urban Realm," in *Explorations in Urban Structure*, ed. Melvin Webber et al. (Philadelphia, 1964), 79.
53. Ibid., 405.
54. Sharon Zukin, *Landscapes of Power* (Berkeley: Univ. of California Press, 1991), 4–5.
55. Margaret Drabble, *The Realms of Gold* (New York, Fawcett, Popular Library, 1975), 111, 118.
56. Drabble, *Radiant Way*, 255.
57. Quoted in Myer, *Margaret Drabble* 108, 109, 130.
58. Drabble, *Radiant Way*, 198. It seems significant that Drabble suddenly uses the French word *louche* (shady, ambiguous, shifty), to describe a form of othering, that renders the alien suspect by labeling it as foreign. It also seems that she sees this poverty as a staged enactment, intended to bring its actors into collision with the law.
59. Ibid., 325.
60. Ibid., 324–25.
61. Ibid., 107–8.
62. Ibid., 21.
63. Ibid., 195–96.
64. Ibid., 26.
65. Ibid., 111–12.
66. Zukin, *Landscapes*, 5.
67. Drabble, *Radiant Way*, 176.

68. Ibid., *Natural Curiosity*, 173–76.
69. Ibid., 240.
70. Elizabeth Grosz, "Bodies-Cities," in Colomina, *Sexuality and Space*, 250–51.
71. Drabble, *Natural Curiosity*, 235.
72. Ibid., 200.
73. Drabble, *Radiant Way*, 281.
74. Myer, *Margaret Drabble*, 142.
75. Margaret Drabble, *The Gates of Ivory* (New York: Viking, 1992), 292–95.
76. Ibid., 460.

4. Monika Maron's Dissection of the Scarred Body Politic

1. Didier Eribon, *Michel Foucault* (Paris: Flammarion, 1989), 13.
2. Monika Maron, *Flugasche* (Frankfurt: S. Fischer, 1981), 36. Monika Maron, *Flight of Ashes* (London: Readers International, 1986), 24. All quotes are from these editions.
3. Monika Maron, *Stille Zeile 6* (Frankfurt: S. Fischer, 1991), 194–95 (translation mine).
4. Michel Foucault, *Discipline and Punish*, 187, quoted in Hubert Dreyfus and Paul Rabinow, eds., *Michel Foucault: Beyond Structuralism and Hermeneutics* (Chicago: Univ. of Chicago Press, 1982), 159.
5. Hans-Joachim Maaz, *Der Gefühlsstau: Ein Psychogramm der DDR* (Berlin: Argon, 1990), 85–87, (translation mine).
6. Maron, *Flugasche, 16–17.*
7. Maron, *Flight of Ashes*, 8.
8. Maron, *Flugasche*, 57.
9. Maron, *Flight of Ashes*, 40 (translation mine).
10. Maron, *Flugasche*, 43, 121 and *Flight of Ashes*, 90.
11. Maron, *Flugasche*, 12.
12. Maron, *Flight of Ashes*, 5 (translation mine).
13. Maron, *Flugasche*, 8.
14. Maron, *Flight of Ashes*, 3.
15. Maron, *Flugasche*, 17.
16. Maron, *Flight of Ashes*, 8–9.
17. Maron, *Flugasche*, 65–66.
18. Maron, *Flight of Ashes*, 46–47.
19. Maron, *Stille Zeile 6*, 196–97.
20. Ibid., 172–73.
21. Ibid., 176.
22. Ibid., 66.
23. Maron, *Flugasche*, 153.
24. Maron, *Flight of Ashes*, 117.
25. Dreyfus and Rabinow, *Michel Foucault*, 153; quotation is from Foucault, *Discipline and Punish*, 136.
26. Maron, *Flugasche*, 113–14.

27. Maron, *Flight of Ashes*, 84.
28. Monika Maron, *Die Überläuferin* (Frankfurt: S. Fischer, 1986), 179.
29. Maron, *The Defector*, trans. David Marinelli (New York: Readers International, 1987), 131.
30. Maron, *Flugasche*, 109–110.
31. Maron, *Flight of Ashes*, 80–82.
32. Dreyfus and Rabinow, *Michel Foucault*, 188; quotations are from Foucault, *Discipline and Punish*, 200.
33. Maron, *Flugasche*, 120, 122.
34. Ibid., 232–33.
35. Maron, *Flight of Ashes*, 89–91.
36. Ibid., 179–80.
37. Maron, *Überläuferin*, 55.
38. Maron, *The Defector*, 37.
39. Maron, *Flugasche*, 147–49.
40. Maron, *Flight of Ashes*, 112–14.
41. Cf. *golem*, *New Columbia Encyclopedia*, William H. Harris and Judith S. Levey, eds, (New York: Columbia Univ. Press, 1975), 1104c.
42. Maron, Überläuferin, 140.
43. Ibid., 144.
44. Maron, *The Defector*, 104.
45. Maron, *Überläuferin*, 60, 63 and *The Defector*, 40, 43.
46. Maron, *Überläuferin*, 62 and *The Defector*, 42.
47. Maron, *Überläuferin*, 129.
48. Maron, *The Defector*, 93–94.
49. Maron, *Überläuferin*, 26.
50. Maron, *The Defector*, 14.
51. Maron, *Flugasche*, 71.
52. Maron, *Flight of Ashes*, 50–51.
53. Maron, *Überläuferin*, 50 and *The Defector*, 33.
54. Maron, *Flugasche* 78 and *Flight of Ashes*, 56.
55. In July 1988, for instance, theater in Berlin had regressed to propagandistic potboilers, such as a Soviet comedy that was being performed in a theater right in the center of East Berlin whose German title was advertised downtown on a huge banner: "Ich will endlich ein Kind" ["I want a baby—finally!"]. Women were no longer being admitted as students in scientific disciplines like engineering.
56. Maron, *Überläuferin*, 51.
57. Ibid., *The Defector*, 33.
58. Ibid., *Stille Zeile 6*, 125, 129.
59. Translation mine.
60. Maron, *Stille Zeile 6*, 154–55.
61. Translation mine.
62. Maron, *Stille Zeile 6*, 218–19 (italics mine).
63. Translation mine.
64. Maron *Überläuferin*, 116 and *The Defector*, 83.
65. Maron *Überläuferin*, 144 and *The Defector*, 104.

66. Maron, *Überläuferin*, 188 and *The Defector* 137.
67. Ibid., 193.
68. Maron, *The Defector*, 141.
69. Maron, *Überläuferin*, 191–92.
70. Maron, *The Defector*, 140–41.
71. Kurt Hager, in *Der Spiegel* Nr. 22 (Hamburg, 1987), 55.
72. Maron, *Stille Zeile 6*, 117, 217.
73. Cf. *Überläuferin* 216; *Defector*, 159. Maron mentions a theater troupe who perform the *Antigone* and who are walking around the city in search of a new place where they can perform their play.
74. Maron, *Stille Zeile 6*, 182.
75. Maron, *Stille Zeile 6*, 206–7.
76. Maron, *Stille Zeile 6*, 57.
77. Maron, *Stille Zeile 6*, 215.
78. Maron, *Flugasche 72, Flight of Ashes*, 51–52, *Überläuferin*, 84, and *The Defector*, 59.
79. Maron, *Überläuferin*, 156 and *The Defector*, 113.
80. Maron, *Überläuferin*, 84.
81. Maron, *The Defector*, 59–60.
82. H. Cixous, *"Coming to Writing"*, 49–51 (italics mine).
83. Maron, *Überläuferin*, 127–28, 178 and *The Defector*, 92, 130.
84. Maron, *Stille Zeile 6*, 80.

Conclusion: Managing Alterity

1. Jana Sawicki, *Disciplining Foucault: Feminism, Power, and the Body* (New York: Routledge, 1991), 63.
2. Ibid., 63.
3. Chambers, *Border Dialogues*, 72.
4. Michael Sorkin, ed., *Variations on a Theme Park: The New American City and the End of Public Space* (New York: Hill & Wang, 1992), xv.
5. Sylviane Agacinski, "Another Experience of the Question, or Experiencing the Question Other-Wise," in *Who Comes After the Subject?*, ed. Cadava et al., 16.
6. Chambers, *Border Dialogues*, 80.
7. Chambers, *Migrancy, Culture, Identity* (London: Routledge, 1994), 31.
8. See also M. Christine Boyer, *The City of Collective Memory: Its Historical Imagery and Architectural Entertainments* (Cambridge: MIT Press, 1994), 489–91. Boyer develops an interesting critique of Jameson's claim that the postmodern city is unmappable and that therefore orientation and critical consciousness become impossible. Boyer focuses her attention on the postmodern city as radical artifice, with many highly theatrical historicized festival marketplaces, which rescript the observer's role into that of a tourist/consumer's. However, she asserts that agency is still possible, and that, keeping the materiality of the city's construction in mind, we may expose the rules of its construction and penetrate the artificial neutrality of its underlying discourse.

BIBLIOGRAPHY

Primary Sources

Drabble, Margaret. *The Gates of Ivory*. New York: Viking, 1992.

_____. *Jerusalem the Golden*. New York: Fawcett, Popular Library, 1967.

_____. *The Middle Ground [1980] New York: Bantam, 1982*.

_____. *A Natural Curiosity*. New York: Viking, 1989.

_____. *The Radiant Way*. New York: Viking, 1987.

_____. *The Realms of Gold*. New York: Fawcett, Popular Library 1975.

Duras, Marguerite. *Un Barrage contre le Pacifique*. Paris: Gallimard, 1950.

_____. *The Seawall*, trans. Herma Briffault. New York: Harper & Row, 1986.

Maron, Monika. *The Defector*, trans. David Marinelli. London: Readers International, 1987.

_____. *Flight of Ashes*, trans. David Marinelli. London: Readers International, 1986.

_____. *Flugasche*. Frankfurt: S. Fischer, 1981.

_____. *Stille Zeile 6*. Frankfurt: S. Fischer, 1991.

_____. *Die Überläuferin*. Frankfurt: S. Fischer, 1986.

Rhys, Jean. *After Leaving Mr. Mackenzie* (1930). London: Penguin, 1988.

_____. *Voyage in the Dark*. London: Penguin, [1924] 1986.

Secondary Sources

Bartky, Sandra. *Femininity and Domination: Studies in the Phenomenology of Oppression*. New York: Routledge, 1990.

Baudrillard, Jean. *La Société de Consommation*. Paris: Denoël, 1970.

Beauvoir, Simone de. *The Second Sex*. New York: Knopf, [1949] 1971.

Benjamin, Walter. *Illuminations*. New York: Schocken, 1978.

Berger, John. *Ways of Seeing*. London: BBC, 1972.

Bordo, Susan. *Unbearable Weight: Feminism, Western Culture, and the Body*. Berkeley: Univ. of California Press, 1993.

Bourdieu, Pierre. *Outline of a Theory of Practice*. Cambridge: Cambridge Univ. Press, [1972] 1977.

Boyer, M. Christine. *The City of Collective Memory: Its Historical Imagery and Architectural Entertainment*. Cambridge: MIT Press, 1994.

Bunyan, John. *The Pilgrim's Progress*. London: Oxford Univ. Press, 1960.

Butler, Judith. *Bodies That Matter: On the Discursive Limits of Sex*. New York: Routledge, 1993.

————. *Gender Trouble: Feminism and the Subversion of Identity*. New York: Routledge, 1990.

Cadava, Eduardo, Peter Connor, and Jean-Luc Nancy, eds. *Who Comes After the Subject?* New York: Routledge, 1991.

Chambers, Iain. *Border Dialogues: Journeys in Postmodernity*. London: Routledge, 1990.

————. *Migrancy, Culture, and Identity*. London: Routledge, 1994.

Cixous, Hélène. *"Coming to Writing" and Other Essays*, ed. Deborah Jensen. Cambridge: Harvard Univ. Press, 1991.

Colomina, Beatriz, ed. *Sexuality and Space*. New York: Princeton Architectural Press, 1992.

Connolly, William. *Identity/Difference*. Ithaca: Cornell Univ. Press, 1991.

Davis, Wade. *Passage of Darkness: The Ethnobiology of the Haitian Zombie*. Chapel Hill: Univ. of North Carolina Press, 1988.

Deren, Maya. *Divine Horsemen: The Living Gods of Haiti*. New York: Documentext/McPherson, 1970; video 1985.

Der Spiegel. Hamburg: Augstein, 1987.

Douglas, Mary. *Purity and Danger*. New York: Praeger, 1966.

Dreyfus, Hubert, and Paul Rabinow, eds. *Michel Foucault: Beyond Structuralism and Hermeneutics*. Chicago: Univ. of Chicago Press, 1982.

Druxes, Helga. *The Feminization of Dr. Faustus: Female Identity Quests from Stendhal to Morgner*. University Park: Pennsylvania State Univ. Press, 1993.

Eagleton, Terry. *Ideology: An Introduction*. London: Verso, 1991.

Emery, Mary Lou. *Jean Rhys at "World's End": Novels of Colonial and Sexual Exile*. Austin: Univ. of Texas Press, 1990.

Eribon, Didier. *Michel Foucault*. Paris: Flammarion, 1989.

Foucault, Michel. *Discipline and Punish: The Birth of the Prison*. New York: Vintage, 1977.

Gaensbauer, Deborah. "Trespassing and Voyeurism in the Novels of Virginia Woolf and Marguerite Duras." *Comparative Literature Studies*, vol. 24, no. 2 (1987), 192–201.

Gardiner, Judith Kegan. *Rhys, Stead, Lessing and the Politics of Empathy*. Bloomington: Indiana Univ. Press, 1989.

Gates, Henry Louis, ed. *"Race," Writing and Difference*. Chicago: Univ. of Chicago Press, 1986.

Giddens, Anthony. *Modernity and Self-Identity: Self and Society in the Late Modern Age*. Stanford: Stanford Univ. Press, 1991.

Goffman, Ervin. *Encounters: Two Studies in the Sociology of Interaction* (New York: Macmillan, [1961] 1985.

Gregory, Chris. *Gifts and Commodities*. London: Academic Press, 1982.

Habermas, Jürgen. *Towards a Rational Society*. Boston: Beacon, 1970.

Hyde, Lewis. *The Gift: Imagination and the Erotic Life of Property*. New York: Vintage, 1969.

Irigaray, Luce. *Le sexe qui n'en est pas un*. Paris: Minuit, 1977.

――――. *Le Temps de la Différence*. Paris: Le Livre de Poche, 1989.

――――. *This Sex Which Is Not One*, trans. Catherine Porter. Ithaca: Cornell Univ. Press, 1985.

Jameson, Fredric. *Postmodernism Or, The Cultural Logic of Late Capitalism*. Durham: Duke Univ. Press, 1991.

Jonaitis, Aldona. *Chiefly Feasts: The Enduring Kwakiutl Potlatch*. New York: Univ. of Washington Press, 1991.

King, Anthony. *Urbanism, Colonialism and the World-Economy*. London: Routledge, 1991.

Kloepfer, Deborah Kelly. *The Unspeakable Mother: Forbidden Discourse in Jean Rhys and H.D.*. Ithaca: Cornell Univ. Press, 1989.

Lukács, György. *History and Class Consciousness*. Cambridge: MIT Press, 1971.

Maaz, Hans-Joachim. *Der Gefühlsstau: Ein Psychogramm der DDR*. Berlin: Argon, 1990.

Marini, Marcelle. *Les Territories du Féminin: Entretiens avec Marguerite Duras*. Paris: Editions Minuit, 1977.

Mauss, Marcel. *The Gift: The Form and Reason for Exchange in Archaic Societies*. New York: Norton, [1950] 1990.

Myer, Valerie Grosvenor. *Margaret Drabble: A Reader's Guide*. New York: St. Martin's Press, 1991.

Olalquiaga, Celeste. *Megalopolis: Contemporary Cultural Sensibilities*. Minneapolis: Univ. of Minnesota Press, 1992.

Ortner, Sherry, and Harriet Whitehead, eds. *Sexual Meanings: The Cultural Construction of Gender and Sexuality*. Cambridge: Cambridge Univ. Press, 1981.

Popp, Adelheid. *Jugend einer Arbeiterin*. Berlin: Dietz, 1983.

Rhys, Jean, *After Leaving Mr. Mackenzie*. London: Penguin, [1939] 1988.

――――. *Good Morning, Midnight*. New York: Norton, [1939] 1986.

――――. *Smile Please: An Unfinished Autobiography*. New York: Harper & Row [1979] 1980.

Robert, Paul. *Le Petit, Robert: Dictionnaire de la langue française*. Paris: Sociéte du Nouveam Littré, 1969.

Rorty, Richard. *Contingency, Irony and Solidarity*. Cambridge: Harvard, Univ. Press, 1989.

Savitch, H. V. *Post-Industrial Cities*. Princeton: Princeton Univ. Press, 1988.

Sawicki, Jana. *Disciplining Foucault: Feminism, Power, and the Body*. New York: Routledge, 1991.

Sharpe, William, and Leonard Wallock, eds. *Visions of the Modern City: Essays in Art, History, and Literature*. Baltimore: Johns Hopkins Univ. Press, [1983] 1987.

Showalter, Elaine. *The Female Malady: Women, Madness and English Culture*. New York: Pantheon, 1985.

Sophocles. *The Oedipus Cycle*, trans. Dudley Fitts and Robert Fitzgerald. San Diego: Harcourt, Brace Jovanovich, 1977.

Sorkin, Michael, ed. *Variations on a Theme Park: The New American City and the End of Public Space*. New York: Hill & Wang, 1992.

Spain, Daphe. *Gendered Spaces*. Chapel Hill: Univ. of North Carolina Press, 1992.

Squier, Susan Merrill. *Women Writers and the City: Essays in Feminist Literary Criticism*. Knoxville: Univ. of Tennessee Press, 1984.

Stallybrass, Peter, and Allon White. *The Politics and Poetics of Transgression*. Ithaca: Cornell Univ. Press, 1986.

Thomas, Nicholas. *Entangled Objects: Exchange, Material Culture, and Colonialism in the Pacific*. Cambridge: Harvard Univ. Press, 1991.

Tison-Braun, Micheline. *Marguerite Duras*. Amsterdam: Rodopi, 1984.

Tracy, Laura. *Catching the Drift*. New Brunswick: Rutgers Univ. Press, 1988.

Turner, Victor. *From Ritual to Theatre*. New York: Performing Arts Journal Publications, 1982.

Whitford, Margaret. *Luce Irigaray: Philosophy in the Feminine*. London: Routledge, 1991.

Willis, Sharon. *Marguerite Duras: Writing on the Body*. Urbana: Univ. of Illinois Press, 1987.

Young, Iris Marion. *Justice and the Politics of Difference*. Princeton: Princeton Univ. Press, 1990.

Zukin, Sharon. *Landscapes of Power*. Berkeley: Univ. of California Press, 1991.

INDEX

Books in the Kritik series